SNUBBED
A Basketball Season of Triumph, Crisis and Despair at St. Bonaventure University

By Brian Toolan

Printed in The United States of America

ISBN: 978-0-9978317-1-9

Snubbed: *A Basketball Season of Triumph, Crisis and Despair at*

St. Bonaventure University /Toolan-1st ed.

1. St. Bonaventure, Olean New York. 2. Basketball. 3. Sports.

4. Society. 5. NCAA.

Cover photograph: Jaylen Adams flexes his muscles after Bonnies' victory at Dayton. (Associated Press)

Back cover: Marcus Posley crumples to the floor in closing minutes in loss to Davidson in Brooklyn. (Associated Press).

NFB/Amelia Press
<<<>>>
119 Dorchester Road
Buffalo, New York 14213
For more information please visit
nfbpublishing.com

To my family.

SNUBBED

TABLE OF CONTENTS

FOREWORD

Nov. 13, 2015: Basketball weather has arrived in Western New York. A heavy and cold rain pours for the second day. Fat, grey clouds press on the hills and hang even more deeply in the valleys. Hail accompanies the rain. The wind whips off Lake Erie in gusts of 60 miles an hour. In this rugged and remote place, St. Bonaventure University will open its 96th season of men's basketball on this night.

Another 352 college basketball teams, each a member of one of the 32 basketball conferences that comprise the National Collegiate Athletic Association's Division I for basketball, are also beginning their 2015-16 seasons at this time. A tiny percentage of those schools, maybe a dozen, maybe 15, no more than that, have reasons to believe they could win the national championship on April 4, 2016.

St. Bonaventure is not one of them.

Many more schools --- and their players, their coaches, their fans, their alumni --- hope their teams have seasons that will earn them entry to the NCAA Tournament. Sixty-eight teams will have their hopes answered.

11

Most will come from the so-called power conferences, the Atlantic Coast Conference, the Big East, the Big 10, the Big 12, the Southeastern Conference, the Pac-12. But March becomes a magical month because the winner of each of the conferences --- particularly the smaller conferences, the one-bid conferences such as the Ivy League, the Middle Atlantic Athletic Association, the Missouri Valley Conference, the Southern Conference and the Horizon and Patriot leagues --- receive an automatic bid, allowing for sometimes stunning upset victories that bring a riveting charm to the tournament, and there isn't an abundance of charm in sports these days. The whole thing is a carnival lasting weeks for college sports fans and the millions who fill out brackets in their workplaces each year.

St. Bonaventure is a member of the muscular Atlantic 10 Conference. The smallest member of the 14-school conference. It has the smallest enrollment, the smallest endowment, the smallest budget for the men's basketball program. It is located in Olean, N.Y., an inconvenient place, with a small, economically challenged population and harsh winters. By any measure one could apply, the Bonnies are seriously outgunned by their conference rivals, some of them major public universities, others wealthy private colleges, all of them located in major markets. All these schools have advantages that Bonaventure lacks ... in most cases, in the extreme.

Those are the challenges that confront the school and its men's basketball team, but there are strengths as well.

St. Bonaventure has a gilded basketball history. Its teams have played in the NCAA Tournament six times, in 1961, 1968, 1970, 1978, 2000 and

2012. The Bonnies have gone to the National Invitation Tournament 14 times, and won the tournament in 1977. The greatest season in the history of St. Bonaventure was the 1969-1970 campaign. The team won the prestigious Holiday Festival at Madison Square Garden, pounding highly ranked Purdue and its All-American guard Rick Mount in the title game. The Bonnies went to the Final Four in 1970, a season in which they were ranked as high as No. 2 in the nation. The star of that team, a first-team All-American and No. 1 choice in that year's NBA draft, Bob Lanier, played 14 seasons of pro ball, was an NBA all-star six times and is in the Naismith Memorial Basketball Hall of Fame in Springfield, Mass.

Lanier remains the most significant player in the history of the program. Many people believe, certainly all Bonaventure faithful believe, that the school would have been the national champion in 1970, if not for Lanier having been injured in the late moments of a rout of Villanova in the East Region championship game in Columbia, S.C. The Bonnies went to the Final Four in College Park, Md., and lost a close game in the national semifinals to Jacksonville University, led by future NBA star Artis Gilmore. Lanier was considerably better than Gilmore. If Lanier had played, the Bonnies would have beaten Jacksonville and played for the national title against perennial championship contender UCLA ... a UCLA team that no longer had Kareem Abdul-Jabbar and did not yet have the services of the hugely talented Bill Walton. It was a beatable UCLA squad. But not for Jacksonville, which fell to the Bruins in the title game.

St. Bonaventure remains the smallest college ever to make the Final

Four.

Reaching for 1970 to establish your school's high-water mark is tell-tale in and of itself. But that is the scale of things when you are not Michigan State or Louisville or North Carolina, and you are St. Bonaventure, located in hardscrabble Olean on New York's Southern Tier, and the closest thing to a real city is Buffalo 70 miles to the north. And college basketball has been radically made over in the past five decades in favor of the huge schools in huge conferences doted on by national television.

The Bonnies made the NCAA Tournament in 2000 and lost in double overtime to Kentucky in a first-round game. And in 2012, the team won the Atlantic 10 Conference Tournament and the automatic bid to the NCAA tourney. The Bonnies were a 14th seed and led most of the way in a first-round matchup with a nationally ranked Florida State team, before losing, 66-63. The star of that team, Andrew Nicholson, was drafted by Orlando in the first round of that year's NBA draft. He played four seasons with the Magic and now is with the Washington Wizards.

St. Bonaventure won the National Invitation Tournament in 1977.

The lore of the Bonaventure basketball program is rooted in a long-ago era, when smaller colleges in the East, places such as Providence, Holy Cross, Duquesne, Niagara, La Salle, Fairfield and others, recruited terrific players from basketball hotbeds in Philadelphia, Washington, New York and Boston. Those days are gone for a number of reasons. African-American ballplayers had found homes at Catholic colleges when some major conferences nationally were not even recruiting blacks. Catholic high schools, once feeders for the Catholic colleges in the East and Midwest, have closed at an alarming rate in the last 15 years. High-quality players are now identified by recruiting services when they are in grade school, creating an unsavory and wide-open marketplace. And these young players have a clear sense of where their best opportunities for exposure reside, resulting in, say, a good player from Nassau County, Long Island ending up in Ames, Iowa or Fayetteville, Ark., and not nearby St. John's.

So those advantages are gone for Bonaventure's basketball program and for programs like it. If a history of success is to lift the Bonnies and the university these days, it will have to be a new one, something built today.

The Bonnies have had success under Head Coach Mark Schmidt. The 2015-16 season will be his ninth in Olean. He inherited a shattered program when he arrived and has steadily built the Bonnies into a winning team in the A-10. Building on that success, however, will be an even stiffer challenge.

Nonetheless, the school has one asset that continues to serve it, something gauzy enough to be difficult to describe but real enough that it can't be ignored: St. Bonaventure University places a firm emotional grip on the people who come to know it. Students love being there. Brilliant professors arrive and stay for 40 and 50 years. Alumni cherish the place. Pete Thamel, now with ESPN.com, wrote this for a piece in the New York Times when the Bonnies won the A-10 Conference Tournament and were heading for Nashville for their first-round game in the NCAA Tournament four years ago:

Every university in America — from Maine to Hawaii — has a proud alumni base. But if you have ever shared a cubicle or a lunch room with a St. Bonaventure graduate, you will be exposed to rare levels of loyalty and partisanship. Schmidt jokingly and endearingly calls it a "cult."

That loyalty was manifest in Nashville in March of 2012. Bonaventure supporters were as obvious a presence in the town as the loyalists from Florida State, the University of Texas and Cincinnati. They camped out for two days in one of the larger bar-restaurants on Nashville's non-stop entertainment row. One Bonaventure alum, a high-ranking executive with Delta Airlines, freed up a plane to fly fans from Buffalo to Nashville at a cut-rate cost. On game day, buses loaded with Bona alums residing in North Carolina, most of them employees in Charlotte's robust financial industry, made the 400-mile trip overnight, arriving just in time for a 9 a.m. beer blast in a Nashville honky-tonk. You could not get in the place. Tipoff for the Bonaventure vs. Florida State game was noon.

Why such affection for a small college? Maybe a remote place enfolds those who spend time in it. Maybe it's the campus, which is spread over 500 acres and is distinctively beautiful. Not august like Columbia or classic like Princeton or commanding like Penn State, but beautiful in its setting and its architecture, some of it older but striking, some of it freshly built but gorgeously blended, and for the way the campus seems to represent the humanistic values of its Franciscan founders.

The influence of the Franciscan friars, their belief in the goodness and worth of every individual, their devotion to lives spent serving others, their academic heft, contribute to the aura of the place. A friar trudging through snow to teach a class, his wind-whipped brown robes stark against an all-white landscape, is, well, a hell of a thing to see. In the hearts and minds of people who have come to know it, Bonaventure is a place bless-ed. An institution that inspires a lifetime of loyalty from the people it has touched.

There are 29,000 living alumni of St. Bonaventure University, and since it is human nature that people want their choices and backgrounds and experiences to be ratified, a heavy burden falls on the men's basketball program: It is, by far, the greatest marketing tool, the readiest endorsement for the worth of the place. It shouldn't be like that, of course, but it is. Re-sources are limited at a small school; for example, I don't ever recall see-ing even a modest advertisement for St. Bonaventure in one of the several college special sections the Sunday New York Times publishes each year. Basketball brings St. Bonaventure's name to significant markets, places like Philadelphia, New York, St. Louis, Richmond, Washington, Charlotte. Bas-ketball gets the school on regional and national telecasts. Basketball can reach prospective students, or their parents. It can make alumni dig deeper for donations.

Thus, there is a pressure for the school's sports teams, especially men's basketball, to draw attention to the university, so that it stays healthy, that it remains secure, that it has a future simply because it has benefited so many others. And it is a different kind of pressure than what bears down on, say, the football coaches and players at the University of Mich-

17

igan when they run out of the tunnel at the Big House in front of 100,000 fans, all of whom really just want their allegiance to be repaid with a victory. If Michigan didn't win a football game for five years, there would still be 45,000 students there, still only three of every 10 applicants would be admitted, the faculty would still be world-class and Ann Arbor would remain a classic college town. None of those ingredients exists in Olean.

Pressure abounds at St. Bonaventure University these days. It has always been a small college, but too-few students have created a financial crisis. Undergraduate enrollment used to be about 2,200. It was only 1,687 in the first semester of 2015. Tuition is the primary revenue-generator for most schools, so the consequences are considerable, threatening. Demographics indicating a sharp decrease in the population of college-aged students, the costs of a college education, crushing student debt, a sluggish economy and stalled wages have combined to make these trying times for many colleges to attract students, especially the small, private colleges. That puts St. Bonaventure in a bull's-eye.

Industry experts and academics are predicting a number of these schools will shut down. One administrator predicts 30 percent of these schools will not exist by 2024. Public universities, significantly less expensive in many cases, are more of an option for students and their parents these days. St. Bonaventure is in the same region as the huge and prosperous University at Buffalo, and state colleges in nearby Geneseo, Brockport and Fredonia, all part of the widely respected State University of New York system.

Large endowments will help other private schools to ride out the conditions. St. Bonaventure's endowment is tiny, about $62 million. For a sense of scale, A-10 rival St. Louis University has an endowment of $1 billion.

The situation resulted in the Bonaventure administration and its board of trustees to do what once would have been unthinkable: Consider leaving the top tier of college sports, the NCAA Division I level, and instead compete at the less-costly Division II or Division III level. Instead of the opportunity to meet Kentucky or Florida State in the NCAA tournament, instead of playing conference foes the rank of George Washington or Dayton or Massachusetts or Virginia Commonwealth, the Bonnies would tangle with the Rochester Institute of Technology or Keuka College. It would save money. But it would topple St. Bonaventure from whatever toehold it had created for itself in the world of college sports. It would assure the legacy of its basketball program would recede and be lost to the mists of time. The school's top officers and its board of trustees, after long and intensive research, decided in the spring of 2015 to remain in Division I. Basically, they decided what would be lost would be unaffordable.

So that was the atmosphere in which Mark Schmidt and his assistants prepared the Bonnies for the 2015-16 basketball season. Schmidt no longer is simply the coach of the smallest school in the Atlantic 10 Conference, he is now the coach of the third-smallest program in all of Division I. Only Presbyterian College and Wofford College, both in South Carolina, have fewer undergraduate students, and those schools play in conferences that are dwarfed by the firepower of the Atlantic 10. The other 350 Division I basketball schools are larger, richer and have more students. Most of them are exponentially larger.

This proposes to be a different sort of college basketball book. It will spend little or no time considering the plights of Indiana or Duke, the wardrobes of coaches such as Jay Wright and Rick Pitino, the obsequious pronouncements of Dick Vitale, or the tiresome drama of how many Big 10 Conference teams should be stuffed into the NCAA Tournament field of 68. Instead, it concentrates on one team, one coach, one school and a season that unfolds amid a crisis.

Location, size, finances and the powerful schools that comprise the Atlantic 10 Conference assure that St. Bonaventure would be an underdog in any season. After the decision to remain Division I, the stakes are higher this season for Mark Schmidt, who might just have the toughest job in college basketball yet is coming off back-to-back 18-win seasons. An argument can be made that no coach in the nation does more with less. Schmidt is likely the best coach in the history of St. Bonaventure basketball. In fact, given what he confronts, he might be the best coach anywhere.

One last thing: I am a graduate of St. Bonaventure. I was there from 1968 to 1972, the finest of times for Bonnies basketball. From time to time, I will draw on my own Bonaventure experiences and familiarity, in the hope of lending perspective.

CHAPTER 1:
TO KNOW MARK SCHMIDT

The thing you notice when you first meet Mark Schmidt is his size. He is taller and stronger than he appears to be when kinetically stalking the sidelines during a game, arms waving, his go-to blue blazer astir as he fast paces his half of the court and delivers loud and non-stop instructions to his players. He looks like a Division I athlete, someone who played from 1982 to 1985 on very good teams at Boston College, when the Eagles were a force in the Big East Conference, three times went deep in the NCAA Tournament, and filled the Conte Pavilion in Chestnut Hill, Mass. Schmidt describes himself as just "a role player" on those squads.

The next surprise is his demeanor: outgoing, friendly, witty, quick with a smile. From afar, it seems Schmidt is only dutiful as it regards dealing with the media, that he tolerates it because it is part of the job, but not anything he enjoys. Steve Mest, the sports information director at St. Bonaventure, makes this point: "Do you know who (Schmidt's) favorite coach is? Bill Belichick." Nonetheless, Schmidt, while always pressed for time, is good to be around.

Schmidt's office is part of a warren of rooms tucked above the rest of the athletic offices a floor below in the sprawling Reilly Center on the campus. His assistant coaches have offices on the other side of a stairway. Schmidt's own office is a large and comfortable one, with a big desk, so that Schmidt --- who is not much for e-mail or computer programs --- has room to sketch plays on paper. This amuses his assistant coaches, until it is time for them to force feed to the players the groaning playbook of four continuing offenses versus a man-to-man defense, three continuing offenses versus a zone and some 80-plus set plays.

The room is well-appointed and includes the kind of keepsakes that end up in the workplace of a head coach in most any sport. On a long table behind the desk is a box of Flutie Flakes, with a photo of the star quarterback on the front of the cereal box. Schmidt actually roomed at BC with Doug Flutie and Gerard Phelan, the passer and receiver in one of the most dramatic scoring plays in college football history. To get to Schmidt's office, one must be cleared by his secretary, the able and amiable Bobi Cornelius, and then through the workspace of Matt Pappano, the young director of basketball operations and the go-to guy on many aspects of the program. So the suite is a self-contained command center and you get the feeling Schmidt likes its isolation, because there is little room for wasted motion in Mark Schmidt's world.

The 2015-16 season will be Schmidt's ninth at St. Bonaventure. It might not have happened. His alma mater interviewed him for its head coaching job after Boston College dismissed Steve Donahue in April of 2014. But the job went to Jim Christiansen, who had been the head coach of Ohio University. If Schmidt was disappointed with the decision, he doesn't show it. Asked if he enjoys living in Olean his answer comes quickly and emphatically: "I love it up here," he said. "No one bothers me, no one messes with me. I have a small group of friends who I play golf with. I have a house on a golf course. My wife's family is in Pittsburgh, so it is easy for her to see them."

Schmidt is the father of three sons, one of whom, Nicholas, the oldest, plays basketball at Alfred University, an hour's drive east from Olean. Derek and Michael play for Olean High School's basketball squad. Schmidt's salary these days is about $650,000, which goes a long way in a place where the average per capita income is a bit over $25,000.

Schmidt's coaching career began at St. Michael's College in Winooski, Vt., just outside Burlington. He was paid $6,300 a year. He was there two years. He then made the incremental job moves that most any aspiring assistant coach must do: Two seasons as an assistant at Penn State, one season at Loyola University in Baltimore and seven seasons at Xavier University, where he coached the big men, including All-American Doug West, and learned about life as well as basketball from head coach Skip Prosser, a formative influence in Schmidt's career.

In 2001 Schmidt left Xavier to become head coach of Robert Morris University in Pittsburgh. The Colonials play in the Northeast Conference, a one-bid conference as it regards the NCAA Tournament. The team was 12-

18 in Schmidt's first year, and his best record there, 17-11, was in the 2006-07 season, his final year at Robert Morris. His time with the Colonials was not a staggering success overall, but as he has managed at St. Bonaventure, his program steadily improved. Heading in to the final season, his record for the previous five years was 65-79. The team was 15-14 in 2005-06 and lost in the NEC semifinals. Robert Morris returned four starters in Schmidt's last year in Moon Township and a writer for the Beaver County Times, John Perrotto, raised the possibility that a strong season could lead to other schools eyeing Schmidt:

"Mark Schmidt is in his sixth year at RMU, and this year may be his ticket out. If he can win with a tremendous group that he's put together, Schmidt could be moving up the coaching ladder. But he's not the type to coach for another job. However, he probably didn't envision his first head-coaching job would be his last, so he likely has at least thoughts of moving on."

His last season at Robert Morris included a win at home over Duquesne and victories at Canisius and Marshall.

Perroto's prediction was on target. Schmidt received a phone call from Steve Watson, the athletic director at St. Bonaventure, who was looking for a head coach. Watson had fired Anthony Solomon after four impossible seasons ... impossible because Solomon, an assistant coach at Notre Dame, agreed to take control of a flat-out disaster in the wake of "the welding certificate scandal" that broke in March of 2003. The school had admitted an athletic forward from a junior college in Georgia. But he did not earn an associate's degree. He earned a certificate in welding. Everyone up the chain of command strenuously argued against giving the player a scholarship, that the player was ineligible. The president of the university, Robert Wickenheiser, decided the player was eligible to play. Wickenheiser, Jan van Breda Kolff, the head coach, and Gothard Lane, the athletic director, were all dismissed by the board of trustees. Key players left for other schools to escape the penalties Bonaventure received for admitting and playing an academically unqualified player. Solomon took over a ravaged program and his four-year tenure was abysmal. The ashes of the program were still red hot when Watson called Schmidt.

Schmidt was in a hotel room in Atlanta when Watson called. They were both in town because it was the Final Four weekend, which is a must-attend event for all flavors of basketball types. The National Association of Basketball Coaches holds a convention at the Final Four site each March. Watson asked Schmidt if he could go to Watson's hotel room to discuss the Bonaventure opening.

"I didn't bring a lot of clothes," Schmidt recalled. "So I walked over in a sweat suit. I didn't know anything at all about Steve Watson. When he opened the door, I said to myself 'holy shit.' The guy is 6-foot-9. We just started talking, and the longer it went on, the more it became like two friends talking.

"I became more and more comfortable with him. Our personalities meshed."

Watson heard good things from several different people before he called Schmidt. But beyond those endorsements, the thing that impressed Watson was Schmidt's devotion to his family. "At a place like St. Bonaventure, that stuff is important," Watson said. "Very quickly, I knew we weren't just hiring Mark, we would be hiring Mark, Anita and the three boys.

Most of what Schmidt knew about St. Bonaventure was the result of his being at Xavier University, a longtime Atlantic 10 Conference rival. The teams played each season, and Schmidt had made the trips to Olean and the Reilly Center. Schmidt had made one other visit to Bonaventure. Robert Morris played the Bonnies in Solomon's first game as the head coach. Solomon's team won, one of the 24 victories he compiled in four years.

"The place was packed," Schmidt said. "The little guy, Marques Green, ran all over the place and had a big game." Green was a tiny point guard, maybe 5-foot-6, recruited out of Norristown, Pa., who embarrassed opposing guards with his incredible quickness, made all of his teammates look good by driving the lane and dishing off, and could nail three-point shots all night. Green made real the phrase "ankle-breaker." He was that quick, that hard to defend. Green had 17 points, six rebounds, eight assists and just three turnovers in 39 minutes when the Bonnies clobbered Connecticut, 88-70, three nights after Christmas in 2001. The nearly 17,000 fans of the Huskies started exiting the Hartford Civic Center with about eight minutes to play. And that was a superb UConn team, which included future NBA players Emeka Okafor and Caron Butler and advanced to the Elite Eight in that year's NCAA Tournament.

As Watson and Schmidt continued to talk in the next few days,

Schmidt became more comfortable. Schmidt contends he was unbothered by the fact that he wasn't the first choice for the job, that Will Brown, the head coach at the University at Albany, had very publicly been discussing the position with Watson and then turned down the offer to coach the Bonnies, deciding to stay at Albany. The notion that Albany, a State University of New York campus and a member of the America East Conference, was a better coaching situation than storied St. Bonaventure and the A-10 was a hard jolt and a stinging insult to fans of the Bonnies. That negative impression would be noted by others who were knowledgeable about or involved in college basketball: coaches, athletic directors, media, analysts, recruiting gurus and potential recruits. It took a toll and assured Bonaventure's recovery would be hugely challenging. It must be noted that Brown has dominated the America East in recent years and taken Albany to the NCAA Tournament five times since 2006, including the 2013, 2014 and 2015 seasons.

Schmidt remembers being unmoved by it all. "Why should I care?" he recalled. Schmidt retained his interest in the job, and the budding relationship with Watson was the key factor.

"I felt like he would have my back," Schmidt said of Watson. And he recalled another thing Prosser had once told him. "It isn't where you are coaching," Schmidt said. "It is who you work for."

Prosser also told Schmidt that Bonaventure was once a great program and there was no reason it couldn't be good again. Schmidt became the head coach of the St. Bonaventure men's basketball program in the spring of 2007.

Schmidt's record after eight seasons in Olean is 124-123.

Being a coach of any kind was not a long-held dream of the young Mark Schmidt. He played basketball at Bishop Feenan High School, located in Attleboro, Mass., and founded in 1961 by the Sisters of Mercy. His career on the court as a Shamrock earned him a place in Feenan's athletic hall of fame.

He was recruited to Boston College by the legendary Coach Tom Davis, who left BC after Schmidt's freshman season to take the head-coaching job at Stanford. Davis was succeeded by Gary Williams, another remarkable coach, who had BC ranked as high as No. 11 in 1983, No. 6 in 1984 and No. 12 in 1985, Schmidt's last season at Chestnut Hill. Williams left for Maryland, his alma mater, at the end of the 1985-86 season. He made Maryland a national power and won the 2002 national championship.

Schmidt entered BC's college of arts & sciences as a freshman. In one of those meetings that all freshmen must endure, Schmidt was asked by a guidance counselor what he wanted to do professionally. "I said I wanted to make a lot of money," Schmidt remembered. He transferred to the school of business and majored in marketing. "I never once thought about coaching," Schmidt said.

Life being what it is, Schmidt did not have a job after college and surely wasn't making any money. He took a job stacking Bayer aspirin on supermarket shelves. "The key was making sure that the Bayer brand was at eye level on the shelves," said Schmidt. So he was back at home and decided to do substitute teaching, including at Bishop Feenan. He was soon roped in to being an assistant coach for the football and basketball teams. Being a basketball coach clicked. "It became my passion," Schmidt said. "I couldn't wait for the bell to ring to end class and get to the basketball team."

A series of connections resulted in the offer of an assistant coaching position at St. Michael's College, a Division II program on a pretty campus outside bustling Burlington and a location that hardened Schmidt for Olean winters. His $6,300 salary included selling advertisements for the programs distributed to fans at the basketball games. There was one proviso and it came from a priest at the college: Bars were not allowed to buys ads.

"If you have ever been to Burlington," Schmidt said, of the state's largest city and home to the University of Vermont, "you know there are hundreds of bars. I couldn't sell them ads." Strapped for cash, Schmidt's mother paid his car loan.

But his time in Vermont would provide a life-altering bit of good fortune. Schmidt was standing in line at a fast-food restaurant in Burlington when he saw a guy, someone he had met recently at a wedding in New York City. That fellow invited Schmidt to join him skiing and then on to a house party in Burlington. At the party, with a group of friends, was Anita, an industrial engineer sent to Burlington by her company to help manage a project. A relationship blossomed.

Mark Schmidt and Anita Bacho were married on Sept. 7, 1991.

Schmidt's ninth year at St. Bonaventure presents several testy challenges. For the first time in seven seasons, he will not have a major presence inside, a quality big man. Andrew Nicholson improved in huge increments over his four seasons, which ended in 2012 with his being named Atlantic 10 Conference Player of the Year. When the Bonnies defeated Xavier in Atlantic City that year to win the conference tournament and a trip to the NCAA Tournament, Nicholson had a commanding performance, scoring 28 points, grabbing 14 rebounds and recording eight blocked shots. Nicholson is likely the second-best big man in the school's history, second only to Bob Lanier, whose signature is scrawled on the Reilly Center court.

In Nicholson's final season he had a young and raw freshman teammate, Youssou Ndoye, a 6-foot-11 native of Senegal, who was off everyone's radar. Schmidt found him at a prep school in northern Maine. Schmidt recalls people laughing when Ndoye was offered a scholarship. Ndoye was hungry, and he watched and learned from Nicholson in the one year they were teammates. Ndoye improved with each season and by his senior year was a double-double per game in points and rebounds and the best shot-blocker in the conference. Schmidt described Ndoye as a gym rat and a "sponge" as it regarded instruction and practice. Ndoye is now in the NBA's developmental league and signed by the San Antonio Spurs.

Schmidt does have two big men on this season's roster, the 6-10 redshirt center Jordan Tyson, and a 6-9 freshman, Derrick Woods, who is strong and runs the floor well. Schmidt and David Moore, the assistant coach who works with the big men, believed Tyson was much improved and ready to be the starting center. But Tyson tried to play through what he believed was a sprained wrist only to discover it was a torn tendon.

It required surgery. So Tyson would miss at least a good portion of the non-conference schedule as he rehabbed his injury. They hoped to get him some minutes before conference play began.

The coaches also believed they had a starter and a big-time scorer in Courtney Stockard, an athletic 6-foot-5 guard who put up points and also rebounded well at Allen Community College. In his second year with Allen, which plays in the well-regarded Kansas Jayhawk Community College Conference, Stockard averaged 23 points. Schmidt had recruited Stockard to replace the graduated Andell Cumberbatch, another big guard, a decent scorer and the best defensive player on last year's team. But Stockard broke his foot in practice in October, and had to be redshirted for the 2015-16 season.

So before the season even started, the team was smaller, younger, less experienced and lacking depth.

Schmidt also would have a new boss. Tim Kenney is the new athletic director, replacing Steve Watson, who moved on to the AD job at Loyola University in Chicago. Kenney had been an assistant AD at the University of Massachusetts, so he arrived in Olean already holding Schmidt in high regard for how he has improved the men' basketball program. Kenney also walked in to the buzz-saw of a university reconsidering if it could afford to be Division I and joined every other ranking administrator at the place in having to trim budgets. Schmidt and Kenney genuinely seem to like one another. Schmidt said he credits Kenney for having "new ideas."

Kenney's motto is, "Ideas trump finances." That's good news, because there is not a storehouse of finances at St. Bonaventure.

Finally, the 2015-16 Atlantic 10 men's basketball conference looks to be a slow crawl through barbed wire. The good teams are better than a season ago and the weaker teams seem much improved. Conference play will be a meat-grinder.

CHAPTER 2:
'WE HAVE TO PLAY FAST'

St. Bonaventure entered the 2015-16 season coming off back-to-back seasons of 18 wins. That is no small thing given the challenges the Bonnies face. Only four teams in the A-10 had managed at least that many victories in the previous two seasons. The others include Virginia Commonwealth, which had 26 wins in each of those campaigns. Dayton won 26 in the 2013-14 season and 27 the next year. George Washington had 24 victories at the end of the 2014 season and 22 the next season. Richmond won 19 and 22 games in those two seasons.

That Mark Schmidt's ninth season in Olean would begin with an overall winning record is rather remarkable given the ugly thicket he walked in to when he accepted the job in the spring of 2007.

Bonaventure finished seventh in the conference last season, and then beat La Salle in the A-10 tournament before losing a close game to Dayton in the next round. The overall record was 18-15. The Bonnies were 10-8 versus conference opponents.

In a poll of Atlantic 10 coaches, Bonaventure was picked to finish in eighth place in the 14-team league in the 2015-16 season. The coaches expected Dayton to finish first, followed by Rhode Island, Davidson, George Washington, Virginia Commonwealth, Richmond, St. Joseph's, St. Bonaventure, La Salle, Massachusetts, Duquesne, St. Louis, George Mason and Fordham. An online outfit called collegesportsmadness.com rated the Bonnies preseason at No. 83 in the nation. Eighty-three in a field of 353 Division I teams isn't all that bad, but six A-10 teams were rated higher, with Dayton the best at No. 38.

The only Bonaventure player to receive a preseason honor from the conference coaches was guard Marcus Posley, who was selected to the second team.

Before his operation for the torn tendon in his wrist, Jordan Tyson was expected to be the starting center. Dave Moore, the assistant coach who works closely with the inside players, believed Tyson, who had added weight and muscle to his 6-foot-10 frame, was much improved from his freshman year, when a broken jaw suffered in practice led to his being redshirted for the year. Schmidt also expected Tyson to be the starting center. So before the season began, Tyson would either be unavailable for much of the non-conference schedule or miss another season entirely. Derrick Woods, an athletic but unpolished freshman, would now get some minutes in the post.

The loss of Tyson would ripple through the rest of the roster: Dion Wright, an athletic and skilled senior but just 6-foot-7, would spend a lot of time as the virtual center. Denzel Gregg, 6-foot-6 and entering his junior season, would see significant minutes as an undersized power forward. The loss of Courtney Stockard, expected to be a tall third guard, meant that the Bonnies would have three small guards playing together in stretches. Jaylen Adams, who might very well have been the A-10 rookie of the year in the 2014-15 season if he had not injured his hand midway through the conference schedule, would be the starting point guard, his natural position. But he would, at times, move to a shooting-guard position --- not a problem, because Adams is a fine shooter, including from behind the three-point arc. A scintillating prospect, Nelson Kaputo, a 6-foot freshman from Toronto, would be used as a point guard for stretches, as he, Adams and Posley would form a three-guard unit.

Kaputo was recruited by Assistant Coach Jerome Robinson, who played guard at Bradley University. Along with speed, the ability to drive and a good outside shot, including from behind the three-point arc, Kaputo showed another attribute that impressed Robinson. "I was watching his team from Toronto play a team from Detroit, and it was a war," Robinson recalled. "At one point, Kaputo goes in to the lane and gets hammered. He loses one of his front teeth. He has a big gap showing. And he was on his hands and knees looking for the tooth. His coaches tried to take him out of the game, but Kaputo refused to leave. So the kid is tough."

Kaputo is also high-energy, outgoing and very well-spoken. His major is journalism and mass communications and he wants to be a sports broadcaster. And that seems entirely plausible. Kaputo was ranked as one of the best point guards in Canada and he was considered a very good recruit by the Bonnies' staff. He is also a left-hander, which is sometimes hard to watch when the player is a point guard, kind of like trying to cut your hair in a mirror. Robinson believes that can be an advantage.

"A left-handed point guard can be an advantage on drives in to the lane," Robinson explained. "Defenders are conditioned to react to right-handers. They are used to moving to their left on defense. Defending a left-hander is different."

A rotation that would have Kaputo, Adams, Posley, Gregg and Wright on the floor for much of the time would give Bonaventure a fast and athletic lineup. It would also be a Lilliputian lineup, which could be challenged on defense by teams with big guards who would shoot over them or muscle past them on drives, and be pounded on both the offensive and defensive boards by bigger, stronger forwards and centers.

That was the calculus that confronted Schmidt: Would speed and offensive firepower overcome a lack of size and a lineup that would be more dependent on freshmen, Woods and Kaputo, than imagined? And it would be a short bench. Idris Taqqee, a strong 6-foot-4 guard, was a fine defensive player and a good rebounder who saw time last season as a freshman but was not much of a scorer. LaDarien Griffin, a 6-foot-6 freshman from Florida, would be eligible but would be unlikely to get much playing time.

For Schmidt and his three assistant coaches, the formula would have to be team speed and an ability to make the game be played "between the foul lines," as Schmidt described it. There would be no Youssou Ndoye to secure the paint, no one to stymie opposing guards who beat their defenders or muscular forwards who might force their way to the rim or dominate the rebounding.

"We have to play fast," Schmidt said. "We have to play the game between the foul lines, not below them." This would be akin to hockey these days, where offense is created by the speed and decision-making that happens between the blue lines, rather than just dumping the puck in to the corners and chasing after it, grappling for the puck and hoping it finds its way to the stick of a teammate set up on the crease.

There were other keys. Avoid foul trouble. And get a combined 55 points each contest from Posley, Adams and Wright. Gregg has to be a significant contributor. Schmidt has taken to describing Gregg as "the X-factor." The coach used that term in a number of preseason interviews. Schmidt also said Idris Taqqee must "make his presence known, whether it is some points, forcing turnovers or on defense." The coaches liked Taqqee last season, and he played some meaningful minutes as a freshmen. He was a good enough football player in high school and at prep school that he drew some interest from Southeastern Conference schools.

Gregg spent the summer in 2015 in Indianapolis, working on his strength and conditioning and playing ball. The work seemed to make a difference. Some of his teammates believed Gregg had markedly improved over the summer months and that he would be a difference-maker this season. A finance major with hopes of being a money manager and investor, Gregg is a fine athlete, fast and able to elevate. Schmidt is serious about the talk of Gregg as the "X-factor." The coach mentioned it in an interview at the Atlantic 10 Conference pre-season media event, and you had the feeling Schmidt had a target audience of one --- Gregg. It let the Syracuse native know there was pressure on him to perform.

Everyone seemed sold on the strategy. Robinson, the second-year assistant coach, was confident because of the combined strengths of Posley, Adams and Wright. Assistant Coach Steve Curran shared Schmidt's concerns about interior defense. And the most critical personnel were nearly ebullient. Posley recalled that Dayton flourished the season before with a small lineup, "and if Dayton could do it, we can do it." Adams said that the injuries to Tyson and Stockard meant, "We play fast, play aggressive defense and stay out of foul trouble." And Wright said he was confident about the season, and that defense was imperative. He also added: "Since I am an undersized five, I'll use my speed to beat my man to the spot, and not play behind him."

Schmidt chooses not to be expansive with the media. In fact, he admits to telling what he terms "half-truths," accurate information but delivered in doses so scant he surrenders nothing much strategically. But at the Atlantic 10 Conference media day in Brooklyn just before the start of the season, Schmidt did have interesting things to say. When it was remarked that Schmidt has managed to compile a winning record in his first eight years at Bonaventure, he credited getting "good players but under the radar, guys other coaches might see as not big enough, not strong enough." He said he values players who have character and who can overcome adversity. He offered Ndoye as an example: "People laughed when we gave

Youssou a scholarship," Schmidt said. "But he is a sponge. He is in the gym every day. He went from being laughed at to the San Antonio Spurs."

Schmidt also said this year's team needs Posley to be "a great leader." He also said Posley needs to raise his shooting percentage. "We need a big year from him," Schmidt explained. "He can be a really good player." Also mentioned was Wright, saying he epitomizes the kind of player Schmidt has been able to find, that he was under-recruited and that "he has worked his tail off." Schmidt called Wright "one of the 15 best players in the league."

Ben Howland, who was the head coach at Pitt and then UCLA, which he took to the national championship game in 2006, was a color commentator for the NBC Sports Network in the 2014-15 season. Howland now is in his first season as the head coach at Mississippi State. He came to Olean to do a conference game and was very impressed with Wright ... partially for the fact Howland never heard of Wright, who grew up in Carson, Calif., about 15 miles from the UCLA campus. Howland marveled at the job that Schmidt has done in getting players to a place as small and out-of-the-way as Bonaventure.

The ability to recruit players that were passed over by other DI programs and turn them in to solid performers, the kind of athletes that have made Bonaventure very competitive in a conference as daunting as the Atlantic 10, has been a hallmark of Schmidt's tenure. It has to be, given the size of Bonaventure and its location. And his players improve over the seasons under the coaching of Schmidt and his assistants. The Bonnies rarely sign a highly recruited athlete, a four-star or a five-star player, as adjudged by the online recruiting sites that dissect a 16-year-old kid as if he were a frog in a biology lab.

Andrew Nicholson is a classic example of Schmidt luring an under-recruited player and transforming him, over the course of four seasons, in to the best player in the conference and a first-round selection in the 2012 NBA draft. Schmidt is also an excellent tactician, finding opponents' weaknesses and exploiting them while maximizing the strengths of his own players. Schmidt is an X's and O's junkie. The strategizing is probably the aspect of the job that he most relishes.

So that was the cast that Schmidt and his coaches readied for the season. The team faced an 11-game non-conference schedule, one that would not require the Bonnies to play anywhere but in the state of New York. The parochial quality of the non-conference slate caused disappointment and hand-wringing from some fans, especially the ones that populate the online community known as the Bona Bandwagon. The schedule included no ranked teams, no marquee names, with the exception of a game at the Carrier Dome versus Syracuse, and the Orange were expected to struggle some this season.

Supporters fretted that the non-league schedule would hurt Bonaventure's strength-of-schedule rating, which is a critical ingredient as it regards at-large bids to the NCAA Tournament and the National Invitation Tournament. It also meant that the Bonnies would not get the exposure that would come from visiting, say, Notre Dame or Ohio State or Florida, playing in front of tens of thousands of fans and, certainly, regional or national television. In other words, new opportunities to exhibit Bonaventure basketball, to catch the attention of high school coaches and quality young players in markets that know little or nothing about a small Franciscan school in New York's Southern Tier that plays in a big-time conference and dreams big dreams.

Schmidt defends the non-conference schedule, claiming most of those teams will be strong contenders in their various conferences, top-flight teams.

The season would begin at home on the late afternoon of Saturday, Nov. 7 with an exhibition game against Mansfield University, a Division II school in the north-central mountains of Pennsylvania. The Mounties bus up to Corning and then head west on Interstate 86, which everyone still calls Route 17, for two hours. It is a manageable trip, and Mansfield has been the exhibition opponent for the Bonnies for a number of seasons now. What happens next is rarely pretty, but the Mounties get to play against a Division I opponent, in a large venue and in front of a crowd that is bigger and more boisterous than what they draw when they play, say, at East Stroudsburg or Millersville or any other member of the Pennsylvania Collegiate Athletic Conference. This visit was about as ugly as it gets, with Bonaventure winning, 108-48.

The starting lineup surprised some folks. Posley, Adams and Wright were joined by Woods and sophomore Idris Taqqee. Gregg was the first forward to come off the bench and Kaputo was the first guard. He would score 11 points. He was 3-for-7 from the three-point line and provided four assists.

It was 21-4 with less than eight minutes gone when Jaylen Adams scored on a dunk. It was 58-19 at the half. The Bonnies had 24 points in the paint, 13 second-chance points and 23 points off turnovers. In the second half, it was 70-20 at one point, 85-31 at the 10-minute mark, and 94-40 with five minutes to play. All nine Bonnies played, with Griffin getting 14 minutes and Caleb McGuire, the team's only walk-on, scoring four points. The Wright-Adams-Posley troika combined for 42 and Denzel Gregg had 23.

After the game, Schmidt allowed that "we didn't play the Lakers," but he liked that everyone saw action and that the Bonnies played at the kind of pace that will be required.

Not much was discussed in Schmidt's press conference about Derrick Woods and defense. Woods played 26 minutes and scored 12 points, including going 4-for-4 from the foul line. He had nine rebounds, five of them offensive rebounds, a very good display, especially so since Woods did not have the benefit of summer strength and conditioning training and summer scrimmages. Instead, he was in summer school back in Pennsylvania to make himself eligible for the 2015-16 season.

But Woods, who clearly would have to provide key minutes, had problems defensively. He fouled out and had real trouble guarding Mansfield's Matt Tamanosky, a 6-foot-5, 240-pound sophomore forward who went 8-for-11 from the field, almost all of that in the lane and while being played, for the most part, by Woods. Tamanosky had 17 points in 33 minutes. Asked about Woods and his defense the next day, Schmidt said, kiddingly, of the Mansfield player: "That guy wouldn't have scored on me."

CHAPTER 3:
REMAINING DIVISION I

The decision that St. Bonaventure University would remain a Division I program in athletics and a member of the Atlantic 10 Conference was reached and announced in the spring of 2015. However, the decision was preceded by years of angst and bitterness and, in some pockets of the institution, framed thusly: What matters most to the university? A mid-major basketball program or a thriving academic environment that sustains its faculty and attracts high-achieving students? Because St. Bonaventure cannot afford to have both.

Rigid? Maybe. A gross exaggeration? Probably not.

For years, members of the faculty and school administrators had chafed as their salaries stagnated. One long-tenured professor said the faculty is aged because they can't afford to retire. This is a condition on a number of college campuses these days, some of them good schools. At St. Bonaventure, one irritant became an open conversation: The rising salaries for athletic coaches, especially the basketball coaches, Mark Schmidt and Jim Crowley, whose women's basketball program has achieved in an almost

45

unimaginable fashion, making the women's Sweet 16 in the NCAA Tournament of 2012, the same year the men's team won the A-10 Tournament title and an automatic bid to the NCAAs.

People on campus have been giving voice to the tension created by academics and administrators being underpaid and the basketball coaches being rewarded with large boosts in salaries for years. Barry Gan, who earned a doctorate at the University of Rochester, came to Bonaventure in 1984 and has been a member of the Faculty Senate since 1988, including as its chairman.

He expressed unhappiness with Schmidt's salary weeks after the coach hit campus in the spring of 2007.

"I and other faculty were outraged at the reports of the salary that was currently being offered," Gan said in a letter to the school president. He said he saw the figures in the Olean Times Herald. While members of the Faculty Senate did vote on Gan's motion to decry the new coach's salary, it was simply to see where the senators stood on the issue. Ten of the faculty supported Gan's position, and three others declined to vote yea or nay.

"I don't think there's anything the Faculty Senate can do," Gan said. "Contracts are signed, offers have been made and commitments have been made. I was simply interested in making a point."

Both the Buffalo News and the Olean Times Herald reported that Schmidt signed a seven-year contract worth $2.1 million when he left Robert Morris University to take the job as the Bonnies' head coach in the spring of 2007.

"There are people who work for the university who qualify for food stamps because they're paid so low," Gan said. "It's the apparent hypocrisy of the university when they say they don't have the money for this or that."

Gan's anger came after faculty members were advised in a letter from the school president, Sr. Margaret Carney, that there would be no faculty raises because of budget restraints. An enrollment shortfall was identified as the reason for the frugality. Schmidt's salary, which would have averaged about $300,000 annually, if correctly reported, would have been considerably more than what the president of the university was making at the time, about $125,000. Of course, nowadays it is no huge surprise to discover that football and basketball coaches earn more than their university presidents. It makes no sense, of course, if priorities were even roughly in order, but that's the situation presently.

Eight years later, just about the time the university was deciding that Division I was the best future for the school, the issues were still the same. They were captured in a three-part series by Shawn Campbell, who was about to graduate with a journalism degree from St. Bonaventure in May of 2015, and it centered on the tensions resulting from a tiny, underfunded college competing in a conference as powerful as the A-10. Campbell produced the report as his senior capstone project and it appeared in the Olean Times-Herald on three consecutive Sundays, beginning on May 18, 2015.

Gan was quoted early in that report, and it regarded the fact that St. Bonaventure spent $9.5 million on its sports programs in 2013-14, according to a U.S. Department of Education data analysis. According to Gan, that figure represented one-seventh of the university's overall budget.

"My guess is that there's probably no school in the country that spends one-seventh of its budget on athletics," Gan told Campbell. Gan might be right. An analysis in 2009 by two economists, Jonathan Orszag and Mark Israel, indicated athletic budgets amount to about 6 percent at most universities.

Gan was not the only dissident on campus in 2007, and the tensions over the funding for Division I sports, especially basketball, remained eight years later. Dr. Denny Wilkins, a journalism professor, and a basketball fan often in attendance at games, has had serious concerns about the imbalance for a decade. "Faculty and staff have had no or barely cost-of-living increases in compensation for years," Wilkins told Campbell. "So they look at spending on athletics, it's a symbol. You throw in Division I athletics and a university that is trying to find another thousand students for fiscal sustainability, and you have to ask questions about the priority of Division I spending."

Dan Collins is a 1973 graduate of St. Bonaventure, a middle infielder on the baseball team during his time there, and today the vice president for corporate communications at Corning Inc. His affection for the place is matched by actions and financial contributions. Collins is a vice president of the board of trustees. He is a season-ticket holder for men's basketball games, making the two-hour drive from Corning to Olean on weeknights and weekends.

Collins was long a fan of horse racing, so in 2005 he founded Bona Venture Stables. The organization sells partnership shares in thoroughbreds, and Collins actively manages the operation. Collins has brought both Crowley and Schmidt up to Saratoga during the summer racing season. One of Collins's horses was named Nicholson, in honor of the 2012 A-10 player of the year, and Schmidt and the racehorse were introduced. "Schmidt is not all that comfortable around horses," Collins recalled. "He's kind of nervous around them."

For Collins, the psychic wear-and-tear of the rightness of Division I for a school the size of St. Bonaventure can be traced back to March of 2003, when the NCAA ruled that the Bonnies had been playing all season with an ineligible player and forced that all the wins that season be forfeited, except for one. The immediate aftermath of that was the forced resignation of the school's president, Robert J. Wickenheiser; the departures of the athletic director, as well as the head coach at the time, Jan van Breda Kolff, and the refusal by the team's players to finish out the season. Alumni were devastated. The suicide of Bill Swan, the chairman of the board of trustees, that August was the most anguishing consequence. The next four seasons, under the new head coach, Anthony Solomon, a good man who took on a near-impossible mission, were disastrous. Perhaps a certain what's-the-point malaise was overtaking the program and the school at that point. This was the mess Schmidt walked in to more than nine years ago.

Division I athletics had been "the elephant in the room," as Collins described it, for too long. Collins would know; he has been a board member for 14 years. Finally, in 2014, the university undertook a nearly year-long examination of remaining Division I or dropping down to the less-expensive Division II or III. A committee of board members and administrators, dubbed the Bluebird Committee, was created to study the question and report back to the top-ranking officers and the trustees. The committee was co-chaired by Bob Daugherty, the board's president, and board member Colette Dow.

The process was complicated, of course, but according to Collins, it boiled down to what would be lost by leaving Division I and the Atlantic 10 versus what would be gained by dropping to DII or DIII. Certainly, leaving DI would save some money. For example, Bonaventure travels to far-flung Atlantic 10 sites such as St. Louis, Charlotte and Richmond on behalf of non-revenue sports such as baseball, women's lacrosse, and men's and women's soccer. Much money is spent traveling on behalf of recruitment for DI athletes, especially men's and women's basketball. And, as it regards attracting many more student-athletes, enrollment would be steadied whether these were DI athletes or DII, DIII and club sports athletes.

The money saved from dropping from Division I could be applied to other needs, such as salaries for staff and faculty. And the idea of expanding the roster of sports, whether as a DII or DIII school, would still attract student-athletes who want to compete beyond high school. At least theoretically, enrollment could still expand through athletics while expenses were greatly reduced from the DI level.

Some of the DI expenses were the result of what Collins termed "the nationalizing of conferences." And he is right. On the largest scale, this is evidenced by the conference shuffling that has redrawn the map for big-time college football, and it tugged college basketball along with it. Rutgers now plays Minnesota and Northwestern in the Big 10. Pitt is in the Atlantic Coast Conference, figuring out how to beat North Carolina State and Virginia, and not Penn State or Georgetown. Utah is in the Pac-12. West Virginia, nothing but an eastern school, has no conference foe closer than Ames, Iowa. Most of the other Big 12 teams are in Oklahoma and Texas. Some historic and regional rivalries have been wiped away and travel budgets have ballooned, all in the chase for television dollars and national football championships.

Some of that is clearly evident in the Atlantic 10 Conference. Virginia Commonwealth, Richmond and Davidson, located in North Carolina, were not original A-10 members. Nor was St. Louis. Their arrivals have greatly enhanced the status of the conference, but the enlarged footprint means more expense for sports travel than years ago. It is most obvious in men's and women's basketball, but A-10 softball, women's lacrosse, and men's and women's soccer and swim teams are hurtling between St. Louis and Amherst, Mass., Richmond and Rhode Island.

What would be surrendered by leaving Division I and membership in the A-10 was also quantified, and it was sobering. There is revenue sharing in the Atlantic 10. Real dollars. There is regional and national television money. Collins described that revenue as "considerable." Ticket revenue would be shattered; there would never be 5,400 people in the Reilly Center for a Bonaventure game against, say, Gannon University.

The committee's work also accommodated critical but spiritual implications. There is little chance of overestimating the importance of basketball as the glue that binds alumni. Without big-time basketball, alumni giving would drop, and significantly, the committee projected. Lost also would be the connectedness between the school and its graduates. And might that mean, in a short amount of time, that those alumni would stop urging their children that Bonaventure should be on their short lists for college consideration?

Then there is the question that Tim Kenney raised, just about the time he was talking to Bonaventure about the job as athletic director: "Who do you want to be your peers?" Collins and his committee raised the same question. There must be some value, some measurable benefit to be grouped with institutions such as George Washington University, Davidson College and the University of Richmond. Or Catholic institutions such as St. Joseph's, Dayton and St. Louis, and major research universities such as UMass and Virginia Commonwealth.

The committee considered the benefits and detriments of switching to the Middle Atlantic Athletic Conference, where Niagara, Canisius and Siena, so alike Bonaventure in mission and geography, compete. But the MAAC does not have the geographic reach, the television exposure nor the marketing opportunities that the A-10 provides.

Thirty percent of Bonaventure's enrollment comes from outside New York State, a point made by Carney in a letter to alumni and the school community in the spring of 2015, after the DI decision was finalized. Is it fair to assume some of those students are drawn to the place because of the exposure provided by being a member of the A-10? The committee considered that point, and believed major college basketball was an incentive for prospective students, especially beyond New York State. The number of out-of-state students at Niagara, for example, is only 10 percent, according to Collins.

In the end, the committee reported to the board of trustees that there would be short-term benefits if the university dropped from Division I, but over time, those savings would erode and the greater benefits of Division I and membership in the A-10 would have been sacrificed. The committee recommended remaining Division I in athletics, and the board approved that recommendation.

Division I athletics brings 250 students to the school, according to the committee's report. Expanding DI athletics could raise that figure to 300 in short order and to 400 long-term, the committee determined. How? Suggestions have included a men's lacrosse program, expanding the swim teams and a track program that concentrates on distance events. Kenney was stunned when he learned, shortly after his arrival as the AD, that the women's lacrosse team had a roster of just 20. Kenney thinks it should be somewhere around 40. Again, many of these student-athletes would be receiving partial scholarships. Their presence brings positive revenues from tuition and fees. And their numbers would add to the vitality of the place. There are too many empty dorm rooms, entire floors in some cases, and vacant space once devoted to academics.

Club sports is viewed as another way to attract student-athletes, and strengthening these sports would be another manner of attracting students who played sports in high school and who might be unlikely to compete even at the DII or DIII levels. At one time or another, Bonaventure has listed a roster of club sports that included women's field hockey, men's and women's basketball, men's ice hockey, men's and women's lacrosse, men's and women's running teams, ski racing for men and women, and men's and women's volleyball.

Men's rugby has become a high-profile club sport at Bonaventure, including seven-man rugby, growingly popular at colleges nationwide. There are established conferences for many of these club sports.

The club sports have been "formalized," as faculty member Denny Wilkins described it, with the appointment of a club sports director and the availability of training and strengthening coaching for these athletes. There are some concerns that the school doesn't have the locker room space and other facilities for these added sports, Wilkins said.

Whatever the drama surrounding the DI decision, whatever relief it brought basketball-crazed students and alumni, whatever disappointment it meant for faculty who believe the university's priorities are out of whack, it does not alter one essential reality: Studies upon studies have found that most colleges do not make money from their athletic programs. The revenues spent on sports do not bring substantial profits, or any profits at all in many cases.

As Carney pointed out, athletics bring students to the college that might not be there otherwise, and expanding the sports program might bring even more students. But beyond that, the athletics program does not produce profits.

Kenney, the AD, described the benefits of sports as "non-quantifiable." It brings the school some recognition. There is a quasi-marketing benefit to sports.

If there are any benefits to a university in the way of more applicants or more generous giving by alumni based on winning football and men's basketball programs, they are scant, a Cornell University economist, Robert H. Frank, reported in 2004. Another report, this one in 2010, reported only 14 athletic departments nationally had operating profits. Even in the Southeastern Conference, home, at least these days, to the most consistently powerful football programs, athletics require support from university general funds.

Lastly, studies have debunked what has been called "the Flutie Effect," the notion that Doug Flutie's miracle touchdown pass that beat powerful Miami of Florida in 1984, somehow transformed Boston College. BC already was a rich school that annually had far more applicants than spots available for admission 30-some years ago. The benefits of winning college sports programs were the less-tangible things: school pride, publicity, marketing, keeping tight connections with alumni.

Some ever-hopeful Bonaventure supporters have long embraced the notion that if the Bonnies could achieve what Gonzaga University and Butler University have accomplished in college basketball in the past decade or more, then the future would be blindingly bright. And maybe it would. But Gonzaga and Butler have some assets that do not show themselves in Olean.

Gonzaga has nearly 5,000 undergrads and another 2,400 post-graduates studying in one of seven colleges and schools that comprise the university, including a school of engineering, a law school and a school of nursing and human physiology. Gonzaga bestows both masters and doctoral degrees. Spokane might be difficult to get to from most of the U.S., but it is a city of 208,000. Gonzaga's endowment is $186 million.

Butler, with an endowment of $191 million, has 4,100 undergraduates and offers 18 masters programs and a doctorate in pharmacy. Butler's hometown, Indianapolis, is robust and large enough to have hosted a Super Bowl.

In 2010, Butler's men's basketball program had a .02 percent profit. Gonzaga, the same year, had expenses of $3,053 million but showed a profit of about $1 million. The Zags fell in the second round of the NCAA Tournament in 2010, but Butler made it to the title game, losing by two to Duke.

CHAPTER 4:

SEEING ORANGE

No matter the relative strength of the non-conference schedule, there was pressure on St. Bonaventure to play well before conference games commenced. It was a bit more intense than in other seasons, and for a variety of reasons. In the absence of the injured Jordan Tyson, and given the reliance on the fresh-faced newcomer, Derrick Woods, Bonaventure had to truly perform, and not simply play fast. All the key players loved the notion of a fast-paced style of play, but now there had to be clear evidence that they could do it, that it would be a season-long trademark.

The Bonnies needed to crank out victories, but they also had to prepare themselves for the rigor of the A-10 schedule. Given the question marks that were Tyson and Woods, rebounding and interior defense had to come from others, especially Dion Wright and Denzel Gregg. Both were athletic, but would they hold up in the lane, where physicality and sheer size usually prevail. And the short bench meant that the Bonnies did not have a lot of personal fouls to waste.

The coaches expected, and required, a big-time senior season from Marcus Posley. Jaylen Adams had played wonderfully as a freshman a season ago, starting immediately and showing that he was both a scorer and an assist-making point guard, but his season-ending injury amid conference play assured he did not have a full season of experience.

The non-conference schedule would determine just what kind of a contributor the freshman Nelson Kaputo would be, given that he was straight out of high school in Toronto. Wright could be counted on to score and rebound, and he improved year-by-year in his previous three seasons. But Gregg, the dubbed X-factor, would have to contribute at levels that were not required when he was a freshman and sophomore.

Idris Taqqee was a pleasant surprise as a freshman, tough and athletic at 6-foot-4, and displayed he was good defensively and as a rebounder. But how much offense might he provide in a season when the team lacked a seasoned big-man?

There is the game plan, and then there is the executing of the game plan, and the non-conference challenges would force answers.

BINGHAMTON

Binghamton University provided the first real game of the season, arriving in the Reilly Center on the night of Nov. 13. Binghamton plays in the America East Conference and had a rough season a year ago, starting several freshmen. Binghamton hosted the Bonnies last season and played them very tough in the first half and early in the second half, before

Bonaventure pulled away for the win. Schmidt pointed out those freshmen are now sophomores, and that he expected it would be a good game. He was right.

Woods and Wright each picked up two fouls in the first half, limiting Woods to eight minutes of play and Wright to 14. Binghamton forward Dusan Perovic was the reason for much of that. He had six points and four rebounds in the first half, and his team stayed with the Bonnies on the boards. Nonetheless, Bonaventure made a run, stretching a 14-11 lead at the 11:02 mark to a 30-19 lead with 2:23 left in the half. Jaylen Adams and Denzel Gregg sparked the Bonnies' offense. But Binghamton chewed up that lead quickly, getting a pair of three-pointers and a couple of free throws to make it 30-26 at the half.

This was evidence of another Bonaventure failing that would show itself during the non-conference schedule, an inability to put opponents away when it had the opportunity. Schmidt has an indelicate term to describe a team's killer instinct, one with roots in the Irish Republican Army, according to the coach. "We could have curbed them," he likes to say. Curbing is forcing an enemy or a victim to bite down on a sidewalk or roadway curb, and then stomp the victim's head from behind. The result, when the curbing has been properly applied, does nothing good for the enemy's dental work.

Binghamton flirted with an upset for much of the second half. Wright, Woods and Denzel Gregg spent most of the 20 minutes toiling with foul problems. The Bonnies surrendered the lead to the Bearcats at the 18:30 mark. It was still a 40-40 game with 11:05 to go. A nice feed from Nelson Kaputo to Wright gave the Bonnies a 48-42 lead, but in the last seven minutes, Woods and Wright would shuttle between the bench and the floor because they both had four fouls.

Binghamton closed it to 50-48 on free throws from Justin McFadden with 5:24 to go, but free throws from Woods and a three-point shot from Kaputo made it 55-48 with 4:50 left. Wright's two free throws made that 57-48 with 3:35 to play and the Bonnies won it 63-53. Gregg ended the night with 15 points and 11 rebounds, and Wright had 20 points and nine rebounds. Kaputo played well in his first game, getting seven points and five assists in 23 minutes. Forwards Perovic and Willie Rodriguez combined for 23 points for the Bobcats, who lost the rebound battle 43-37. Missing in action was Marcus Posley, who was just 2-for-10 from the field, one-of-five on three-pointers, for five points. Binghamton helped a bit with 19 turnovers.

Afterward, Schmidt told reporters that he thought Kaputo was the star of the game, for providing a lift when the Bonnies needed it. He also said Binghamton was a team on the rise: "Those freshmen are sophomores now."

SYRACUSE

Ah, Syracuse. This is one New York school that Bonnie fans love to hate, and this season, in just the second game, brings the opportunity to sting the place. Bonnie loyalists hate it because the Orange never board buses and make the easy trip over to Olean for a game in the Reilly Center. They hate Syracuse Coach Jim Boeheim because he doesn't schedule the Bonnies on a regular basis. They hate him because he has forgotten that 35 years ago, when there was no Big East Conference and no Carrier Dome and Syracuse had not won national championships, Bonaventure and the Orange would occasionally encounter one another. And every five years or so, when Syracuse and the Bonnies do play these days, Syracuse wins, further agitating Bonnie fans.

They hate Syracuse and Boeheim because there is absolutely no reason for the coach or the institution to spend much time thinking about the Bonnies, let alone create an annual home-and-home series. In fact, any kind of a relationship beyond a non-conference visit by the Bonnies to the Carrier Dome once every five years or so is wishful thinking.

It has been 17 years since college basketball split like a cell and created high-major college basketball programs and mid-major programs. Syracuse is about as high-major as it gets. Bonaventure is a mid-major, along with other eastern Catholic basketball schools that weren't invited in to the Big East Conference when Dave Gavitt, the pied-piper from Providence, organized it in 1979. For much of the time before the Big East came along, Bonaventure wasn't in a conference. It was an independent, as was the case with most eastern schools. All of that has changed.

The latest collegiate sports convulsion, one of very recent vintage and dictated singularly by big-time college football, the one that has Utah in the Pac-12 and Rutgers in the Big 10 and UConn in with a bunch of bandit schools in some creation called the American Athletic Conference, and Notre Dame playing in the Atlantic Coast Conference, but not for football, joined by the likes of Pitt, Boston College and, yeah, Syracuse, assures the moat that separates royalty from pretenders in college basketball is wide and deep.

And all of that is okay because it must be, and the Bonnies fans should be pleased that their school is in a tough-as-nails conference these days, more than holding its own against powerful state universities and glamorous private institutions, and getting on regional television. But many fans are not, and that says something about high aspirations, or delusions. Beating Syracuse every now and again, when the schools do meet, is a more realistic goal.

So on an unusually balmy Tuesday night, thousands of Bonnies fans trooped in to the colossus that is the Carrier Dome, joining the hometown fans to make for a crowd of 21,379 --- or about six home games worth of fans at the Reilly Center --- to play Syracuse.

Things started very well. Bonaventure opened a 19-8 lead with 11:51 to play on a three-pointer from Posley. They led 24-16 on a Kaputo three-pointer. Then Wright made it 27-16 on a three-point shot that just beat the buzzer on the shot clock. All the while, the Bonnies were doing a good job on the boards and on interior passing that led to baskets inside. A basket by Woods gave Bonaventure a 32-21 lead with 3:20 to play. Syracuse chipped away to make it 35-29 at the half.

There were moments when it appeared that the Bonnies should

be leading by more, when Denzel Gregg, playing in his hometown, was helping Wright score on the inside and Adams and Kaputo were hitting three-pointers. It was an impressive first half nonetheless, especially as it regarded offensive rebounding by the Bonnies, Wright and Gregg in particular.

Bonaventure led 40-31 on a score from Woods, and a jam by Gregg on a pass from Posley provided a 45-35 score with 15:30 to play. But that would be as good as it got. Syracuse extended its zone and the Bonnies were slowed. The sharp offensive sets that had given them a couple of 11-point leads were blunted. The fast breaks of the first half and the interior passing that allowed Wright and Gregg to score inside went missing. Instead, the Bonnies passed the ball aimlessly around the perimeter, rarely getting an opportunity to drive or a good look for a shot.

It took to the 8:34 mark before the Orange took the lead 57-54 on a three-point play. A three-pointer from Jaylen Adams cut the Orange lead to 61-58 with 6:08, but Syracuse pulled away from that point and cruised to a 79-66 win.

Syracuse guards Michael Gbinjie and Trevor Cooney played well in the second 20 minutes. For the game they combined for 41 points. Forward Malachi Richardson helped inside and ended up with 15. For the Bonnies, Adams had 16 points, Wright had 13 and Gregg had 11 points and eight rebounds.

In the postgame interviews, Boeheim said: "I thought St. Bonaventure played great." Generous remarks from Boeheim, who would soon begin a nine-game suspension for improprieties in the program he has guided for decades.

Schmidt said he felt that Syracuse "kind of exposed us defensively in the second half," but he also said "if you get 24 offensive rebounds (as the Bonnies did) you are doing something right." Schmidt, correctly, said Bonaventure lost the game on defense, not because of its offense. The Orange had 50 points in the second half.

Schmidt concluded that if the Bonnies could play as they did in the first half, "We have a chance to be pretty good."

CHAPTER 5:
THE REGION

It is beautiful country, the western stretch of the Southern Tier of New York State. The Allegheny Mountains begin their northeast-to-southwest course and cut through southern Cattaraugus County and plunge in to northwest Pennsylvania. The Allegheny River runs through the valley of this range of mountains. The region is a festival for hunters, fishermen, hikers and skiers. Autumn comes early, and is particularly distinctive in this location. Spring comes late. Summer is mellow. Winter locks the place up, but no one who lives there seems to mind it much. Maybe because that's basketball season. Maybe because Western New Yorkers are sturdy, dependable folks.

The river runs behind the athletic fields of St. Bonaventure University, and the mountains begin to rise just beyond, so close that when you stand in the middle of the campus, it almost seems as if they are an arm's reach away. The setting melds with the architecture to create the beauty of the school's campus. It is a serene, almost contemplative place, maybe exactly what the Franciscan friars had in mind when they founded it more than 150 years ago.

The school straddles the line between the twin towns of Olean and Allegany. Olean has the look and the feel of a small city. Allegany sits more like a village. Together they are home to the university. With the exception of the occasional, low-grade town-and-gown hassles, it is a truly symbiotic relationship. The region's residents are devoted fans, and many are season ticketholders to the basketball games. Local residents often send their kids to the university. The students shop at the malls and stores and frequent the restaurants and bars, and some of those are standouts. More than 500 faculty and staff buy homes, settle in to the community, pay taxes, spend dollars.

The remote location is something of a challenge as it regards recruiting Division I-quality athletes, especially basketball players. It is a bit remote. It is not urban or even suburban. It is not particularly multicultural. Nonetheless, great ballplayers have been coming to Bonaventure for decades. Mark Schmidt and his assistants have been remarkable in finding hidden gems, luring them to the campus and convincing them that the school and its geography, the opportunity to earn a degree and play in the Atlantic 10 Conference is all there for them. Hometowns for this season's roster are as far-flung as California, Georgia, Florida, Missouri and Illinois, and as near as Syracuse. The women's basketball team also ranges far to find players. Good players are primarily interested in where they have the best opportunity to be coached, get playing time and win. And if a player from, say, Newark or Cleveland is put off by the location, his mother is liable to overrule him, seeing the place as safe, devoid of the dangers that lurk in many urban settings.

Schmidt and his coaches have made this process easier for themselves by creating a winning program over the past nine years. Schmidt even has a riff on it: "Other coaches used to say, 'Ah, Olean is a hard place to get to, but once you are there, you probably will win.' "Now they say, 'Olean is a hard place to get to, and you will have a hard time winning when you do get there.'"

But there is trouble on the home front these days, and it is a dilemma that goes far beyond luring athletes to the school. The places that used to reliably feed the enrollment at St. Bonaventure have lost large percentages of their populations, and the people who remain are getting older. These locations have been pipelines to the college, and they are running dry.

Buffalo and Rochester are particularly problematic. Between 1950 and 2000, Buffalo lost nearly 50 percent of its residents. A city created on industry that grew to 580,132 people became home to just 292,684 these days, according to New York State census data. Rochester's population slumped to 219,713 from 332,488. Buffalo had been a thriving steel town, and it sits on Lake Erie, so it made it easy to move product to markets. So much of that is gone today. Kodak propped up Rochester. That has diminished. Niagara Falls was a city of 102,390 in the 1960s, and today has a population just over 50,000.

The hits to Buffalo and Rochester are particularly troublesome for St. Bonaventure. Many students, in any era, were from those two regions.

Western New York is by far the hardest hit region in New York State as it regards lost residents. But Syracuse, in central upstate New York, another place that fed students to St. Bonaventure, is also struggling. Its population dropped from 220,853 in 1950 to 147,306 in 2000, a loss of 33.2 percent, according to census studies. The Mohawk Valley, home to Troy, also has been gushing population.

The state's population growth in the past 20 years or more has been primarily northward out of the New York City metropolitan area. Rockland and Orange Counties are fast-growing. The rest of the Mid-Hudson area is swelling. Even as far north as Saratoga has added population. Long Island is jammed.

New York's Southern Tier stretches from Broome County in the east to Erie, Pa. Drive west on Route 17 (someday to be officially I-86, if federal highway standards are ever met) and thriving communities used to show themselves like a string of Christmas lights pulled taut: Binghamton, Owego, Elmira, Corning, Olean, Jamestown. All of these places sent waves of students to Bonaventure, lots of them coming from Catholic schools that served those locations. Binghamton's population was 85,000 in the early 1950s. Today, Binghamton has just 46,000 residents. Elmira has lost 38 percent and Corning 39 percent of their residents. Jamestown's population has declined from 43,000-plus to about 31,000 these days.

New York State labor experts blame the loss of manufacturing jobs as a key reason for population decreasing in the hardest-hit locales. Others believe it is at least partially the result of a general migration from the

North and Midwest, to regions in the South and West. These theories are not disconnected.

There is a bubbling stew of factors that is making enrollment decline a crisis for colleges, especially smaller private institutions. In the case of St. Bonaventure and other schools in less populous locations, economic conditions are an aggravating factor.

It is an 80-mile drive from the Buffalo International Airport to Olean, and most of it requires heading south on NY Route 16, which can be slow-going. Steve Curran, one of Mark Schmidt's crackerjack assistant coaches, knows that journey, and he dislikes it. He often goes to the Buffalo airport to wait on a basketball recruit flying in there. Then he and the player drive south through Erie County and pick up Route 16 around East Aurora and head in to Cattaraugus County and down to Olean. If it is daylight, Curran has one concern.

"I keep looking for Confederate flags hanging from porches or in the back of pickup trucks," he explained. That's because his passenger, the recruit, is usually African-American. A day later, after the player has met the other coaches, worked out with the team, and stayed with some of the players in their dorms or townhouses, Curran has to haul the player back to the airport, and then turn around and make the drive back to Olean and home.

"By that time, it's often 1 in the morning," said Curran, a New Englander who played at Merrimack College in North Andover, Mass., and hopes to be a head coach at some point, maybe at his alma mater. "I hate that drive."

Make that trip in the daylight and you pretty much get a look at the rural impoverished. There are farms, and a few seem fairly substantial. Some belong to the Amish, who seek a smidgen of tight Route 16 for their horses and black carriages. There are a few quaint small towns. Holland is pleasant, Franklinville is another, so is Hinsdale. For the most part, however, this is a two-lane boulevard through hard times, sparsely populated and challenged. It does not mean at all that the residents are not worthy people, great parents, dependable neighbors. The region does not look starkly different than the small towns or semi-rural stretches where many of us were raised, where lives were well-lived, the right values were exhibited despite little means.

There was a magazine story more than a few years back that described the challenges of getting basketball recruits to Murray State University in Kentucky, usually a contender in the Ohio Valley Conference. If recruits could tolerate the lengthy drives from a large airport such as Nashville or a smaller field such as Paducah, they would like what greeted them when they finally arrived on campus, no matter how remote it might be. What confronts Curran and the other Bonaventure coaches is not all that different, though Murray State has more than 11,000 students. But the town of Murray is only slightly larger than Olean.

That is pretty much one of the challenges of recruiting high-quality ballplayers to Olean. If they can shrug off the journey from Buffalo to Olean, see the beauty of the campus, meet the coaches and prospective teammates, see a ballgame and understand the fan support the team receives from students and residents, then the coaches have a chance to make them Bonnies. If the recruit and his family are driving up from New York or Philly or the Washington area, the sparsely populated terrain west of Corning on Route 17 is hard not to notice.

No matter the way a recruit or any other student gets to the Bonaventure campus, especially from the huge metropolitan regions in the Northeast, the journey can be an issue. That is why declining populations in Western and Central New York mean more challenges for the university.

Olean, the largest town in Cattaraugus County, and the county itself, are losing residents. Olean had 15,347 residents in 2000. In 2013, data indicated that figure was below 14,000. Household income is just $37,471 --- 20 percent below the median household income for all of New York State. The average cost for a home is just a bit over $70,000. Twenty percent of the population is 62 or older. Per capita income for 2013 was just $24,396. Olean's population peaked in the early 1950s at just under 23,000.

So Olean, built on timber, and then oil, and then a railroad town, is losing population, and the population that remains is aging and incomes are low. The trends are similar for the rest of the county, which lost 3 percent of its population in the past five years. Basically, major sources of enrollment for St. Bonaventure historically are, these days, far less able to provide potential students.

Amid these challenges, the City of Olean has undertaken a transformation of its downtown. North Union Street, the heart of the downtown area, now has a series of roundabouts that will slow vehicle traffic on behalf of wide bike lanes and streetscape. Incumbent businesses are being remodeled, new businesses are opening, including a Tuscan restaurant with a handsome exterior, and the old Olean Business School building is being redone as the Olean Business Incubator, to attract entrepreneurs who might provide new commerce and expand employment.

The village of Allegany, part of the Town of Allegany, had 1,816 residents in 2010, according to census data. That number had dropped below 1,800 in 2014. It has a pretty main street, flanked by merchants, restaurants and bars.

There is a population drain south of the New York state line as well. The city of Bradford, Pa., just a 20-minute drive from Olean, was an oil boom town in the late 19th century. In the 1930s, more than 19,000 people resided there. These days, 8,500 people call it home, and that is nearly a 7 percent drop since the 2000 census. The counties that comprise Pennsylvania's northern tier are among the least-populated in the state, counties such as Warren, McKean, Potter, Tioga and Bradford. Deer hunters from around the state are drawn to the region. New residents, not so much.

Bonaventure's coaches have spread themselves around the area. Schmidt, his wife, Anita, and three children live in Olean. Matt Pappano, a Bonaventure grad and the director of basketball operations, and his wife, Lauren, live in Olean. So does Assistant Coach Dave Moore, his wife, Erica, and their daughter. Assistant Coach Steve Curran and his family, wife, Melissa, and their three children, live in Allegany. The newest assistant coach,

Jerome Robinson, lives in Portville with his wife, Beth, and their three children.

The true romantic among the assistant coaches would seem to be Moore. A woman who brought an aged relative to the Reilly Center to see games usually sat just behind the Bonaventure bench. She caught Moore's eye. At one game, Moore believes it was late in what would be a victory over Duquesne, Moore introduced himself by scribbling his name and contact info on a stat sheet and passed it to the young woman. The woman, named Erica, as he discovered, responded that evening. So Moore's time in Olean has been amply rewarded, in ways far beyond just being a key member of a winning basketball program.

CHAPTER 6:

EARLY CONCERNS

LOYOLA

When asked if Loyola University of Baltimore, due in the Reilly Center on a Saturday night, presented many worries, Mark Schmidt was quick with an answer: "They are good. They have players who would start for us." One of them was a senior guard named Tyler Hubbard, and he proved that Schmidt wasn't just being polite. Hubbard was 7-for-12 from the field and all seven of his goals were three-pointers as the Greyhounds did their best to make things uncomfortable for Bonaventure.

The first 20 minutes, however, were a big dose of comfort for Schmidt and his team. Marcus Posley rediscovered his scoring touch and his 14 points in the first 20 minutes, along with the inside punch of Dion Wright, who had 11, gave the Bonnies a comfortable lead at the half, 50-34.

This was the offensive whirlwind that Schmidt and his coaches anticipated, the one that wasn't around for the last 10 minutes in Syracuse. Posley hit two from distance in the first half but he also was scoring on drives and getting to the foul line. Bonaventure outrebounded Loyola 19-12, with Wright providing seven of those. Loyola shot well, 13-for-24, 6-for-10 of them three-pointers, but the Bonnies turned them over eight times and created five steals.

This was the formula Schmidt and his coaches were seeking: high-octane offense, sweat and toil on defense. Outside shooting from the guards and points in the interior from Wright, a very tough matchup because of his quickness and touch around the rim. The defense, unfortunately, disappeared in the second half. Loyola took full advantage and made things uncomfortable.

A drive inside and a made free throw by Wright gave the Bonnies a still-comfortable 62-47 edge with 13:18 remaining. Then the Greyhounds got hot. A tip-in by Eric Laster made it 62-52. Another score inside, this time by Franz Rassman, made it 67-59. A pair of free throws from Andre Walker cut it to 67-61 with 9:28 to go. Posley hit a jumper and was fouled to push the Bonnies up 71-61, and a three-pointer by Jaylen Adams gave the Bonnies some breathing room at 77-66 with 6:45 left. Adams and Posley did enough scoring to provide the Bonnies with comfortable leads the rest of the way. The final was 94-82.

Posley would finish with 26 points and was 10-for-10 from the line. Adams had five points in the first half but would finish with 16. Nelson Kaputo had 11, and Denzel Gregg played well in the second half, ending with nine points and four rebounds.

Loyola had five players in double figures and went 11-for-21 on three-pointers. The Bonnies hit on 30 of 54 field goals for the game and went for 44.4 percent from distance. It was the first thing Schmidt noted in his press conference, and it wasn't really a compliment.

"Thank goodness we shot 55 percent from the field and 44 percent from threes, because if we didn't, we would have lost," he said. "At this level, and the teams we are about to play, we can't allow a team to shoot 53 percent from the field."

It was defense, Schmidt had said in Syracuse, that cost his team the game against the Orange. And he was right. So three games in to this season, was this an early pattern or a critical inability that would cost the Bonnies dearly moving forward?

The Loyola coach, G.G. Smith, was not surprised that his team rallied in the second half. "I've been in these games many a time," he said. "The other team's going to relax, so they are going to give us a chance to get back in the game."

While he was bothered by his poor shooting and lack of overall scoring in the first two games, his breakout against the Greyhounds wasn't a surprise to Posley. "I knew it would happen sooner or later. I've just been in the gym, continuing to shoot, so it happened for me tonight," he explained. "I had a good game, but we still have a lot of work to do."

Smith, the Loyola coach, had kind words for Adams. "With Jaylen, we know him from being from Baltimore," Smith said. "We've seen him play a lot. He's really good. He just knows how to run the team."

CANISIUS

The Koessler Athletic Center, squeezed into the 72-acre campus of Canisius College near West Main Street in downtown Buffalo, has been a house of horrors for St. Bonaventure of late. The last time the Bonnies won there was the 2002 season. The 2,100-seat arena has been spruced up, with new lighting and seat backs replacing bleachers in the past couple of years, and it was packed on this night, the Tuesday before Thanksgiving. Canisius had lost on the road to Hofstra but then scored solid wins at home against Lehigh and Cornell. The Golden Griffins had shown they can put up a lot of points, so no one in the Bonaventure contingent expected this to be anything but a dogfight between rivals.

Bonaventure and Canisius are ancient foes, two-thirds of the unofficial Little Three Conference, which includes Niagara. Back when few Catholic schools in the East belonged to conferences, the Little Three rivals played each other twice each season. But now, with the Bonnies in the Atlantic 10 and Canisius and Niagara in the Middle Atlantic Athletic, the teams can only manage one meeting each season. But the rivalries remain intense.

For the Bonnies, playing Canisius now means going up against Coach Jim Baron, one of the stars of the 1977 Bonaventure team that won the NIT. Baron also coached the Bonnies for nine years, reviving the program and taking his teams to the NIT twice and to the NCAA Tournament in 2000, when it lost a double-overtime, first-round game to Kentucky. Baron had put together a very solid program at Bonaventure but the university president at the time, Robert J. Wickenheiser, sought a coach with a higher profile, or so it was rumored, and he urged Baron's departure. Baron went on to coach the University of Rhode Island for 11 years, before being fired. Then he moved on to Canisius.

This is Baron's third year as the coach of the Griffins, and he and Mark Schmidt greeted each other warmly in the minutes before this game began. Coincidentally, Wickenheiser, who remained in the Olean area after being fired over the recruiting scandal, would die three days after this game. He was 72.

Canisius is a bittersweet rival these days, and because of Baron. There are staunch fans of the Bonnies who still have a difficult time casting Baron as an opponent, as the enemy. For others, their dislike for Canisius --- and Niagara --- makes Baron nothing but the enemy, something they got used to when Baron was the head coach at Atlantic 10 rival Rhode Island.

Among the things that Schmidt had stressed before the season began was that the Bonnies had to avoid foul trouble. The starting five plus Denzel Gregg were the only known commodities, given the injuries to Courtney Stockard and Jordan Tyson. The next men off the bench, if needed, would be raw and untested freshmen. So of course, Dion Wright had two fouls in the first five minutes and the team committed six fouls overall with 11:56 still to play in the first half.

Minutes later, Idris Taqqee was tagged with his second foul. So Wright, Taqqee and Jaylen Adams were on the bench with foul trouble and freshmen Derrick Woods, Nelson Kaputo and LaDarien Griffin were in the game.

This is precisely what Schmidt wished to avoid, and Canisius was ahead, 14-11. But Woods was playing really well. He was rebounding and also scoring, including a dunk, a layup and two made free throws. When Kaputo hit a three-point shot he trimmed the Canisius lead to 17-16. Late in the first half, Griffin scored inside. The three freshmen bought time for the Bonnies as they managed the foul troubles of Wright, Adams and Taqqee.

In the meantime, Posley was on a rampage. He would end the first half 5-for-9 from the field, including one three-pointer, and went 7-for-7 from the free throw line because of drives to the basket. His 18 points in the first 20 minutes gave the Bonnies a 41-38 halftime lead. With Adams limited to just 11 minutes in the first half, the three freshmen, led by Woods' nine points, provided a combined 14 points. Neither Wright nor Taqqee scored in the first 20 minutes, but Gregg contributed seven points.

Canisius guard Malcolm McMillan forced enough fouls in the first half to get to the line 11 times and converted 10 of those shots. Forward Phil Valenti had eight points for the Griffins.

Posley kept up his pace in the second half. He hit a three-pointer to give Bonaventure a 55-47 lead and a layup by Wright made it 57-50 with 12:55 to go. But Canisius answered with three-point baskets by Jermaine Crumpton and McMillan.

Wright would score 13 points in the second half and a dunk off a feed from Kaputo pushed the Bonnies to a 64-53 lead with 9:51 on the clock. But that did not last long, as Kassius Robertson hit a three-pointer and McMillan hit two free throws to pull Canisius within 65-61. When Crumpton scored on a tip-in it was a 69-69 game with just 1:47 to play.

The Bonnies would win this game from the free throw line and their aggressive play inside was a key. Posley, Wright and Adams all went 2-for-2 from the line as the clock wound down. When Taqqee was fouled going for a rebound, his two made free throws put Bonaventure ahead 77-71 with 12 seconds remaining. The final was 77-73, and it was a well-earned victory for the Bonnies. Canisius was a handful.

Baron said after the game that his team had "too many missed opportunities."

"He made shots and he made plays," Baron said of Posley, who ended the game with 35 points. "We had to stop their guards. We did a good job on Wright. But Posley was the difference. We need guys to step up that way."

Posley was matter-of-fact regarding his play. "I'm a senior. I have to be a leader," he said. "More experience comes down to playing better." Schmidt agreed: "You are only as good as your seniors ... meaning Dion and Marcus. The Canisius gym is so small, you need seniors to lead the younger players."

Schmidt called Canisius "an attacking team, a very good offensive team." The coach was also pleased that Bonaventure outrebounded the Griffins by five and had 10 more points off fast breaks than the opponents.

This is the kind of game that Bonaventure must have if it is going to have a successful season and hold up under the pressure of the conference schedule. It was also a good way to head in to Thanksgiving Day. The team and the coaches planned a holiday banquet in the Olean area that would include at least some of the coaches' and players' families.

The day will likely be a bit sweeter for the three freshmen, Woods, Kaputo and Griffin, who were thrown in to a taut game, a rivalry game in a difficult venue, and made valuable contributions. It wasn't by design, maybe, but it was a real test and could provide dividends as the season progresses.

HOFSTRA

Tim Kenney grew up on Long Island and he has enough ties to the place that he knew, before the season even opened, that St. Bonaventure would have a stern early-season test in Hofstra. "They will be a load," Kenney said. And he was correct. The Pride knocked off Florida State in the Virgin Islands tournament, then dropped a pair to South Carolina and Indiana State.

Schmidt and his coaches knew a lot about Hofstra, beginning with the coach, the wise-cracking Joe Mihalich, who had given the Bonnies a tough time when he was the Niagara coach. Schmidt likes Mihalich, and threw an arm around his shoulders when they met before the game. Mihalich escaped Niagara with two terrific guards, Juan'ya Green and Ameen Tanksley, both from the Philadelphia area, and they gave Hofstra real firepower.

Derrick Woods started but quickly had two fouls and headed for the bench. Denzel Gregg replaced him. The Bonnies were missing some easy chances in the early going but managed to open a 10-point lead, 29-19, on a basket and free throw from Posley. A score by Dion Wright maintained that lead but Wright had two fouls on him with more than six minutes to go in the half.

Scores from Tanksley and Green and a three-point shot by Denton Koon, a 6-foot-8 forward who earned his degree at Princeton and was using his last year of eligibility with Hofstra as he worked on his graduate degree, pulled the Pride to within five, 42-37, at the half.

For the 3,229 fans who made it to the Reilly Center this afternoon, it was a good game to watch. Both teams were playing at a sprint. Koon managed 11 points in the first 20 minutes and Tanksley had nine. Denzel Green had done a nice job replacing Wright. The junior had 11 points and six rebounds. Posley had 15 and Adams had 12. Woods would leave the first half with three fouls. Hofstra's Green had just five at the half, but the pace of the game practically assured he'd get in a rhythm and make a mark.

In fact, Green was a monster in the second half. His jumper gave Hofstra a 51-50 lead with 14 minutes to play. Moreover, Hofstra was taking control inside. Two layups by Malik Nichols and a drive and free throw from Tanksley pushed Hofstra to a 66-59 lead with 9:04 left. When Koon hit a three-pointer and Rokas Gustys scored inside the Pride were up 73-60 and this one was slipping away from the Bonnies.

Bonaventure did answer on back-to-back three-pointers from Adams and Nelson Kaputo to trail by just 81-80 with 37 seconds left. But Tanksley and Green kept getting sent to the foul line and never missed. Each converted four free throws in the last half-minute and Hofstra had an 89-83 win on the road.

Bonaventure fell to 3-2, and with upcoming games at Buffalo, home against Ohio and Vermont, and a trip to Siena, this non-conference schedule was beginning to look challenging, just as Schmidt maintained.

The box score was transmitting an array of alarms. Tanksley finished with 24 points and Green had 23. Posley and Adams both had four personals, which meant they were having difficulties defending the Hofstra guards. Koon finished with 14 points. The Pride went to the foul line a ridiculous 33 times and made 28 of those shots. That is where the game was won. The Bonnies also were outrebounded, 41-36. Adams had 24 points and Posley added 22. Dion Wright had 10 points and 10 rebounds.

So offensively, this game should have been winnable. Adams, Posley and Wright had a combined 56 points, a key goal. But, at this point, the team is a mess defensively in the second half of games. Another portion of the preseason formula for winning was to avoid fouls. That didn't happen on this day. Wright was out for much of the first half with two fouls. Woods would have his three first-half fouls and Denzel Gregg would eventually foul out.

The absence of these players for serious stretches, especially in the final 20 minutes, explains Hofstra's second half performance: 52 points, dominant rebounding, numerous trips to the foul line. The Bonnies had played just five games and twice gave up 50 or more points in the second half.

Schmidt bemoaned --- again --- the problems on the defensive end.

"They beat Florida State because they have good players," Schmidt said in the media room. He called Hofstra an NCAA Tournament team. "It's just disappointing that we couldn't give a better defensive effort in the half-court."

While the provincial quality of the Bonnies' non-conference schedule alarmed some supporters, the head coach had no problems with it and was making no apologies. Schmidt described it as the toughest non-conference schedule in his nine years at the school.

"The teams we have played and will play are at the highest levels of their conferences," Schmidt said, in an interview after the first six games and a record of four wins and two losses. Leaning back in the chair at his desk, he added that given the Bonnies' talent level at the moment, "There are no nights off." He also said the difference between high-major teams and low-major teams are big men. "Everyone can find guards," he said. "Everyone has good guards."

Bonaventure saw a bundle of those guards in its first five games in the season, and they unveiled some of the team's challenges. Defensive woes were at the top of Schmidt's list. "The team is young," Schmidt said. "We aren't good on the ball," allowing guards to penetrate and exploit the Bonaventure defense. He reminded that Ndoye, a muscular 6-foot-11, a looming presence, covered for those lapses last season, discouraging guards from storming down the lane because of his ability to block and alter shots.

The size and strength of the lineup were also resulting in major foul difficulties for St. Bonaventure. Schmidt said the Canisius game was a perfect example, when Wright, Woods and Gregg were on the bench at various times and LaDarien Griffin was inserted, and did well, scoring a key basket and grabbing a couple of rebounds in 10 minutes of time in the charged atmosphere of a Little Three game and a packed house in Buffalo. But that is hardly a formula for success for this team.

Schmidt also described what he termed "a leadership gap." He said: "We only have two seniors. Marcus has only been here one full season. And Dion needs to use all his energy and intelligence on his being as good as he can be. Everyone else is a junior or younger."

The absence of a clear leader, someone who takes control of situations and through talent and a strong personality wills the team out of tough situations, is a problem. That shortcoming has impacted the team and its performance in the early season.

Schmidt also said that Jordan Tyson was expected to be back in time for the South Carolina State game on Dec. 19 in Olean. Schmidt wasn't quite sure of what Tyson would be able to deliver, but there was one thing that gave the coach some comfort: "If anything, he gives us five more fouls," said Schmidt. "We've had chronic foul trouble without Jordan."

CHAPTER 7:
A WINNING STREAK

When Mark Schmidt claimed his team's non-conference schedule was hardly a cakewalk, then the four-game stretch that began with a game at Buffalo, followed by home contests against Ohio, Vermont and South Carolina State was probably on his mind. Buffalo, Ohio and Vermont are solid almost every year, and as for South Carolina State, well, the Bonnies have a habit of losing to these under-the-radar Deep South colleges.

UB lost its coach, Bobby Hurley, to Arizona State after the 2014-15 season and he took the star guard with him. But the Bulls had top guards in Lamonte Bearden and Jarryn Skeete and a big but rather untested interior. Nat Oats replaced Hurley as coach, and it was Oats who recruited most of the roster. And no one can look past a team that won 23 games a year ago and was 12-6 in the Mid-American Conference, which is no cakewalk in any season

Ohio and the Bonnies have played some memorable games. The Bobcats always have deadly shooters and capable big men, but this team is young, with six freshmen and four sophomores. The Columbus Dispatch preview of the Bobcats had them pegged for a 9-9 league mark and a third-place finish in the MAC's East Division.

Vermont is always a contender in the America East Conference, and this year is no different. The Catamounts are seen as a top contender for the league title, along with Albany and Stony Brook. If Vermont has an edge, it would be star guard Trae Bell-Haynes.

BUFFALO

This began as a basketball game desperately seeking some rhythm. And it went undiscovered for an entire Wednesday night before a crowd of 4,192. Dion Wright played well at the start, scoring 10 points to give Bonaventure a 14-12 edge with 10:30 to go. Then Posley hit a three and freshman LaDarien Griffin scored on a drive and later hit two free throws to give the Bonnies a 25-22 edge. Griffin was in there because of foul trouble … significant foul trouble. By halftime, Derrick Woods had three fouls and Wright and Denzel Gregg each had a pair. Unfortunately for Griffin, he too would have three fouls in five minutes.

When Wright hit a hook shot and Adams drove for a basket, the Bonnies led 29-23 with 4:25 left in the half. But the Bulls would not go away. Subs Blake Hamilton and CJ Massinburg each scored on drives and Buffalo cut the lead to 33-32. Wright, who would have 16 points in the half, scored inside and then Nelson Kaputo hit a three-point goal and the Bonnies led 38-33 at the half.

Amid the skittish environment, both teams shot high percentages, but not from behind the arc. Buffalo was 0-for-7 from three-point range and Bonaventure hit just 2-for-14 from distance. The Bonnies were 6-for-6 from the foul line, but the rash of fouls by Wright, Griffin, Woods and Gregg helped the Bulls get to the line 18 times in the first 20 minutes. But they made just 11 of those.

If you were a Bonaventure supporter, you would have to be concerned with the inside play. Buffalo outrebounded the Bonnies 18-13, and UB had seven offensive rebounds. The foul trouble and the task of staying on the boards with Buffalo would hamper Bonaventure in a grind-it-out game like this one, and on the road. And someone besides Wright would have to join in the scoring. Almost all of the Bonnies' 22 points in the paint were from Wright.

Despite it all, the Bonnies surged in the first 11 minutes of the second half. A rebound and dunk by Woods made it a 42-35 game. Then Posley, on a nice feed from Gregg, extended the lead. In successive trips, Idris Taqqee and Wright contributed eight points on four scores inside that gave the Bonnies their biggest lead of the game at 54-45 at the 9:01 mark.

From that point forward, the Bonnies went stone cold. Wright, who would finish with a career-high 26 points, hit jump shots at the 7:24 and 6:15 marks. The second one made it a 58-50 Bonaventure lead. If not for Buffalo's own offensive flaws, this would have been a loss for the Bonnies. Roddell Wiggington made a free throw to pull within 58-51. The Bulls, while grabbing rebounds on the defensive end, managed to miss four shots and turn the ball over twice. By the time Ikenna Smart scored on a dunk to make it a 58-53 game, only 3:23 remained.

Time was not a huge problem for Buffalo. Bonaventure could not score, but they fouled enough to get UB to the line and Lamonte Bearden drove for a layup to cut the Bonnies' edge to 58-56. And when Wigginton made two free throws, the game was tied 58-58 with 37 seconds to play.

Schmidt took a 30-second timeout with 33 seconds to go. He wanted his team to have the last shot and he wanted to leave the Bulls as little time as possible to tie the game or win it on a last possession. For one of the few times in the game, the plan worked. The ball found Posley above the foul line and he hit a soft jumper to give the Bonnies a 60-58 lead with 10 seconds remaining. The assist was provided by Wright. Bearden's layup attempt with one second left was blocked by Woods.

By any measure, it was an ugly win. The Bonnies had only two players in double figures: Wright with his 26, and his team needed all of them, and Posley with 13. The Bonnies got to the foul line just nine times, and made eight. Buffalo shot 32 free throws, thanks to the foul-prone Bonnies, but only made 19 of them. Bonaventure was 2-for-21 on three-point shots, a tick over 9 percent. Buffalo was worse: 1-for-13.

They key for winning this game was probably provided by Buffalo with its 21 turnovers. The Bulls took only 44 shots for the game, because of the turnovers and the 32 trips to the foul line.

There clearly is a link between committing so many fouls and the quality of your defensive play, and those numbers had to look lousy to

Schmidt. Gregg, the X-factor, as Schmidt calls him, provided just two points in five minutes and fouled out midway through the second half. Jaylen Adams, who was a non-factor, something Schmidt can't afford, had six points despite playing 37 minutes with serious foul trouble. Derrick Woods saw 26 meaningful minutes despite his four fouls, and had five rebounds, four points and one block, the play that sealed the game.

In a conversation the next day, Schmidt rattled off the things that concern him. "The team is young and not good on the ball (defensively)," he said. They have size problems inside, meaning Woods, who is prone to foul, gets more minutes than he should be receiving at this point in his freshman year.

"Canisius and Buffalo are big examples," Schmidt said. "Gregg, Dion and Derrick sat with fouls in the first half." He said the difference in free throws against Buffalo was evidence of the shaky interior play.

Schmidt did have one piece of good news. He expects Jordan Tyson to be ready to play against South Carolina State in a couple of weeks. "If anything, he gives us five more fouls," he said, without any sign of a smile. "We are in chronic foul trouble without Jordan."

OHIO AND VERMONT

These two teams are almost a matched set: Dangerous guards and able big men. Capable of hot streaks of shooting. Ohio U. has long been a well-regarded program and a force in the tough Mid-American Conference. Vermont has become a mid-major standout in the last 15 years and was previewed as one of three teams likely to win the 2016 America East Tournament and the automatic bid to the NCAA that comes with it. The two programs are usually well-coached, and evidence of that is Mike Lonergan going from Vermont to George Washington and Jim Christiansen leaving Ohio for Boston College.

Ohio came in to its game against Bonaventure with a 5-2 record that included a 90-81 loss to Florida State. Vermont arrived with a 4-5 mark but bombed Niagara, 85-67, for one of its victories.

If the Bonnies could handle both of these schools, they would have non-conference wins that look appreciable if a post-season tournament is a possibility and it would raise Bonaventure's record to 6-2, with only South Carolina State, Siena and Niagara between Mark Schmidt and his best non-conference record in nine seasons.

The similarities between Ohio and Vermont extended to their performances against the Bonnies. Ohio fell, 81-68. Vermont left Olean an 80-68 loser. Too much Jaylen Adams was the difference in both contests, along with strong second-half defensive efforts that allowed the Bonnies to open substantial leads.

Adams dropped 22 points on Ohio and a career-best 28 on Vermont. His accuracy in each game was remarkable: The sophomore was 5-for-7 from behind the arc against Ohio and 7-for-10 against Vermont. Adams had six assists against the Bobcats and seven assists versus the Catamounts.

Even the sound bites from the two coaches were the same. "I'm sick of Adams," said Ohio's Saul Phillips. This is just his second season as coach of the Bobcats but Adams has nailed him twice. As a freshman, Adams had 26 in a win at Ohio.

"We didn't want to give Adams the threes," said Vermont coach John Becker, "yet we did." He added: "We stunk defensively."

Bonaventure needed strong second halves to capture both of these victories. The Bonnies led Ohio 37-35 at the half. "Our 2-3 zone in the second half helped us cool down their shooting," Mark Schmidt said. He also was pleased that the Bonnies held Ohio to just three three-point goals in the second half. Ohio had six three-pointers in the first half. The Bonnies also turned the Bobcats over 13 times, good for 20 points and a telling factor in the margin of victory.

Phillips was complimentary of Schmidt's ability "to get so much from a team with such little depth." He then added: "I'm impressed with St. Bonaventure."

Adams had a lot of help in this game. Marcus Posley had 19 points and Dion Wright added 14 points, including going 8-for-9 from the line, and grabbed 12 rebounds. The Bonnies also outrebounded the lanky Bobcats, 37-32.

"We're usually a better rebounding team in the trenches," Phillips said, "but that battle was won by St. Bonaventure."

The Bonnies opened leads of 36-25 and 41-29 against Vermont, but the Catamounts came on strong late in the first half to trail just 43-37 at intermission. Then they came out hot in the second half, and made it a 45-45 tie. But the Bonnies put together two runs of their own, the first was started with Adams hitting his fifth three-pointer of the game to push his team on an 11-2 burst. With Bonaventure leading 62-55, Vermont was hit with an 11-1 surge by the Bonnies that gave them their biggest lead, 73-56, with 7:02 to play.

Kurt Steidl, a big guard with a soft shooting touch, had 19 points for the Catamounts, who placed four players in double figures. But the scoring droughts in the second half were killers. Adams got help from Dion Wright, who had 16 points and seven rebounds, and Denzel Gregg, with 10 points and seven rebounds. Missing in action for Vermont was forward Ethan O'Day, a preseason first-team pick in the America East, who had just two points and four rebounds for the night.

Posley did not have a big night scoring, just eight points, but he had six assists and four rebounds, all on the defensive end and helping to cool Vermont for long stretches in the last 20 minutes.

"Bonaventure stopped our run in the second half," said Becker, "and came back, like good teams do."

"We can't let teams back in the game," Schmidt said. "We didn't defend well but we rebounded."

If the wins over Vermont and Ohio are telling, it would indicate the Bonnies firepower will give them a chance in lots of games moving forward, including in the A-10. The play from Wright, in particular, is critical, especially if the team can stay on the boards with the muscular interiors that they will face in the conference.

Ohio and Vermont were tough tests, even in the Reilly Center, and the Bonnies managed to pass them.

SOUTH CAROLINA STATE

More than 3,300 fans assembled on the Saturday before Christmas to see the Bonnies play their first game in 11 days because of a break for exams. Jaylen Adams would be among the spectators. He was suspended for one game for a violation of team rules and sat on the bench. The opponent was South Carolina State, a member of the Mid-Eastern Athletic Conference. The Bulldogs were expected to be a contender in the conference. They entered the game with a 5-6 record, and it included a lopsided loss at Duquesne in the previous game. SC State did play well at Kansas State in a two-point loss.

This was not a riveting spectacle. And that was a good thing. The Bonnies have had misfortunes with teams from the MEAC, like a loss at home to Maryland-Eastern Shore a year earlier. The Bonnies went through the motions for much of the time in that game, were down 12 at halftime, pulled to within one on a put-back by Youssou Ndoye in the final minute but fell 82-80 to the Hawks.

There was no drama in this one. The Bonnies led 17-6 in the first seven minutes. A drive and foul shot from Marcus Posley put Bonaventure up 20-9 with 10:50 to play and it was 36-11 when Derrick Woods scored on an assist from Nelson Kaputo, who played all 40 minutes in the absence of Adams. The score was 41-20 at the half and Posley had 16.

The Bonnies seemed to lose interest in the second half but didn't pay much of a penalty for it. The lead remained at 20 points most of the way and the final was 64-45. Lackluster would be the most generous appraisal of Bonaventure's play in the second half.

Posley finished with 26 points and was 5-for-14 on three-pointers. Wright had his usual productive game with 14 points and 10 rebounds. Idris Taqqee had nine rebounds and Kaputo had 12 points, seven assists and seven rebounds. Denzel Gregg had 10 rebounds. A good time was had by all.

Jordan Tyson, injured with a torn tendon in his wrist, made his long-awaited return to play and had two points on free throws and one rebound. Posley said all of his teammates stepped up to cover for the absence of Adams.

South Carolina State shot terribly, and that could be the end result of too much time on the road. The Bulldogs were 17-for-60 from the field and 3-for-20 from beyond the arc.

The fourth straight victory gave Bonaventure an overall record of 7-2 with a game at Siena and a home game with Niagara being all that is left to the non-conference schedule. A 9-2 record would be a nice way to begin the conference action, which is two weeks away.

CHAPTER 8:

BROTHERLY LOVE

<u>SIENA</u>

Jimmy Patsos, the Siena College coach, was wearing a Santa Claus hat when he arrived in the media room after his team beat St. Bonaventure, 73-70, at the big but homely Times Union Center in Albany. This was Siena's third straight victory over its rival to the west, so it would keep the Franciscan Cup for another season and inspire Patsos to deliver his comedy routine, even if you sometimes had no idea what he was talking about.

Patsos, big guy, big personality, opened his monologue by declaring he was The Grinch That Stole Christmas. Apparently, that's because Patsos was grouchy with his team at some point late in the first half because of turnovers. The Saints would rack up 25 turnovers for the game, usually a catastrophe, but the Bonnies would end up turning it over 20 times, so it was a virtual wash.

"I was The Grinch," he said. "At halftime I wasn't very good. I was upset we had thirteen turnovers."

According to Patsos, his players kept assuring him that everything was fine and to settle down and quit bitching and they would take care of the game. As a result of their confidence, Patsos claimed he basically sat on the bench and calmly watched the last nine minutes of the second half without providing much in the way of instruction.

So, his unwarranted anger toward his team made him The Grinch, and he shouldn't have been testy because the players assured him they had things under control, and that's why he was wearing the hat. Get it?

There were some other one-liners and humorous asides, some of them opaque, but he also said that the series with the Bonnies was a great thing and that Mark Schmidt is a friend --- because Schmidt played for Gary Williams at Boston College and Patsos had been an assistant under Williams, and they both survived it --- and that he was almost sorry that Siena had beaten Bonaventure the last three seasons and by a total of just eight points.

When Patsos got up to leave, he said he would keep the hat, adding, "I don't think (Schmidt) will want to wear it."

Siena entered the game with a 7-4 record. The Saints opened their season with away-game losses against Duke and Wisconsin, and they were beaten by Cornell and St. Peter's. But they won their previous two games, against Hofstra and Albany. Those were good wins for the Saints. Hofstra is tough, as the Bonnies discovered, and Albany is an obvious rival, especially since the Danes became a consistent winner.

The game was a tight match, with scores tied on 10 occasions and eight lead changes. But it was not well-played by either team. The combined 45 turnovers speak for themselves. But both squads shot well: Bonaventure was 28-for-60 for 46.7 percent and the Saints went 26-for-55 and 47.3 percent. Each team made six three-pointers.

Siena won because it got to the foul line 24 times, even though it converted just 15 of those tosses, and outrebounded the Bonnies 38 to 27. Bonaventure was 8-for-12 from the foul line. Getting battered on the boards is something that hasn't happened much in the first nine games for Bonaventure. Siena had 19 second-chance points but the Bonnies had 40 points in the paint. Javion Ogunyemi had 15 points and 10 rebounds for Siena. Dion Wright's six rebounds led the Bonnies.

It was an uphill climb all night for Bonaventure. Siena took a 6-0 lead and led 16-11 before Bonaventure cut in to it. With 12 points coming from Jaylen Adams, the Bonnies were able to trim an eight-point Siena lead and be down just 34-32 at the half.

Siena was getting balanced scoring --- five players would finish in double figures, with guard Marquis Wright leading the way with 20 points --- and hurting the Bonnies on the offensive glass. The Saints would finish with 17 offensive rebounds. But there were points in the second half when it appeared the Bonnies could take control. A three-point shot by Marcus Posley gave the Bonnies the early lead in the second half. They led 51-49 after three straight goals from Denzel Gregg, the last one a jam off a terrific pass from Nelson Kaputo.

The game was tied at 56 when Gregg hit a three-pointer and the Bonnies went up 60-56 after back-to-back steals by Adams and Kaputo. When Wright banked in a shot from the lane, the Bonnies led 66-63. Marquis Wright answered with a three to tie the game with under three minutes to play.

Brett Bisping scored inside to give the Saints a 70-68 lead with 34 seconds to go. After a Bonaventure turnover --- they would have three in the last two minutes --- Adams hit two free throws and it was Siena ahead, 71-70. The Bonnies best opportunity to steal the game came next. Siena's Ryan Oliver was fouled with 17 seconds to play and then missed both of the free throws.

Adams tried to determine the game with a drive to the basket but he was whistled for traveling. Was it a good call? So much has become expected of Adams, his game so normally pristine, that this was something of a shock to the considerable Bonaventure contingent amid the crowd of 6,593. Adams looked befuddled but there wasn't a clamorous reaction from the Bonaventure bench. Marquis Wright was fouled and made both free throws to give the Saints the 73-70 margin. A three-point attempt by Dion Wright on a set play missed from afar.

Schmidt wore neither a hat nor a smile to the press conference. Three straight losses to Siena would be grating for someone with Schmidt's competitive drive. "All those losses are tough," he said.

"It was a good game," he termed it. "We had a slow start but we fought back. We didn't close out the game. Three turnovers in the last few minutes. We had 20 turnovers. The effort was there. We did a good job defensively.

But too many turnovers."

Of the travel called on Adams as he tried to make a play in the waning seconds, Schmidt had little to say. "The ball was in the right guy's hands at the end," the coach said. "We didn't execute." Schmidt had good things to say about Gregg's effort, the 12 points and three rebounds. Adams and Posley each had 18 points.

There are unbreakable ties between Siena and St. Bonaventure. Siena's president, Brother F. Edward Coughlin O.F.M., is a Bonaventure grad, a Buffalo guy. The Franciscan friars from both schools know one another well, obviously. The battle for the Franciscan Cup is a fine thing. Nonetheless, there is a chippy quality to the rivalry and it is evident.

Lavon Long, a forward for Siena, was looked at by the Bonnies but, apparently, wasn't offered. So he headed to Siena. Long and Adams are both from Baltimore and know each other well. Long's mother playfully visits the Bona Bandwagon when this game approaches each season, reminding the Bonaventure fans that it is her son and her son's team that has had the upper hand recently.

The Patsos routine for the reporters would have been received with a deep chill, or worse, if it played out before Bonnies' fans. Too much pluck, too much self-absorption, all of it coming at the expense of the losing team. What Patsos likely believed was self-effacing walked right up to the edge of being obnoxious.

The large number of Bonaventure fans in the Times Union Center this night were typically loud and strong-minded, and eager to end this

Siena run of superiority. Nearby sections of Siena supporters took exception. In the final seconds, when it appeared that Siena was likely going to win this game, Siena fans started leaving their seats, heading for the doors and, on their way, hassling the Bonaventure supporters. Two older Siena fans kept mockingly wishing them Merry Christmas. It got testy, nothing more, but there is an edginess. When the Franciscan Cup is presented to the winner after the game, the friars from both schools mingle, and words are spoken that declare the cup never really leaves the unified brown-robed family. For everyone else, there was a winner and a loser on this night. Bonaventure stumbled to 7-3.

The Bonnies' streak of coaches with torn Achilles tendons stretched to a second year. Assistant Coach Dave Moore popped his tendon working out the team before the game. Moore forged on and somehow managed to hop on one foot to team huddles on the court and then back to the bench. The annoying little scooter and then the boot that Schmidt had to endure after his Achilles snapped last season now await Moore.

NIAGARA

The Purple Eagles are struggling. Ever since Joe Mihalich left for the head-coaching job at Hofstra, and took two key players with him, Niagara has been in a swoon. Niagara came in to this game 3-9 and some of the defeats, at Hartford, home vs. Youngstown State, are a measure of how troubled this team is. Head Coach Chris Casey is in his third season and player departures have made it difficult for him to steady the program. The exits continue, however. Romero Collier, a freshman from Syracuse, learned he was academically ineligible in his first semester and left the school.

Niagara played well in spurts and that, along with some sloppy play early by the Bonnies, kept the game close for the first eight minutes. Unfortunately for Casey and the Eagles, Jay Adams had a hot hand early and Niagara had no one who could deal with Dion Wright. The foursome of Wright, Adams, Idris Taqqee and Nelson Kaputo combined for 33 points in the first half, while Marcus Posley went scoreless. The Bonnies opened a 35-23 lead late in the first half but Niagara trimmed that to 35-27 at intermission. The Bonnies nailed seven of 14 three-pointers but turned the ball over eight times.

Guards Cameron Fowler and Emile Black combined for 17 points and were the reasons for Niagara hanging in there. And Niagara got off to a good start in the second half. It was a four-point game with 17:18 to go but Adams hit another three-pointer, Wright turned a rebound in to a score, Kaputo hit another three-pointer and a conventional three-point play by Wright pushed the Bonnies in to a 49-37 lead.

Niagara suffered a long and fallow stretch midway through the second half that allowed the Bonnies to open a 61-41 lead. Niagara kept competing, trimming the deficit to 69-59 with less than four minutes to play. Three-pointers from Wright and Adams made it 80-64. The final was 82-69.

The 8-3 non-conference record is the best in Schmidt's nine years at the school. The win over Niagara was the 132nd in his time at Bonaventure, tying him with Jim Baron. Schmidt seemed unmoved with all of that. The next day he said he doesn't pay attention to those milestones and, anyway, it is a credit to his assistant coaches and the players they have managed to recruit.

"Niagara put us on our heels," he told reporters, which was more generous than accurate. "I thought we played better defense after that. In the second half, we came out a bit soft again. We caught ourselves, got it up to 21, and then got soft again.

"Give them credit, they fought back. With the teams we are about to play, we can't afford to do that. When you have a team down, you have to knock them out."

Schmidt did like the fact that so many players provided serious minutes and points. "We have unselfish players, guys who are sharing the ball. We have guys who understand what it takes to score points," he said.

Wright finished with 28 points, including hitting 2-for-4 on three-pointers. Adams ended with 16 and Kaputo had 14.

The loss at Siena interrupted what would have been a terrific stretch after the loss to Hofstra. But an 8-3 mark instead of 9-2 is a trifling thing when compared to making noise in A-10 play. The non-conference performance showed the Bonnies have strong offensive skills and rebound well for their size (largely the 6-foot-7 workhorse who is Wright). What they get in the way of rebounding and interior defense from Derrick Woods and Jordan Tyson will be both interesting and critical.

The A-10 is likely stronger this season than any time since Xavier departed for the Big East. It is probably fair to say that the only taste of action for the non-conference schedule that would approximate what the A-10 will serve up most nights was the second half against Syracuse. That did not go well, and this season's Syracuse team is young in key spots, shadowed by the program improprieties that will cause Jim Boeheim to miss nine non-conference games, and could struggle in its conference this season.

CHAPTER 9:

AGAINST ALL ODDS

Maybe size and resources are overrated. Consider the University of Louisville and Coach Rick Pitino. In June of 2015, the university extended Pitino's contract through the 2025-26 season. His annual salary of $4.48 million was raised to just under $5.1 million. Pitino will also benefit from a total of $7.5M in retention bonuses that would be paid in installments once every three years. The total value of the deal, if Pitino is still the head coach at the start of the 2025 season, when he will be 73, is $50.93 million.

But Pitino and Louisville won't even go to the NCAA Tournament in 2016. That's because the university decided to penalize itself for allowing female "escorts" and "dancers" to visit the residences of the basketball players, and charm even the high-schoolers who were on campus on recruiting visits. A noble gesture, this self-imposed penalty, but certainly absurd and grating to the Louisville hierarchy, given the investment the school had made in the head coach. Pitino said he had no idea this kind of lechery had infected his program and his players and recruits, even though it was happening right on campus. The entrepreneurial woman who ran this service even hustled out a tell-all book about it.

Certainly, there is a correlation that indicates investments in collegiate men's basketball programs pay dividends. But how to rate that as a predictor of success? Louisville ($16.4 million), Kentucky ($16.1 million) and Duke ($14.1 million) spent more on their basketball programs annually than the rest of the nation's 353 NCAA Division I schools, according to a 2014 study by an online outfit called Basketball State. Mike Krzyzewski was paid $7.3 million in the 2015-16 season plus another $1.25 million as a bonus for the team's title-winning campaign the prior season. The No. 4 spender was Syracuse. The fifth-most spend-happy school, however, was Oklahoma State, and the Cowboys' performance so far in the 2015-16 season has resulted in calls for the head of Travis Ford, their coach. Oklahoma State has gone dancing in recent seasons but has disappointed its fans by early exits from the tourney.

The rest of the Top 10-spending programs were, in order, Minnesota, Indiana, Marquette, Georgetown and Auburn, which threw $10.25 million annually at its program. The coaches' salaries are a big portion of each of the budgets. These are good times for coaches named Pitino. Richard Pitino is the Minnesota head coach.

The comparative budgets do offer surprises. Michigan State, always a powerhouse, often a Final Four participant, is only the 11th most-expensive program. Pitt ($9.1 million) spent more than Kansas, UCLA or Connecticut. Wisconsin's spending is less than Arkansas spends. Virginia Tech and

Gonzaga spend about the same --- $6.1 million. Penn State, whose basketball team is not flourishing and plays before thousands of empty seats in a monster of an arena on campus, spends more than Notre Dame, LSU and Xavier, perennial Top 25 outfits. So paying more than $5 million or $6 million a season does not assure annual Top 25 rankings. But it does in a lot of cases.

So it begs the question: How important are expenses, coaches' salaries, arena revenues, enrollments and endowments to success in college basketball? At that moment when the buzzer sounds, the referees move to center court for the opening tap and two groups of five players assemble themselves, do resources matter all that much? In college football, certainly, resources matter more. And you need 50 or more highly dependable players on the roster. But in college basketball, three very good players, another three or four steady players, and a style of play can be equalizers, right?

Coaching in all of its dimensions must be seen as a vital quality. Otherwise, the best-paid coaches would always win. Villanova has been rated No. 1 for much of the 2015-16 season, but Coach Jay Wright is being paid $2.48 million. Villanova's overall budget was $7.3 million in 2014. Modest numbers compared to some national powers. Perhaps, as some politicians maintain, the U.S. economy and uneven tax laws assure that there exists a monstrously wealthy top 1 percent of wage-earners. What is the ratio in college basketball? Because 28 schools had bigger budgets than Wisconsin, but the Badgers made back-to-back trips to the Final Four in recent seasons. When was the last great season at Auburn?

What drives salaries for college basketball coaches is their ability to lure the great players that bring great seasons. Certainly that is the case with the biggest-spending college basketball budgets, because the salaries of the coaches are a huge percentage of those budgets. The men's basketball budget at Duke in 2014 was about $14.2 million. Coach K's base salary for the season just concluded was a bit more than half of that. That ratio diminishes substantially when you get in to the region of the mere mortals of coaching. Iona College, for instance, spent $2.16 million on the men's basketball program in 2014. Coach Tim Cluess was paid $501,638 for the 2015-16 season, according to USA Today. And that is just one example.

If you include the place a Division I university resides as one of its attributes, then St. Bonaventure is the poorest member of the Atlantic 10 Conference. And if salary is the measure of success, then Mark Schmidt is doing a masterful job: Winning the 2012 Atlantic 10 Tournament, taking first-round foe Florida State, a three-seed, down to the wire, winning 18 games in both the 2013-14 and 2014-15 seasons and coaching the Bonnies to what would seem to be an acceptable and exciting season in 2015-16, at least in the early goings.

Forbes magazine already ranked Schmidt as the Division I coach with the greatest value --- as it regards salary vs. victories compiled --- after leading the Bonnies to the 2012 NCAA Tournament. Schmidt's salary in 2013 was listed as $328,465. In May of 2014, according to the Buffalo Business Journal's analysis of Form 990 of the Internal Revenue Service, the

Bonnies' coach made $516,702 and received an additional $61,646 from donors and university-related organizations.

Schmidt's base salary rose to $615,000 in 2015 and other monies pushed it to about $650,000, according to sources. At least as it regards the coach's salary, Bonaventure has rewarded Schmidt for the program he has built. But as a matter of scale, Schmidt's salary and the school's overall budget for men's basketball are dwarfed by what the schools in the Power 5 conferences spend, let alone most of the 13 other member schools of the A-10.

Institutional prerogatives also come in to play. The eight universities that comprise the Ivy League are among the richest institutions, but their budgets for men's basketball are comparatively small. Harvard spent $1.375 million in 2014. Princeton spent $1.1 million, and Yale just $836,226. The U.S. Military Academy allotted $675,070 for its men's team in the Patriot League. There is basketball and then there are higher priorities.

Basketball can be a profitable endeavor for a university, but it is by no means assured. According to a March 2010 study by CNN.com that measured revenues, expenses and profits or losses for all Division I college basketball programs, Duke University had revenues of $11.8 million, expenses of $13.8 million and losses of $2.03 million. But, the study stressed, Duke, the top-ranked team heading in to that season's NCAA Tournament, had reported profits of $4 million to $5 million from men's basketball in prior years. The university said it had since shifted revenues to the non-sport-specific classification. That same year, Indiana University made

$8.2 million in profits from its men's basketball program. Providence, for instance, reported revenues of $6 million, expenses of $4.6 million and a profit for that season of more than $1.4 million.

In 2010, St. Bonaventure had basketball revenues just a bit more than $2 million, expenses of $1.963 million and a profit of $41,588. Duquesne made $644 in profits that season. Many schools report equal revenues and expenses and $0 for profit or loss.

By almost every measure, St. Bonaventure has far less to work with than its 13 rivals in the Atlantic 10 Conference. The Bonnies are dead-last in all categories, and by a distance. Yet, the program has grown steadily as it regards wins-and-losses. The 2012-13 season was disappointing. In the final regular-season game, a home game, the Bonnies fell to Fordham and failed to make the conference tourney. But the next two seasons were fine efforts, with 18 victories each year, including two wins in the 2014 A-10 Tournament, one of them being the Jordan Gathers jumper that knocked off a very good St. Louis team, and a win in the 2015 conference tourney.

So how does one measure the strength and stature and vitality of a university? And do so at a time of shifting demographics, concerns over student debt, political chatter about making public universities tuition-free, growing online educational options, and curriculums that make graduates highly employable, and at some cost to a traditional liberal arts education?

These are challenges that confront all colleges, and especially smaller private schools in non-urban settings, or so we are learning. But some metrics would apply to almost any college or university. Enrollments, acceptance rates, graduation rates, endowments, fields of study, locations would seem to apply to most or all universities. If a school is flourishing as it regards these criteria, it should be easier to assemble a high-quality men's basketball program, or one would think.

How does St. Bonaventure University compare to the other 13 universities that comprise the Atlantic 10 Conference? Here are the measurements:

Davidson College, situated on a beautiful 665-acre Georgian campus just outside of Charlotte, is highly competitive as it regards admissions, with an acceptance rate of about 26 percent. It was founded in 1831. Total cost for attending is about $61,000. It reported an endowment of $682.5 million in 2015. It's budget for men's basketball was $1.97 million, but that has risen since Davidson joined the Atlantic 10 Conference in the 2014-15 season. Head Coach Jack McKillop was paid $400,000 in the 2014-15 season, according to the Charlotte Observer. McKillop has been at Davidson for decades. The Belk Arena, built in 1989, seats 5,300.

The University of Dayton is located on a 338-acre campus about two miles from downtown Dayton, the sixth largest city in Ohio. The city has lost population but the metro area has about 840,000 residents. The larger Cincinnati region is just an hour's drive south, and Dayton has long attracted students from Pennsylvania, New York, New Jersey and New England. Founded by the Marianist Fathers in 1850, the university has 8,550 undergraduate students and another 2,520 graduate students, including some in doctoral programs. The school's endowment is $519 million. The UD

Arena, with seating for 13,500, was built in 1969 but refurbished in 1998 and again in 2002. Coach Archie Miller was paid $693,000 in the 2015-16 season. The men's basketball budget is just over $5 million.

Duquesne University would seem to be similar to St. Bonaventure, but there are wide differences. Duquesne has 5,743 students and 4,505 postgraduate students in nine schools of study, including a law school. Its endowment is $260 million. The school has a 49-acre campus on Forbes Avenue in Pittsburgh, a neighborhood known as The Bluff. Pittsburgh, of course, is a major-league town. The Dukes' basketball program had expenses of $3.5 million in 2015. The head coach, Jim Ferry, has a seven-year contract with a base salary of $600,000 per season and incentives that could drive that to $740,000 each year, according to the Pittsburgh Post-Gazette. The team plays in the Palumbo Center, a 4,400-seat building constructed in 1998.

Fordham University, operated by the Jesuits, has 8,855 undergraduates and nearly 6,500 graduate students. It has campuses in the Bronx and at Lincoln Center in midtown. Obviously, the university resides in a huge metropolitan setting. Fordham had a freshman class of 2,211 in 2015. The faculty numbers 731. The school's endowment and other investments total $721 million. Coach Jeff Neubauer is in his first year on Rose Hill after 10 very successful seasons at Eastern Kentucky. Neubauer's predecessor at Fordham, Tom Pecora, who was fired, made $705,000 in his last season, 2014-15. Fordham's budget for the men's basketball team is $3.99 million. The venerable Rose Hill Gymnasium, built in 1925 and presently the oldest on-campus arena in the country, seats 3,200.

George Mason University, which joined the Atlantic 10 in 2013, has more than 21,000 undergraduate students and more than 34,000 students when graduate students are counted. The nearly 700-acre main campus is in Fairfax but it has two other campuses in Virginia and a campus in South Korea. George Mason is the largest university in Virginia. Its campus in Fairfax is just outside the District of Columbia. George Mason was originally a branch of the University of Virginia. It did not become an independent state-related university until 1972. That accounts for the fact that despite its size, George Mason has an endowment of just $70.2 million. A 2014 report by the Washington Post said Mason's endowment is dwarfed by other universities, in Virginia and elsewhere. The George Mason endowment represents just $1,747 per student, compared to the University of Virginia, with an endowment worth $220,195 per student, according to the newspaper. George Mason has a budget of about $2.8 million for men's basketball. Coach Dave Paulsen has a five-year contract worth $3.5 million. EagleBank Arena is 32 years old and seats 10,000.

George Washington University is located in the District of Columbia in a location known as Foggy Bottom, a mere four or five blocks from the White House. GW has 14,500 undergraduates and more than 11,000 graduate students. St. Bonaventure has a joint 4+4 dual admissions program with the George Washington medical school. After receiving their undergraduate degrees at St. Bonaventure, eligible and aspiring students can be admitted to GW's medical program. There are 2,260 full-time faculty at GW. Its 270,000 living alumni reside in 150 countries. This is one of the most expensive universities in the country. Undergraduate tuition is $48,000, and room and board is $11,500. The school's acceptance rate is just under 40 percent. The university enjoys the vitality of a metropolitan area, including Northern Virginia and Maryland, with a population of 6.1 million. It is also one of the nation's wealthiest metro areas. George Washington's endowment is $1.7 billion. The Smith Center is 30 years old but received a $43 million refurbishment in 2008. It seats 5,000. The men's basketball team has a budget of just about $3 million. Coach Mike Lonergan's contract has been extended through the 2020-01 season. His salary had been about $600,000 per year before the extension.

La Salle University, operated by the Christian Brothers, was founded in 1863. Its campus is centered at 20th and Olney Streets, in a North Philadelphia neighborhood known as Logan. The school has 3,560 undergrads and 2,781 enrolled in graduate or continuing education programs. The university was not fully co-educational until 1970. There are 373 academics. The endowment is $88 million and, much like other schools, including Big 5 rival St. Joseph's, did some belt-tightening in 2015. The university has its own prep school, located in a neighborhood just outside the city. Gola Arena on the campus can seat 3,400 and was built in 1998. The basketball budget is $3.2 million. The university would not disclose Coach John Giannini's salary.

The University of Massachusetts, located in scenic Western Massachusetts in the town of Amherst, has 22,800 undergraduates and 6,500 graduate students. Its endowment is $757 million. There are more than 1,300 full-time faculty at the university. UMass is a major research university, and the Princeton Review claimed UMass-Amherst has the second-best campus food in the nation, for what that's worth. Tuition is $14,000 for in-state students and $30,000 for out-of-state students. The Mullins Memorial Center, home to basketball and ice hockey, seats 10,500. In 2014, the school built a 53,000 square-foot Champions Center, a facility with practice courts, training facilities, offices for coaches, locker rooms and the UMass Basketball Hall of Fame. Both men's and women's squads are centered there. The building's design and construction was overseen by Tim Kenney, an assistant athletic director at UMass at the time and now the AD at St. Bonaventure. Basketball Coach Derek Kellogg had a salary of $994,500 this season and the UMass basketball budget was reported to be $4.2 million.

The University of Rhode Island, which has a renowned Department of Oceanography, appropriate for the flagship university of a place that has Ocean State on its auto license plates, has been around since 1888. Today it has 14,000 undergrads and 2,900 graduate students. The main 1,250-acre campus is in the pleasant town of Kingston, and there are three small campuses elsewhere in the state. The school's endowment was $131.7 million in 2015. The Ryan Center, the basketball arena built in 2002 for $54 million, seats 7,657. Head Coach Dan Hurley signed a new deal with Rhody in 2015 that carries through 2021 and assures a salary of $1 million per season beginning in 2017. He had been making about $650,000, according to the

Providence Journal. The budget for the Rams is $3.9 million.

Located on a stunning 350-acre campus, cleaved by a lake and as much a park as it is home to a college, the University of Richmond is one of the best liberal arts colleges in the country. It has just under 3,000 undergraduates and another 900 or so in postgraduate programs, including at its highly selective law school. Tuition and fees are more than $48,000. The faculty numbers 637. The university is in a suburban neighborhood on the edge of Richmond, the state capital and a city of 215,000. The Robins Center, home to the basketball team, the only one in the nation nicknamed the Spiders, was built in 1972 but totally refurbished in 2013 for $17 million. It is a showplace that seats 7,200, with the four largest video boards in the Atlantic 10, premier-seating and hospitality terraces, and a ceiling painted blue. Coach Chris Mooney agreed to a new contract with Richmond in 2010 that would pay him $700,000 annually through the 2016-17 season, according to a story in the Richmond Times-Dispatch. However, a Form 990 filed in 2014 indicated Mooney was the third highest-paid employe at the U of R, and was paid $1,145,141 that year. Richmond's budget for men's basketball was $4.2 million in 2014, and surely is higher today.

The other Big 5 school in the A-10 is St. Joseph's University, run by the Jesuits, founded in 1851, and located on a 114-acre campus on Philadelphia's City Line Avenue in a neighborhood known as Overbrook. St. Joe's has 219 majors and other programs. It has a joint-degree program with the renowned Thomas Jefferson University Hospital for six medical professions, including bioscience technology, radiological sciences and nursing. There are 301 full-time professors. Undergraduate enrollment is 4,800 and graduate students number 3,234. St. Joseph's also has a prep school. The university's endowment is $216 million. The city, the five Pennsylvania counties that surround it, South Jersey and northern Delaware make the metropolitan region the seventh largest nationally, with an overall population of six million. Coach Phil Martelli's salary has been reported to be $902,000. The school's basketball budget is $4.1 million. The team plays at the modernized, on-campus Hagan Arena, which holds 4,200.

St. Louis University, the western-most member of the A-10, also resides amid a large population base. The school itself is large, with 8,200 undergraduates and 4,600 grad students, which includes the law and medical schools. The campus is urban, just minutes away from the Gateway Arch downtown. The school awards 90 undergraduate degrees and more than 100 graduate degrees. It is also a Jesuit school, founded in 1818. Most undergraduate students reside on campus. The university is in the St. Louis metro region, the nation's 20th-largest. Population growth is outside the city of St. Louis, which is dogged by poverty and crime and losing population to the suburbs. The endowment of $1.076 billion is the third-largest among the 28 Jesuit institutions, trailing only Boston College and Georgetown. More than 60 percent of the school's undergraduates come from outside Missouri. St. Louis also has a campus in Madrid, Spain. Chaifetz Arena, which was completed in 2008 and cost $80 million, seats 10,600. Head Coach Jim Crews is paid "in excess of $854,000," according to the St. Louis Post-Dispatch.

Virginia Commonwealth University is huge and urban. It is a public university with a college of humanities and sciences and 13 different schools of study, from public art to dentistry, nursing, medicine and pharmacy to government and public administration. The main campus is 130 acres in downtown Richmond. There are 24,000 undergraduate students and another 9,000 in graduate programs. VCU has partnerships with 13 international universities, including in Qatar. There are 3,280 on the faculty and 11,000 other staffers in various administrative roles. The endowment is $1.638 billion. In-state tuition is under $13,000, and $31,000 for out-of-state students. Home court for the Rams is the Stuart C. Siegel Center, known as "The Stu," and was built in 1999 for $30.1 million. It has 7,637 seats and the school claims every game since the 2011 season has been sold out. VCU wins at home nearly 86 percent of the time, thanks to a fan base known as the Rowdy Rams. Virginia Commonwealth has the most expensive basketball budget in the A-10: $5.4 million. Coach Will Wade will be paid $1 million in the 2015-16 season, his first. Shaka Smart, his predecessor, was making nearly $1.6 million a year before heading off to the University of Texas.

The Atlantic 10 Conference: Fourteen schools. Four of them large public universities. Ten private universities. Most of them with rich endowments, some of them with law schools, one with a medical school, some of them highly prestigious. Thirteen of them located in large metropolitan areas. One situated in a small, somewhat poor, out-of-the-way location. That is St. Bonaventure, also the smallest and least-wealthy of the schools. The next smallest college, Davidson, has 1,850 undergraduates but an endowment that is 10 times larger than Bonaventure's. Davidson remains small by choice. Bonaventure has less than 1,700 undergraduates because it is in crisis, embattled on numerous fronts. The school most like St. Bonaventure, though unlike in many ways, urban vs. small town being one of the key differences, is La Salle, and its undergraduate enrollment is more than twice the size of St. Bonaventure's.

Resources, enrollment, location, the alumni base … they should matter substantially as it regards sustaining a Division I men's basketball program. And they do. But not all of the time. Otherwise, the Bonnies would not have won the Atlantic 10 Tournament in 2012, and would not have had winning seasons the past two years. Mark Schmidt, his coaches and the players they somehow bring to Olean have made a difference, and this conference season should be interesting. In the end, winning or losing boils down to how one team's top six or seven players match up with the other team's when the ball is tossed at center court. Strategy, style of play matter.

Comparatively, however, surmounting the advantages that Bonaventure's conference foes enjoy is borderline miraculous. And it is accomplished, for the most part, by Schmidt and his assistants, with athletes who often didn't have a whole lot of other options. This against-all-odds quality of the program is what accounts, at least in part, for the fevered Bonaventure fandom.

Two things: The Reilly Center is larger than the arenas of six of

Bonaventure's A-10 rivals, and the support the program receives from students and the nearby community, year after year, is remarkable. Bonaventure seems to be the only school in the conference without a pep band, for what that is worth.

CHAPTER 10:
A GOOD START

DAVIDSON

Everyone seems to like Davidson. Before a conference game was even played, one of the multitude of NCAA Tournament bracket forecasters had Davidson as one of the three teams from the Atlantic 10 Conference that would make the field come March 2016. George Washington and Dayton would also make it. Davidson would be an 11-seed. Seems like bad news for St. Joseph's, which went 10-2 in its non-conference schedule, losing only a game at Florida and to powerful Philadelphia rival Villanova, but the Hawks are likely to continue their season nonetheless. Plus, they have ESPN bracketology savant Joe Lunardi working for them.

There are reasons for Davidson's appeal. The Wildcats won the A-10 regular season the year before, their first year in the league, and went to the NCAA tourney. Jack Gibbs, a high-scoring junior guard and at six feet and 195 pounds built like a bulldog, was one of the best players in the conference and a first-team pre-season selection. Seniors Brian Sullivan and Jor-

dan Barham joined Gibbs to give Davidson a potent backcourt. Bob McK-
illop, who with a full head of white hair looks like a Kentucky colonel but
hails from Long Island, has been Davidson's coach for 27 years and is one
of the most respected coaches in the country. Davidson has a rich basketball history. Stephen Curry, the sharpshooter for the Golden State Warriors
and presently the best basketball player on the planet, is a Davidson grad.

Davidson and St. Bonaventure had a significant meeting in 1970,
when they played in an NCAA Tournament first-round game at St. John's
University's gymnasium on Long Island. This is when the NCAA field was
limited to just 32 teams. The Wildcats were very good, with forward Mike
Molloy and left-handed guard Brian Adrian leading the way. The Bonnies
won, 85-72. Bob Lanier had 28 points and 15 rebounds and Matt Gantt
added 19.

Davidson made the tedious trip to Olean to open the 2015-2016
conference schedule for both schools on Jan. 2. The Wildcats went 8-3
in non-conference play but lost to North Carolina in the Dean Dome in
Chapel Hill, Pitt at Madison Square Garden and DePaul in Chicago --- and
lost by lopsided scores. Nevertheless, Davidson would be a stern A- 10 test
for the Bonnies, even though Sullivan and Barham would miss the game
with injuries.

With the non-conference schedule completed and the game with
Davidson two days away, Schmidt was asked to assess his team and to con-
fide what gives him confidence and what worries him as the A-10 looms.

"Everything worries me," he said. "We have inconsistencies in our effort. We don't have an alpha dog ... no true leader. We play well in spurts, for two and three possessions. We can't have these peaks and valleys."

The conference always assures that toughness will be required. Would the combination of Jordan Tyson, weighed down by the rust of a redshirt season and an injury that caused him to miss all but two games of the non-conference schedule, and Derrick Woods, who showed promising flashes but was just 11 games in to his college career, provide the inside presence the Bonnies would require?

"We are strong from one-through-four. The five-spot is our weakest position," he answered. "We can't just throw the ball in to them for easy baskets. We are too perimeter-oriented. I watched the film when we beat them (Davidson) down there last year ... we'd get the ball in to Youssou ... jump hook, score ... jump hook, score.

"I have plays on my card to get the ball inside but they have Andrew Nicholson's name on it."

Schmidt was asked if the ability to score that Marcus Posley, Jaylen Adams, Dion Wright, Denzel Gregg and Nelson Kaputo have shown --- in spurts --- so far in the season gives the Bonnies "a puncher's chance" in A-10 play.

"Yeah, I like that," he said. "A puncher's chance, yeah. Guys who play with confidence. We have some vets. We have good guard play. Kaputo is a big addition. We can go small. We have to shoot like we did against Niagara."

Then he said of Posley, who scored just six points in the win over

Niagara, "We have to get Marcus back in the fold."

For one night, at least, Schmidt would get everything he wished. With the students still on break, nearly 3,800 came to the Reilly Center on a Saturday night for a game that tipped off at 8 p.m. because of television, and they were loud and engaged by a contest that Chuck Pollock, the venerable columnist for the Olean Times Herald, called "a fantastically entertaining matchup." The Bonnies, playing their best game to date, won 97-85, and it required a near-heroic performance by Jaylen Adams. The sophomore guard from Baltimore, who has a choirboy's countenance and the heart of an assassin, scored 30 points. His line in the box score is remarkable: He was 5-for-8 on three-point goals, 7-for-13 overall and 11-for-11 on free throws. At 6-foot-2, he had six rebounds on the defensive end and four assists. With both teams pushing the pace the whole game, Adams had just two turnovers.

The game was tied at 43 at the half, and Posley had just two points. But he was a force in the second half, forgoing shooting from the outside and instead driving to the basket, contorting his body on some of his shots, and scoring 17 points in the last 20 minutes. He also had four assists and no turnovers.

Bonaventure needed all of that because Davidson kept coming. Gibbs was a big presence. He scored 15 in the first 20 minutes but shot just 6-for-19. But Jordan Watkins, starting in place of Sullivan, had 11 points. Watkins nailed three three-pointers in the first five minutes of the second half to give the Wildcats a 57-51 lead. Wright got two baskets inside, one on a pretty feed from Kaputo, to tie the game at 62-62. But Watkins cooled off and Gibbs went ice cold, though he kept firing away.

The Bonnies were getting terrific defensive play from Idris Taqqee on Watkins and Adams on Gibbs. But Davidson did get points from their big men, Peyton Aldridge, who would end up with 18, and Andrew McAuliffe, who had 11. Wright, who hit a three-pointer as the shot clock went off, gave Bonaventure a 78-75 lead. Wright would eventually foul out. A Posley drive and two free throws pushed the lead to 84-76 with 2:50 to go. Adams and Posley provided free throws to make it 90-82 with 44 seconds remaining.

There were two rows of Davidson fans, dressed in red, behind their team's bench, and they knew this one had slipped away.

This game is basically the blueprint for this Bonaventure team, which is too small, too inexperienced in some key areas, but quick and skillful: Get significant scoring from Adams, Posley and Wright, who combined for 60 points. Get production from the athletic Denzel Gregg, who went for 13 points, including 8-of-8 from the free throw line, five rebounds and four assists in 27 minutes. Get defense, help on the boards and some scoring from Taqqee, who provided five points, six rebounds and, importantly, cooled off Watkins for stretches of the second half. Get something from Derrick Woods and Jordan Tyson, and they did. Woods, who seems more and more comfortable, had 11 points and five rebounds in just 16 minutes. Tyson played 18 minutes and had five rebounds and scored a basket inside to push the Bonnies ahead by six points with 3:20 to go.

It is rather amazing, or maybe sobering, to consider the kind of effort that is required to match that blueprint, and to do it 12 or 13 times in 18 games over 10 weeks if your team is to be of consequence in the Atlantic 10. Even in the afterglow of a superb performance that provides a wonderful start to conference play, that reality nags.

"It was a great college basketball game and a great environment," McKillop said. Last season at Davidson, Posley made the first of his two buzzer-beating, game-winning drives. The second would come in the next game against Virginia Commonwealth at the Reilly Center. "He's a very good player, a senior, mature, experienced, gets to the rim and finishes off, and that's what very good players do," McKillop said.

In his press conference, Schmidt was about as effusive as he would ever allow himself. He said his team made a great effort, a great team effort. He credited Gregg for hitting a key shot, Woods for a strong first half, and declared that Tyson "is getting his legs back underneath him."

Schmidt also said that Posley's big second half, fueled by his drives to the rim, was discussed at halftime. Schmidt added: "Davidson doesn't have a shot-blocker per se, so Posley's drives were part of our game plan."

Buffalo News writer Mark Gaughan tried to articulate what was running through most everyone's heads as it regards the play of Adams. "Jaylen, wow ... the three-point shooting ... are you, like, feeling it?" Gaughan asked. Adams, who never seems particularly impressed with anything, including himself, giggled and provided the only answer possible: "Yeah."

Posley was asked about what he sees in the defense that prompts him to drive to the basket to get his points, what was different in the second half? The pace of the game meant some of Posley's scoring bursts would be in transition, and they were, but his answer left the impression that his bolts inside stem more from confidence and a belief that when he gets in to the lane, he will figure out some way to get baskets and draw fouls. "It's like he said," Posley answered, alluding to Adams, who sat beside him. "You just start to feel it."

GEORGE MASON

Posley brought his skill and confidence with him to Fairfax, Va., for the second conference game, a matchup with George Mason. The Patriots, who have struggled since joining the Atlantic 10, have a new coach, Dave Paulsen, who had been the successful head coach at Bucknell University in the Patriot League. Mason had two stunning wins in a tournament in Charleston, S.C., knocking off Mississippi and Oklahoma State before losing to Virginia in the title game. But the Patriots lost to folks such as Colgate, Manhattan, Towson and James Madison and began A-10 play with a 71-47 bashing by Virginia Commonwealth.

Mason's top player is 6-foot-11 center Shevon Thompson, a third-team preseason pick in the A-10. The Bonnies coaches wondered how Woods and Tyson would manage Thompson, and what the big man's presence might mean for the inside scoring of Dion Wright. But the Patriots also have seven freshmen on their roster, and three of them play a lot of minutes. Moreover, Mason has trouble scoring points.

As in earlier games, Bonaventure held leads at 7-2 and 17-9 but they were squandered. Thompson was having an impact. He was rebounding and drawing fouls. His basket inside cut the Bonnies lead to 29-26, but Posley hit back-to-back three-pointers to provide Bonaventure with a 35-30 lead. It was 37-34 at the half.

Schmidt had to do one of those quickie intermission interviews, where he has to slap on a headset and take questions from the television broadcast team. This is not exactly a passion of his, since it keeps him away from the locker room and the team to discuss second-half strategies. The coach was not thrilled with the first-half performance. He credited Posley's shooting but said the Bonnies were "playing no defense inside." He also said any win on the road in the Atlantic 10 is a good one: "We'll take it if it is a one-point win."

The second half started with Thompson scoring inside and drawing a foul on Woods, his fourth. Thompson missed the free throw. Then the Bonnies began to draw away. Posley scored and added a free throw. Idris Taqqee gave Wright a beautiful feed inside. Posley was fouled behind the three-point arc but missed two of his three foul shots, but it made the score 50-41 with 14:10 to play. Nelson Kaputo hit a three-pointer, and two free throws from Posley made it 55-45 with 11:10 to go. Posley had 24 points at this point and was pretty much owning the game. That was good, because Taqqee, Tyson, Woods and Wright each had four fouls.

Denzel Gregg was a serious presence in the second half, scoring 12 points, including a three-point basket that stretched the lead to 71-58 and a remarkable, no-look, behind-his-head dunk that showed up that night on ESPN's highlights. It deserved to be. The final was 77-58 Bonnies.

With the exception of Thompson, who ended with 14 points and 17 rebounds, all of the Patriots' weaknesses were on display in the second half. They shot just 9-for-30 as Bonaventure used more zone on defense, and Mason turned the ball over 13 times. But the Bonnies did a lot of things right, besides Posley's 30 points and four assists. They outrebounded George Mason 42-41, and had just as many points in the paint, 32. The Bonnies had just eight turnovers. Wright ended with 12 rebounds.

The 2-0 start in the A-10 and the 10-3 overall record is the best for St. Bonaventure since the 1999-2000 season. That team, coached by Jim Baron and led by super guard Tim Winn, went to the NCAA tournament and lost in a heart-breaker to Kentucky in three overtimes. But that club had a roster of players that Bonnie fans will never forget. Along with Winn, there was Peter Van Paassen and Caswell Cyrus. J.R. Bremer was a sophomore and Patricio Prato a freshman. David Capers was a senior and his making three consecutive free throws to extend the game against Kentucky will never be forgotten, and not just by Bonaventure observers. Mark Schmidt's team would not seem to have that kind of luster.

Nonetheless, the Bonnies are surprising people at this point. Paulsen said what others have observed. "That's the thing about them," he told J.P. Butler, the Olean Times Herald beat writer. "At one point, maybe we had a chance to get back in the game, and they ran the shot clock down and the kid (Nelson) Kaputo hit a corner three, and that was like a back-breaker.

So it's not just Adams and Posley … that's a really talented team. A good offensive team, and you really have to be locked in."

MASSACHUSETTS

The Minutemen really have a lot going for them. Huge public university, a striking arena and basketball alums named Rick Pitino, Julius Erving and Marcus Camby. The school used to be able to proudly claim comedian Bill Cosby, who earned masters and doctoral degrees in education there and had very close ties to UMass. Cosby and his wife, Camille, own a 21-acre estate with a main house and four additional structures, pool and tennis court, not far from the campus in Amherst, Mass., and have been using it to hide out since Cosby's avalanche of sexual-abuse cases crashed down on him. UMass publicly announced in 2014 that it had cut ties with Cosby, who had been a heavy donor.

So the Bonnies should not be able to motor in to Amherst and stroll out with a win. But it happened the prior season and happened again on Jan. 9. Bonaventure won, 88-77. Three games in to an 18-game conference regular season should not be the juncture at which one makes sweeping determinations about a team, especially one not named, say, Michigan State or Duke. But the Bonnies are intriguing. Here are the reasons:

They beat Massachusetts fairly easily, opening a 19-point lead midway through the second half. Bonaventure misplaced its intensity for a seven-minute stretch and let the Minutemen crawl within nine points on several occasions, but by then there were only three minutes remaining and it never felt all that dire.

Bonaventure did not even play particularly well overall. They let UMass, which was bombed by Dayton in its previous game, have 16 offensive rebounds. The Bonnies had a grand total of two offensive rebounds. Overall, Massachusetts had a 34-27 advantage on the boards. The Minutemen had 13 second-chance points to Bonaventure's four, and the Bonnies turned it over 14 times. Tyler Bergantino, a senior who did not start in his previous 96 games, had 13 points and hurt the Bonnies inside, and Bergantino is no Shevon Thompson.

Incredible shooting by the Bonnies was the killer difference. They went 28-for-47 from the field and 10-for-18 on three-point goals --- 59.6 percent overall and 55.6 percent on three-pointers. The troika prevailed once again: Adams scored 24 points and did it on a ridiculous seven shots from the field. But he went to the foul line 13 times and converted on 11. Dion Wright finished with 19 points, including a three-pointer, and seven rebounds. Marcus Posley had 15 but was just 3-for-10 from long distance. Adams had eight assists and one turnover. Denzel Gregg had 12 points and five rebounds. Nelson Kaputo was 3-for-4 on three-point attempts and finished with 10.

UMass coach Derek Kellogg was equal parts livid and disconsolate. Before the game, he had warned that he had little time to prepare for the Bonnies because his team played Wednesday night at Dayton and then had to be ready for a noon tipoff on Saturday. That's a fair point. Then while the Bonnies were on the early second-half roll that basically decided the outcome, Kellogg exploded at a call against his club and had to be restrained by his players. By the end of the game, he seemed drained. The TV camera caught him slowly putting on his suit coat and shaking his head before exchanging handshakes with Schmidt.

In the postgame press conference, Kellogg, whose team fell to 8-7 and 1-2 in the A-10, said: "They outplayed us. They executed better on the offensive board. We won a few categories that I was hoping we could win, especially the rebounding. Obviously, it wasn't enough.

"We were 15- for-23 from the free throw line and 4-of-22 from three. And they go 56 percent (from three) and 88 percent from the line. That kind of tells it right there. As a whole, for 40 minutes, they played better basketball at both ends of the floor."

So the formula for success plotted by Mark Schmidt, back in August when t-shirts and basketball shorts was the dress code in the basketball suite at the Reilly Center, was evident once again. This squad can hurt opponents with its firepower, even when not much else is going well. The 55 points Schmidt said he needed each game from Posley, Adams and Wright was there against UMass; they combined for 58 points. Gregg is making an impact, and Kaputo is more than just a freshman substitute, he is the catalyst for a going-small lineup that changes their look and makes defenses adjust.

They have scrapped for wins when they score less than 80 points --- as they did against Binghamton, Canisius and Buffalo --- but it is an uneasy formula, as Siena proved. The other keys were playing up-tempo and clawing on defense, and good defense has hardly been a constant. The Bonnies surrendered 50 points in the second half at Syracuse and 89 at home against Hofstra, and lost. They let Loyola and Davidson score in the 80s at the Reilly Center and survived, but will that really work against Dayton and Virginia Commonwealth?

The end result, at this point, is St. Bonaventure sits alone atop the Atlantic 10 Conference standings at 3-0 and an overall record of 11-3. The season, however, could rest on a 22-day stretch of six games beginning with Rhode Island in Olean on Jan. 13. After that, it is at Duquesne, home with Dayton, at VCU, home with Richmond and then St. Joseph's in Philly.

Seth Davis, the Sports Illustrated writer and CBS-TV basketball analyst, tweeted this the night of Jan. 10, when the weekend's basketball games had wrapped up:

Almost famous. Kentucky, LSU, UConn, Purdue, Wichita State, Cincy, Gonzaga, St. Mary's, Dayton, St. Bonaventure, VCU, USC, Houston @SethDavisHoops.

"Almost famous" because of flirting with the Top 25.

And, for the first time in many seasons, St. Bonaventure received one vote for the Top 25.

Not bad company 14 games in to the season.

CHAPTER 11:

'SELF-MADE MEN'

RHODE ISLAND

The game against Rhode Island, a team many thought capable of winning the Atlantic 10 Conference this season, might better be told from the ending, rather than the beginning. It was a battle, a "man's game" as described by Mark Schmidt, and the Bonnies muscled out a win, 69-64, before a disappointing Reilly Center turnout of just 3,219 on a Wednesday night. It made Bonaventure 4-0 and alone atop the A-10 standings. A heady achievement for a team picked to finish eighth in the league in a preseason poll of its coaches.

The Rams are physical, and Hassan Martin, at 6-7 and 230 pounds, is a bull, as talented as he is muscular. They also are playing without E.C. Matthews, possibly the best player in the league and lost for the year with a pre-season knee injury.

Rhode Island had a 52-47 lead on a three-point goal by sharpshooting Four McGlynn with 9:40 to play. It was 57-56 after Jaylen Adams hit a three-pointer with 7:01 to go. Guard Jarvis Garrett gave Rhody a 64-60 lead on a driving basket and a free throw. Marcus Posley was fouled on a drive and hit both free throws to make it 64-62. Then Denzel Gregg, playing "the best game in his college career," according to Schmidt, nailed a three-point jumper and gave the Bonnies a 65-64 edge with 1:33 to play. Then Gregg scrambled to get a rebound on the Rams next trip down the floor and was fouled. He hit both free throws to make it 67-64 Bonnies with 1:05 to play.

Then it got even more interesting. Jaylen Adams was fouled and his two made free throws gave his team a 69-64 edge with 17 seconds to play. That would be the final score. It was at that point that Dion Wright said something to Martin, who turned around and responded with a shout. Wright grabbed the rebound on Rhode Island's last shot and, facing a TV cameraman positioned under the basket, dribbled the ball in the waning seconds with a sneer on his face.

There were no obvious incidents when the coaches and players shook hands after the game. But a day later, Schmidt was asked about the banter between Martin and Wright. Both Wright and Posley told Schmidt that the Rhode Island bench was hectoring some of the Bonaventure players … "talking shit," as Schmidt explained it. "You suck" was among the taunts, and, according to the two Bona players, Rhode Island Coach Dan Hurley was the source of some of that. According to Schmidt, Marcus Posley, who, as is often the case, was the last player in line for the handshakes, told his coach that Hurley told him "nice game," and then Posley mentioned the taunts --- "the talking shit." Hurley just brushed it off and went on his way.

Schmidt said he had absolutely no first-hand knowledge of Hurley chattering at the Bonaventure players, but he knows of other instances of coaches taunting opponents and he decries it. "I would never do that," Schmidt said. "We (the coaches) are supposed to be the adults."

Hurley's postgame remarks were both gracious and weird. He described the game as "hard-fought," which it certainly was. His team had chances, made too many mistakes, and was not assertive down the stretch, he claimed. Then Hurley noted that the Bonnies shot 16 more foul shots than the Rams, which was accurate; the Bonnies made 26 of 31 and the Rams just 10 of 15. A difference-maker, no doubt.

Then it got a bit strange. "We lost composure down the stretch," Hurley said. "Our highly touted kids didn't play well enough ... compared to the hard-working, self-made guys they have. I don't know if Gregg was a 'top-50,' but he played like it tonight." The "top-50" reference regards recruits who might have been one of the 50 best players at their positions in the nation when in high school or prep school.

This apparently regarded Rhode Island recruiting more highly rated players than St. Bonaventure does. Schmidt did say a day later that he and his coaches tried to recruit Martin, from Staten Island, N.Y., but that Martin indicated he had no interest.

Hurley said that Gregg played as if he were a top-50 player, and noted that the late three-point goal from Gregg, which just beat the shot clock, was the difference in the game. Hurley added again that some of his "highly touted players didn't come to play."

Denzel Gregg was not a top-50 recruit, but he has made himself into a fine player. He went 5-for-6 from the field and 2-of-2 from three-point range. His energy in the paint sent him to the free-throw line 11 times, and he converted on 10 of those shots. He finished with 22 points and five rebounds, including a critical grab after a missed Rhode Island shot in the final minute. He did all of this in just 24 minutes of playing time.

When Schmidt met with reporters, he said: "I'm proud of our men … it was a game for men. I like how we came back against a good, physical, well-coached team." With Gregg sitting next to him in the media room, he gushed about the junior's performance.

The Bonnies had jumped out to a 19-6 lead at the 10:12 mark of the first half when Gregg drove for a basket and then drilled a three-pointer. But the Bonnies were steadily reeled in by the Rams, who were more physical on defense and relentless inside on offense. With 57 seconds left in the first half, the game was tied 25-25. The Bonnies led it 28-25 at the half, but it began to feel like Rhode Island would clamp down on Bonaventure in the late minutes, the way the Rams did last season when they won in Kingston.

That didn't happen. The game was tied at 59 with 5:09 to go. Jarvis Garrett gave the visitors a 61-59 edge at the 4:24 mark and a 64-60 lead on a layup and free throw with 3:39 left. But Rhode Island would not score again. Posley made two free throws and Gregg then hit the bomb that pushed the Bonnies ahead.

The win raised the Bonnies to 4-0 in the A-10. "We are playing hard," Schmidt said, "but we must be better. We were beat on the boards (Rhody had 35 rebounds to Bona's 31, and the Rams grabbed 14 offensive rebounds). We have to get better. You learn how to win by winning."

Dan Hurley, who has turned Rhode Island in to a force in the A-10, is part of the New Jersey coaching clan that includes the patriarch, Bob Hurley, the legendary coach of St. Anthony's High School in hard-scrabble Jersey City, and his brother, Bobby, a star at Duke, an NBA player, and coach at the University at Buffalo until heading to Arizona State for this season.

Some Bonaventure fans remain angry at Bob Hurley, whose tough-love and rigid standards for the under-served kids who play on his championship teams, was captured wonderfully in the book "The Miracle of St. Anthony," written by Bonaventure alum Adrian Wojnarowski. The unhappiness centers on Eli Carter, a highly skillful guard coached by Hurley at St. Anthony's, who committed to St. Bonaventure in 2009 and then de-committed. The fans anticipated that Hurley would have worked hard to convince Carter that a commitment made is one that must be kept, and that a man prospers or withers on his word. Carter would have been a steal for Schmidt and the Bonnies, but instead Carter ended up at Rutgers, assured by the enablers who surround highly sought players that he was "a Big East-caliber player," and someone deserving of a platform loftier than the Bonnies and the Atlantic 10.

In retrospect, it would seem Carter's decision to de-commit from Bonaventure and instead go to prep school for a year and attract better options was a considerable mistake. If he had kept his promise and arrived in Olean for the 2010-11 season, he would have played with Andrew Nicholson for two seasons, the second year being the season that Bonaventure won the A-10 tournament and went to the Big Dance. Eli Carter on that squad would have made for a hell of a team. Instead, Carter would have needed to be wearing an electronic ankle bracelet for anyone to have tracked his college career.

He eventually signed with Rutgers and played as a freshman on a bad team in the 2011-12 season. His sophomore season ended in mid-February with a broken fibula. Two months later, with the leak of a tape of a practice session, the entire Rutgers basketball program exploded when Coach Mike Rice was fired for being abusive to his players. Carter sought his release from the school and it was granted. He was off to the University of Florida.

His first season in Gainesville ended abruptly. He had to redshirt again because his leg injury was hampering his play. He played for the Gators in the 2014-15 season but was largely ineffective. One Florida observer described Carter's play as "exasperating spates of poorer performances." Then, eligible for another season because he was a grad student and could play immediately, he wandered to Boston College, where he played in the 2015-16 season on a weak team. Carter recovered his scoring touch, dropping 31 points against Pitt in one Atlantic Coast Conference game in late January, but the Eagles went nowhere. The team was 7-25 for the year and 0-18 in the ACC. That included a 19-game losing streak. BC played its home games in front of crowds that averaged less than 3,000. Carter would have played before consistently larger audiences in Olean. His checkered, peripatetic college career was done at the end of the season, as long and brutal as a Russian winter.

The day after the victory over Rhode Island the Bonnies sat alone atop the Atlantic 10 Conference. The start to conference play was encouraging. Schmidt was upbeat and expansive that morning in his office, relishing the "intensity" his team showed the night before. He also pointed out that when the Bonnies went small, with Gregg and Wright inside, the Rams had to go small as well, and that was an advantage.

But he made another point, one that would prove prophetic: "This train could go off the tracks at any time."

Schmidt said Duquesne, the Bonnies next opponent in a game to be played in Pittsburgh, needed the win they managed over St. Louis after three straight losses to begin conference play. That led him to describe how losing can become contagious, that it becomes more and more difficult to break a losing streak. "I know coaches who are driven crazy by that," he said, and mentioned how one coach he knew, who was absolutely stricken by a string of losses, couldn't come out of the locker room after his team trailed once again at halftime.

Regarding the current state of his team, Schmidt said sometimes he believes half the roster has attention deficit disorder. "Wright and Posley do everything right three times and all wrong the fourth time," Schmidt complained. He said, not for the first time, he is "infuriated" when a player fails to execute a set play.

These dark moments are on exhibit numerous times in any game, when Schmidt practically walks on to the court, bent at the waist, arms spread wide, brow scrunched in numerous furrows, and bellows at his target: "WHAT ARE YOU DOING?" The player's head sinks, and everyone else is left to feel Schmidt's pain, or worry he is headed for a breakdown. But Schmidt moves on almost instantly, pulling his card of plays from the breast pocket of his blazer and considering his next move.

He was asked about the status of recruitment for next year. "We need a big forward," he answered. "But these days, forwards need to be mobile, fast, like Dion," he added. He thinks the speed of the current game has diminished the need for a classic shooting forward and a classic power forward.

Schmidt was asked if he ever ponders the expectations, the hopes and dreams, of the team's fans, especially the alumni who believe that greatness on the court will hugely benefit the university, and that the stakes are higher now than ever because of the enrollment slump. If Bonaventure were to become a consistent powerhouse, wouldn't enrollment, revenue, prestige and stability follow?

Schmidt considered this, and then answered briskly: "That's not my job. My job is to create a good program."

CHAPTER 12:

THE PRESIDENT RESIGNS

Sr. Margaret Carney, O.S.F., announced her resignation as president of St. Bonaventure University the morning of Jan. 19, the day of the game against powerful Dayton at the Reilly Center. A nun in the Order of St. Francis, a scholar who was dean of the School of Franciscan Studies on campus for eight years, and president of the university for almost 12 years, Margaret Carney will leave office on July 31, 2016. She will turn 75 this year.

Being president of any college or university these days pretty much assures you will have a target on your back. Academia is a messy, knotty world, where very smart people with very strong opinions on complicated issues ranging from the value of liberal arts in the computer- and high-tech age to properly serving multiculturalism to managing expenses when your target audience --- the parents of college-aged students at a time when wages are stagnating --- clamors to be heard. It's like riding a bull on steroids, and Sr. Margaret has taken her lumps. Nonetheless, most people respect her, and they should. She is tough-minded and tireless and, like all college presidents, endlessly hunted for dollars. Evan Dobell, the former president of highly regarded Trinity College in Hartford and a brilliant, quirky, funny man, once told me over lunch after he had taken the red-eye from California at the end of a trip seeking donors, "It's the money ... it's always the fucking money."

Sr. Margaret's presidency began when the scandal-torched men's basketball program was still in ashes and it ended with the enrollment slump. In between, however, much was accomplished, including spectacular construction on campus that made an already striking place even more handsome, modern and high-functioning. On her watch, the Walsh Science Center and the William and Anne Swan Business School were built. The Magnano Dining Center, including a complete makeover of the dining facilities and the addition of Café La Verna, was created. And the Marra Family Athletic Complex, which made over and enhanced what already existed, including installing artificial turf that would make baseball and softball playable in the messy springtime weather, was constructed. It provided vastly improved facilities for baseball, softball, men's and women's soccer, women's lacrosse and the men's and women's club rugby teams.

New fields of study, including a 3-2 pharmacy degree with the University at Buffalo and a degree in cybersecurity, are being launched and other practical, market-ready majors are being considered.

No small thing, the hiring of Mark Schmidt also occurred. And his salary rose steadily to $650,000, making the basketball coach the highest-paid employee of St. Bonaventure. Sr. Margaret and the board of trustees also tackled the question of such a small school competing in NCAA Division I athletics. That months-long study in 2015 resulted in the board of trustees unanimously ruling to stay Division I. Students and alumni cheered the decision. In fact, dropping major college sports would have created a fiery outrage from most alumni.

The decision to remain DI and a member of the Atlantic 10 Conference did not sit well with many faculty and staff, whose salaries have suffered as the university looks to hold down expenses. The decision was warmly received by most others. There is the institution and then, in the minds of most students and grads, there is St. Bonaventure and its basketball program, forever linked. One doesn't live without the other.

I had dinner with Dr. Richard Simpson, an English professor, and an expert in the British Romantics, in Olean in December. He has been an esteemed member of the faculty since he arrived on campus with a fresh PhD. from Kent State University in 1970. Students gravitated to him and his classes as soon as he arrived. Simpson is smart, pleasant, a jazz musician, a wonderful conversationalist ... and, despite being a native of California, a Mormon and a graduate of Brigham Young University, he absolutely gets St. Bonaventure, from what it means to be Franciscan to a basketball program that he followed as a young sports fan on the West Coast. When the university celebrated its 150th anniversary in 2011 and produced a beautiful book on the history of the school, Simpson was asked to write the foreword. It was exquisite, brilliantly capturing and explaining the essence of the place, and the hold it now has on him, someone who traded the West

Coast for Olean, raised two sons there who are now themselves scholars, and held funeral services there a year ago for his beloved wife, Deb. As much as anything, his essay was a long and beautiful prayer for the college.

We talked about the challenges facing the school and the idea of a book on the 2015-16 basketball season amid the enrollment and revenues crises. At one point, Simpson asked me, "What does Mark Schmidt get paid --- $325,000?" I told him it was about $650,000. Simpson paused, and then said, without a trace of rancor, more like bemusement, "I have been here for more than 40 years and never hit $80,000 in any year."

Sr. Margaret's corner office on the second floor of Hopkins Hall, the administration building, is almost unsettling for its neatness. Of course, it would be. Nuns are God's drill sergeants. They bring order to chaos, among many other talents. A proud native of Pittsburgh, she has a black-and-gold Steelers mug on her desk and little else. In an interview, she was asked how to rate the scope of the enrollment crisis on a scale of 1 to 10. She bristled a bit at having to do that kind of intellectual gymnastics, and she should have. The question was meant as an ice-breaker but it was woefully imprecise and ignored the complexities of the situation. She explained that it would "take multiple factors to weather the storm."

The major issue, of course, is the number of students. There are fewer than 1,700 undergraduates. The target number for incoming students in the fall of 2015 was anywhere between 475 to 500, depending on which administrator you ask. Not quite 390 showed up in late August. Tuition is the primary revenue stream for colleges. And the incoming class in 2015 won't provide nearly enough.

"The operating budget is stressed," Sr. Margaret said, but noted that faculty received raises for the first time in three years. One professor said it was a 3 percent raise. "We can't hold the line on salaries," Sr. Margaret said. "The faculty is our greatest resource. We must create new areas for getting students." She mentioned the Pittsburgh area as one place, and she has hosted recruitment gatherings for potential students in New York City and Long Island and Northern New Jersey.

I attended St. Bonaventure from 1968 until 1972, and the number of undergraduates was understood to be 2,000 or a bit more. The incoming class in September of 1968 was larger than the dorm rooms available; a number of freshmen were put up in what was then the Holiday Inn in Olean for a few months, and shuttled back and forth to campus in vans. There were about 550 freshmen, the vast majority males, and some of those had to be guys choosing student deferments over sitting at home waiting to be drafted and sent to Vietnam.

There were far more men than women on campus in those days, at least a 65-35 split, and the place had a harder edge than it does today. Fights were not infrequent. Intramural touch-football games could be war zones; there were always dozens of guys getting around on crutches at any time. Intramural water polo could be total havoc, leaving a bloody, pinkish froth on the surface of the water. If you spent four years there and never had a black eye, chipped teeth, broken bones or dislocated body parts then you simply weren't availing yourself of all the place had to offer. Beer always flowed. Long nights at bars were not limited to Fridays and Saturdays. And most everyone loved the place, including the too-few women students, who handled with grace and good humor the remarkably testosterone-rich environment they were navigating.

My class had large numbers from the Buffalo and Rochester areas, of course, but also from Syracuse and Binghamton. Many students were from Nassau County on Long Island, kids from Catholic high schools in places like Manhasset, Westbury, Mineola and Hicksville. Morris and Bergen counties in New Jersey sent large numbers of students. In fewer numbers, students hailed from Connecticut, Massachusetts and Rhode Island, and from northeast Ohio, including the Cleveland area.

Why have those hotbeds of students dried up for St. Bonaventure? I grew up in northeastern Pennsylvania in a small town 16 miles north of Scranton, a place called Carbondale, and it was as gritty and working-class as the name would imply. If you were thinking of going to college, and most were not, your parents would urge interest in the University of Scranton. Most of those who ended up there from my town were commuters, making the 45-minute drive up and back on Route 6, forced to spend the hours between classes in a lounge in the student center. But they weren't having to pay the costs of room-and-board. For those reasons, "The U," as it was commonly called, held no appeal for me. The campus was a cluster of buildings on a tight and unglamorous campus atop a rise that was five or six blocks from the center of town. The school was and is operated by the Jesuits, and that cut a lot of ice with parents in the Lackawanna Valley. My memory is that the enrollment at Scranton at that time was about the same size as St. Bonaventure's.

Same size, but different in that it didn't have a beautiful campus, wasn't a solidly residential college, wasn't six hours from Carbondale, wasn't located in a state where the drinking age was 18 --- and certainly had no bar on campus, as Bonaventure had (and still has) --- and its basketball team wasn't an ass-kicking powerhouse that was nationally ranked and played before full houses in a campus arena that looked like Madison Square Garden to my eyes.

At the same time that Bonaventure was enrolling fewer than 390 students in the late summer of 2015, Scranton enrolled 925 students --- and that was below the school's target. Scranton has 3,900 undergraduates these days (and 550 graduate students), and 90 percent of them come from Pennsylvania, New York and New Jersey. This is chilling news for anyone concerned with Bonaventure's enrollment. Scranton's campus now spills down those five blocks that had once separated the school from the center of the city. Some of those are handsome office buildings that the school bought, significantly overhauled, and turned in to classrooms and office space. But some of that growth is new construction, glistening, eye-catching architecture. Basically, the University of Scranton, located in a city that is largely unremarkable, losing population, rather poor, and these days laced with drug-trafficking and rising crime, is now a far better option for students from locations that used to be prime geography for Bonaventure. And the Royals of Scranton play Division III sports.

There is another school in Scranton, Marywood College, operated by the Sisters, Servants of the Immaculate Heart of Mary, and many years ago, all women. It was as much a convent as a college for much of its history. My 95-year-old aunt was a novice there as a teenager and now resides in a facility for retired IHM nuns on campus. It has been co-ed for many years now and it managed to enroll 550 freshmen in its 2015 incoming class.

These examples do not surprise Sr. Margaret. "Draw a circle around Scranton," she said. "Most parents don't want their kids going to school any further than a three-hour drive. That makes Scranton accessible to major population centers, and the schools aggressively market that."

But the competition also resides in Bonaventure's neighborhood. The State University of New York at Geneseo, a short drive from both Buffalo and Rochester, primarily an undergraduate college, will admit nearly 1,400 freshmen in the fall of 2016. Overall enrollment is about 5,600. The school has become highly selective. It has 54 undergrad majors and, according to the university, it ranks in the Top 10 nationally for producing graduates who go on to earn doctorates in STEM fields --- Science, Technology, Engineering and Medicine. It costs about half as much as Bonaventure. Students at Geneseo joke about how many kids from Long Island end up there. Bonaventure used to load up on those Long Island kids.

Sr. Margaret believes the university has to find the dollars to market itself more robustly. Another consideration, now that the school is resolutely remaining Division I, is to expand the sports programs. "Athletes equal students," Sr. Margaret said. "It was one of the reasons for the DI decision."

This is interesting, and Tim Kenney, the new athletic director, has discussed it. Bonaventure already has announced it will create outdoor track teams for men and women, primarily for distance events. He was stunned upon arrival in Olean that the women's lacrosse team, which struggles, has just 20 members. He believes they should have about 40 athletes playing lacrosse. And, importantly, the school will consider launching a men's lacrosse program. Upstate New York is loaded with colleges playing lacrosse, and high schools that have lacrosse programs. The sport also has a firm grip in New England, New Jersey, Maryland and Virginia.

Athletes in these sports are often partial scholarship recipients, players who would pay some of the costs of college in exchange for playing Division I sports. In other words, new revenue and a way to expand enrollment.

Bob Daugherty, president of Bonaventure's board of trustees, stressed the transition period between Sr. Margaret's retirement announcement and her departure in July will be marked by continuing progress toward the university's goals. Fixing the perilous enrollment problem is at the top of that list.

"Sr. Margaret and I agree that the next few months are a time to focus more than ever on the many initiatives and strategies under way to lead our charge to grow enrollments by increasing our competitive academic standing and program relevance in the market," Daugherty said in a release. "This focus not only characterizes Sr. Margaret's legacy, but also propels us forward with momentum during this time of celebration and transition."

Before the meeting ended, Sr. Margaret was asked if she was managing to have any fun. "No," she answered. "I knew this job would be a heavy lift when I took it. And it is."

Jaylen Adams calls a play in game at St. Louis University. (Courtesy of St. Bonaventure University).

Marcus Posley splits the St. Joseph's defense on a drive to the basket in Rochester. (Associated Press)

Head Coach Mark Schmidt walks the sideline at the Reilly Center. (Courtesy of St. Bonaventure University).

A Bonaventure cheerleader energizes a packed house at the Reilly Center. (Courtesy of St. Bonaventure University.)

Idris Taqqee (left) and Dion Wright celebrate the triumph at Dayton. (Associated Press)

Coach Mark Schmidt shouts instructions at A-10 Tournament game against Davidson. (Courtesy of St. Bonaventure).

One of several sold-out games at the Reilly Center on campus. (Courtesy of St. Bonaventure University.)

Fans pay tribute to senior guard Marcus Posley. (Courtesy of St. Bonaventure University).

Jaylen Adams drives against St. Louis in a taut game at the Reilly Center. (Courtesy of St. Bonaventure University).

Coach Mark Schmidt reacts to a call in road game versus Dayton. (Associated Press).

Marcus Posley makes the pass against St. Louis that leads to game-winning basket by Jaylen Adams. (Courtesy of St. Bonaventure University).

The unhappy Bonnies' bench during tough loss to La Salle in Philadelphia. (Bob Clark/Olean Times Herald)

Bonaventure guard Idris Taqqee drives against a George Washington player in homecoming victory. (Mike Hastings/Olean Times Herald).

Bonnies guard Jaylen Adams is fouled by a Richmond defender. (Mike Hastings/Olean Times Herald).

Dion Wright drives the lane against Dayton at the Reilly Center. (Mike Hastings/Olean Times Herald).

Mark Schmidt acknowledges Bonaventure fans after beating St. Joseph's in Philadelphia. (Bob Clark/Olean Times Herald).

CHAPTER 13:

A REALITY CHECK

DUQUESNE

When St. Bonaventure came to the Palumbo Center in Pittsburgh a year earlier, it absolutely stole a game from Duquesne. Marcus Posley went off crazily in the final two minutes of regulation to force an overtime after his team trailed by a dozen with less than three minutes to play, and then Jaylen Adams, just a freshman, hit the jumper in OT that provided an almost miraculous victory. The Bonnies handled the Dukes rather routinely in the second meeting at the Reilly Center.

There were no miracles on this Saturday night. The Bonnies hung around, earning a 61-57 lead on an Adams three-pointer and it was only 64-63 Duquesne with 7:59 to go. But the Dukes were getting very hot. They steadily pulled away as the senior backcourt of Micah Mason and Derrick Colter hit shot after shot. The Duquesne lead was 77-66 after a 13-3 run with only 4:14 left, and the Bonnies were cooked.

There were 2,425 fans to see the Dukes improve to 2-3 in the A-10 after the 0-3 start. The crowd looked even smaller than that, frankly.

Gone was St. Bonaventure's unbeaten start in conference play and its perch atop the A-10 standings.

One could decide this was a bad loss … if not for the fact that some worrisome trends for Bonaventure were clearly evident in this game. In other words, maybe this and future defeats would simply be routine losses.

Defense: The final was 95-88, so Bonaventure was a sieve once again. The good news is Mason and Colter will be gone after this season. The bad news is they weren't the only ones who reveled in the Bonnies version of defense. Forwards Eric James, a sophomore, and L.G. Gill, a junior had 16 and 12 points respectively. Much more problematic, Bonaventure allowed Duquesne to shoot 66 percent from the field in the second half; the Dukes made 18-of-27 shots. The failure to make stops made decent performances by a handful of players irrelevant. Denzel Gregg had 19 points in 32 minutes of play. Nelson Kaputo made 3-of-6 three-point attempts and had nine points. The critical threesome of Marcus Posley, Jaylen Adams and Dion Wright, which must provide 55 points each game, according to Mark Schmidt's formula, combined for 54 points.

Rebounding: Duquesne held that advantage by the lopsided count of 49-34. Both teams had 13 offensive rebounds. Wright had 10 rebounds and Gregg had seven, and still it mattered little.

Inside play: Jordan Tyson saw 18 minutes of time and had six points and four rebounds in that stretch. He also missed 5-of-7 free throws. Derrick Woods started but played just eight minutes and was scoreless.

Duquesne had a 46-34 advantage in points in the paint.

Perhaps most dispiriting for the Bonaventure players and coaches was the fact the team made 12-of-28 three-point attempts: 43 percent. And still lost by seven in a game that felt over with about six minutes to go. Posley was human on this evening in Pittsburgh, providing 15 points on 5-for-14 shooting from the field and six assists. But making 12 from behind the arc and losing rather routinely is all the evidence one requires to realize other pathologies are infecting this team. Amid all of the mess, substitutes Gregg, Kaputo and Tyson provided 34 points, and still didn't alter this game in crunch time.

Micah Mason started the season banged up but he seemed fully recovered against the Bonnies. He also saw the victory as a significant one for the Dukes. "It's huge for us," said Mason, who grew up in nearby Natrona Heights, Pa. "We lost three in a row and played three of the toughest teams in the conference, but that didn't define us. We came back and we got better. I think we proved that tonight."

DAYTON

The St. Bonaventure players walked, not ran, off the court at halftime, seemingly in a daze. In the locker room, it was quiet. No one cursed or tossed equipment. There really was nothing to say. The veteran players were the most anguished, slumped over, heads down and silent.

"There was only one voice in that locker room," said Mark Schmidt. "Mine." He described the mood as "somber."

Schmidt went to a blackboard and wrote 0-0. On the scoreboards above the Reilly Center court it read Dayton 45, St. Bonaventure 18. The Flyers came in to Olean, and in front of what then was a season-best crowd of nearly 4,300, absolutely manhandled the Bonnies in 20 minutes. Both teams came in to this key matchup with 4-1 records in the Atlantic 10, and, at least for Bonaventure, a win would have validated its fast start in conference play.

Dayton needed no validation. The Flyers were 14-3 overall coming in, played a much tougher non-conference schedule, and had Dyshawn Pierre, their best player, back in the lineup. Pierre was kicked off the team and ordered not to step on campus in the first semester because of a sexual assault issue. He sued the school and lost, but the lawsuit has been refiled, likely making Pierre the only NCAA basketball athlete with active litigation against the school for which he plays.

These are strange times. The entire Northwestern football team sued the university for not paying the players, arguing the services they supply and the hours they devote to it makes them employees. The suit failed.

The first-half statistics read more like a police report of a savage physical assault, which was pretty much the case: Dayton was 17-for-26 from the field, including 5-for-7 behind the arc. The Flyers outrebounded the Bonnies 22-10. They had 13 assists; Bonaventure had two. The Bonnies were 7-for-28 from the field, 1-for-10 on three-pointers. Dayton shot at a 65 percent clip in the first 20 minutes.

At one point in the first half, this appeared to be a basketball game between two Division I teams. Kendall Pollard scored Dayton's first six points. A drive by Marcus Posley made it a 10-8 game. It was 19-12 in favor of Dayton after Kyle Davis hit a three-pointer and then scored on a drive at the 11:22 mark.

Watching the game at the court level, it was remarkable to view the quickness on the perimeter that Dayton displayed. It made the Bonnies' defense appear to be nailed to the floor.

Steve McElvene scored on a fast break for Dayton with 8:22 showing in the first half, and what followed was devastating for the Bonnies and their fans. In the next five minutes, the Flyers stretched their advantage to 40-15. Pierre and sniper Charles Cooke did a lot of the damage. Free throws by Jaylen Adams made it 40-17 with 3:04 to play in the half. Pierre hit a three-pointer to make it 45-18. The killer stretch was a 19-0 run by Dayton.

Schmidt was glad to be in the locker room. "As a coach," he said, "when nothing is working, you look forward to getting in there. We didn't talk about winning, we talked about gaining respect."

The first five minutes of the second half were unremarkable. Dayton kept scoring, and three-pointers from Cooke and Kyle Davis gave Dayton a 55-25 command with 14:15 to play --- a 30-point bulge. The Bonnies cut it to 58-36 on three-pointers from Kaputo and Posley, and a Posley drive off a feed from Adams. Nonetheless, only 10:16 was left. The Bonnies had outscored Dayton just 18-13 in the second half at that point.

What happened next is memorable. A pair of three-pointers from

Posley and two free throws from Adams, both players more active than earlier, cut Dayton's lead to 62-40 with 7:50 to go. Still, no indication this would remain anything but a resounding Dayton victory on the road.

Another three from Posley and a driving score plus a free throw from Adams, and with both players driven to recover whatever pride was available, cut Dayton's lead to 65-50. Adams made two more free throws and, with 6:03 remaining a 30-point Dayton lead was down to 13.

It was a 10-point game, 66-56, after a pair of free throws from Posley. There was 5:03 to play, and by now the good-sized crowd was in the game. The biggest difference was that Posley and Adams were driving inside, and either scoring or heading to the foul line. Dayton pushed its advantage to 75-61 with 3:17 left on two free throws from Pierre. A three from Pierre made it 78-61. Still, the Bonnies made it 80-72 on two Adams free throws. When Posley dropped a three-pointer with 31.5 seconds left it was 82-75. A deficit of 30 points was trimmed to seven. Most fans were on their feet.

There was never a moment when any realistic observer believed the Bonnies would overcome the wretched first half they had played. But as the clock ticked down, the fans were loudly cheering the gutsy second half played by their team. The final was 85-79, and the Bonaventure players could at least hold their heads up as they shook hands with their opponents. It was the 15th time in the last 16 meetings that the Flyers had defeated Bonaventure.

Two days after the game, Schmidt would say of the Bonaventure supporters: "Our fans get it. I was proud to be the coach of St. Bonaventure.

There was never any booing."

Bonaventure had scored 61 points in the second half against a terrific team. They scored 54 points in a 13-minute stretch at one point. Those are spectacular offensive statistics … even if the opponent was Binghamton. Dayton is loaded and has the record to prove it. Adams and Posley each had four points at halftime. Posley finished the game with 31 points and Adams had 24. Combined, they had 47 points in 20 minutes of play, a scintillating pace, though it will mean nothing in the conference standings. But they accomplished this against a Dayton team ranked No. 11 nationally in the Rankings Percentage Index (RPI), just one more statistical gauge of performance that gets tossed in to the mix but it carries weight when it comes time to pick the field of 68 in the NCAA Tournament. Bonaventure fell to 4-2 in the conference and 12-5 overall. Thoughts of Top 25 votes were dashed by this point.

Dayton's fine coach, Archie Miller, met with the media after the game and said: "If someone said we'd come up here and get a win against this team, I'd take it." He also said he has great respect for St. Bonaventure and Schmidt and that those two guards --- Posley and Adams --- are as good as any pair in the country."

"Bonaventure can beat anybody in the league," Miller added. "We'll take it and move on."

Schmidt brought Posley and Adams with him when he met with reporters. "I thought the last 10 minutes of the first half was when the game was lost," Schmidt said. "I'm proud about the comeback. We were more aggressive and our press worked. Against a good team you have to attack. In the first half, we didn't attack."

Then Schmidt raised the issue of manhood and said it in a way that indicated he has been in a few "knuckles" --- a term in certain Philadelphia neighborhoods for a street fight, if not in Attleboro, Mass. --- himself. "It's like a fight," the coach said. "You can't win a fight if you are backing up. You have to be moving forward to land punches. Our guys went toe-to-toe with them in the second half."

Two days later, Schmidt was still considering what had happened. "They responded," he said of the players. "It was about individual respect and respect for the program."

Schmidt called Dayton a good team with great players. Posley said: "We have to step up and play the way we are capable of playing."

Of the first half, Schmidt described his team as intimidated. He said he knew the younger players might be shaky but he didn't expect his veterans to play that way. "As a coach, I was proud of how we fought back," Schmidt added. "The game is a lesson in life. Dayton has better players, so we have to outwork them."

Anyone walking from the media room after the post-game press conference broke up, and who looked on to the floor of the then-empty Reilly Center, would have seen something intriguing. There was Schmidt, his tie pulled down, his shirttail pulled out, demonstrating a play to Adams and Posley. Still coaching. A few days after the game, he was asked what he was doing.

"Showing them how to attack a ball screen," Schmidt said. "You have to attack their big guy's hip. (Instead) we were being soft."

Two days later, Schmidt was still considering what happened. "They responded," he said again of the players.

Schmidt would also say, "You can't count on outscoring people in this league. It doesn't work. You will lose. Defense is a staple. Offense is fickle. Defense is effort, a commitment. Dayton had too many easy baskets. We have to make them work for it."

These are significant observations by the coach, because most of the Bonnies success to this point in the season has been outscoring opponents. They handled Rhode Island and slipped past Buffalo when the scoring wasn't coming easily. And they gutted out a victory at Canisius. Most of the other victories have resulted from strong offensive play.

VCU

Despite fretting a full-blown snow blizzard that could gum up the Bonnies charter flight to Richmond the next day for a Saturday clash with Virginia Commonwealth, Coach Schmidt was in a pretty good mood. He seems to like to play at the Stuart C. Siegel Center, a 7,500-seat arena, always packed with fans, and a place where the Rams almost never lose. "Have you ever seen a game there?" Schmidt asked. "It's a heck of a scene. They don't have a pep band. They have more like a marching band sitting in the stands. I looked up there one time and they had five trombone players."

The Bonnies flight to Richmond landed safely on a Friday afternoon.

Someone on the Bona Bandwagon, learning the team was on the ground despite a storm that shut down a stretch of the East Coast from the Carolinas to New York City, posted: Deo Gratias.

The weather resulted in a postponement of the game. Instead of playing Saturday, the Bonnies and Rams would square off on Sunday afternoon.

If Dayton isn't the best team in the A-10 at this juncture, then Virginia Commonwealth is. The Rams stood at 6-0 in the conference and 15-5 overall. They were beaten by Duke, Wisconsin, Florida State --- all on neutral courts --- and at Georgia Tech and Cincinnati. The only double-digit loss was to Georgia Tech.

The Rams have lost little despite the departure of Head Coach Shaka Smart, who finally received an offer that could get him out of Richmond. Smart now coaches the University of Texas. Coach Will Wade, a former assistant with Smart and the head coach at Tennessee-Chattanooga for one season, still likes to press and play fast. VCU is hard to handle on the perimeter and in the paint.

Despite not scoring a field goal for the first six minutes and falling behind 7-0, the Bonnies kicked it in to gear. A drive and a free throw by Denzel Gregg cut the deficit to 8-6 with 13:40 left. Melvin Johnson's three-point play made it 15-8 VCU. But two nice baskets by Derrick Woods sandwiched around a Jaylen Adams jumper cut the lead to 17-14. The first half was close the rest of the way, and the Bonnies actually led, 34-33, at intermission.

Marcus Posley went on a rampage in the first six minutes of the second half. He alone scored 16 points, a combination of three-point shooting and drives to the bucket, and gave the Bonnies a 50-41 advantage with 13:40 to play. Bonaventure might sneak out of the Siegel Center and snowy Richmond with the kind of victory that could turn the season. The Rams overall record at the arena is 215-34.

It didn't happen. With Johnson, JeQuan Lewis and Justin Tillman doing a lot of the damage, VCU pulled within 55-54. A three-pointer by Denzel Gregg and a drive by Dion Wright, who played a terrific game, kept the Bonnies in the lead at 60-54. A three-point play by Tillman pulled VCU to 60-57 with 8:30 remaining.

From this point on, three problems plagued Bonaventure: Derrick Woods fouled out. He and Jordan Tyson played a combined 32 minutes and produced a combined six points and six rebounds. Tyson fouled out two minutes behind Woods. Bonaventure had to use its small lineup for the rest of the remaining time, and the Rams took advantage inside. VCU's three-quarter press would produce nine Bonaventure turnovers in the second half. Lewis and Johnson started making things happen offensively.

The game was tied 61-61 with 6:20 to play, but the Rams would pull away. Johnson, Tillman and Lewis --- especially Lewis, a crafty guard --- made the difference. It was 75-67 with 1:40 to go. The final was 84-76.

Lewis, Johnson and Tillman combined for 64 points. The veteran Mo Allie-Cox had 10 points and eight rebounds. Posley finished with 30 points, despite a nagging hip injury. He had 26 in the second half. Dion

Wright had 18 points and 13 rebounds, a hell of a performance on the road and against this team. Denzel Gregg had 11 rebounds off the bench. Jaylen Adams took a bad fall in a collision late in the first half, landing on his hip. He actually missed two free throws that resulted from the play. He had 11 points but didn't seem quite himself after the tumble, though he played 37 minutes.

"I thought we played really hard," Schmidt told J.P. Butler of the Olean Times-Herald. "They made the plays at the end. I thought it was a hard-fought game. They are a really good defensive team and I thought we did a lot of good things. We just didn't finish the way we needed to finish."

Thanks to Wright and Gregg, Bonaventure played VCU even on the rebounds. VCU had 17 points off Bona turnovers, which numbered 12 for the game and nine in the last 20 minutes. The Rams also received 27 points from its bench.

Lewis would finish with 26 points and seven assists. Schmidt thought Lewis was the key to the Rams' victory. VCU announced the attendance as 7,637 --- more than even the listed capacity. They saw a spirited game.

Now 4-3 in the A-10 and 12-6 overall, Bonaventure's season is either on the brink or damn close to it. They would be off this coming week, giving them six days to prepare for a Sunday home game and a national TV audience against Richmond. The Spiders usually torment the Bonnies.

CHAPTER 14:

SEARCHING FOR STUDENTS

Bernard Valento arrived on the St. Bonaventure campus in May of 2015, just about the time the school was discovering that its next incoming class would be alarmingly smaller than expected. It was a painful discovery ... financially, for sure, but also to the institution's self-esteem and plans for the future.

Valento is the new vice president for enrollment. If March is a key month for Mark Schmidt, then May is when Valento will taste victory, defeat or something in between. One year will not measure Valento's performance. His challenge is large and complex, and some things he has no control over, such as the population drain in Western New York and the national demographic dip in the number of 18-to-22-year olds. But a marked improvement over the previous May would be welcome. The time between April 1 and May 1 is the most telling. That is when deposits begin to arrive from students accepting their admission.

It's a big job, and the stakes are huge, but he is a big guy, tall and broad-shouldered, a former college soccer player. Valento is a Minnesota native but knows Western New York. He transferred from a school in his home state to Mercyhurst University in Erie, Pa., to play soccer. He has a masters degree in Career and Human Resource Development from Rochester Institute of Technology. Valento worked in the admissions offices of RIT and Mercyhurst. He was at Brockport State, one of the State University of New York campuses, for 15 years, including as the director of undergraduate admissions, so he knows the network of high school guidance directors in Upstate New York and in the New York City area. He was the vice president for enrollment management at West Virginia Wesleyan University when Bonaventure came calling.

The vice president part of Valento's title is no small thing. It means his position is among the cabinet, one of the nine administrators at the school who report directly to the university president. As athletic director, Tim Kenney is in the cabinet. "It gives us a seat at the table," as Valento says. A hot seat.

Ask enough people, and it becomes apparent that a great deal of institutional firepower is targeted on this enrollment problem. The strategies are collected and fashioned and made actionable in Valento's office, and some of the key tactics are clearly his ideas, but the effort is wide and deep. In the distinctively flat accent that marks a native of the Upper Midwest, Valento rattles off the four main priorities: academic and co-curriculum programming, strong branding, effective marketing and recruitment, and developing new markets for potential students. Beneath all of that, of course, there are the sticky details.

Expanding the staffing in Valento's department is one initiative. Valento is interviewing for a director of recruitment. He has five applicants for the role. He would like to extend marketing the university to high schoolers when they are sophomores, instead of waiting until late in their junior years or early in their senior years. He wants to create the position of alumni outreach coordinator. He is also considering a data director and someone responsible for communications within the admissions department.

Altering the academic offerings is certain to receive a dour reaction from some of the faculty, especially the ones whose disciplines might be in the crosshairs. This is especially tricky for universities, such as Bonaventure, that tout their liberal arts tradition. Maybe some new areas of study, such as majors connected to health care or cybersecurity, or more graduate programs in the School of Journalism and Mass Communications, will come at an unsettling cost to the existing curriculum. But others might not, such as online graduate degree programs in business.

Nevertheless, there is a real tension over how the administration and the faculty will handle curriculum change on behalf of attracting students who would not come otherwise.

Finding new markets for students is an imperative. Seeking students from abroad is one tactic. A particularly interesting endeavor is recruiting young men interested in the priesthood, and providing them a college education as they prepare for the seminary. Valento has this initiative underway. One friar already on the faculty will now report to Valento on behalf of attracting potential seminarians to consider first earning an undergraduate degree at Bonaventure. Seven provinces of Franciscan priests are on board, helping Valento's partner, the Rev. Ross Chamberlain, find recruits. Candidates for the priesthood would still be required to undergo the training after their undergraduate days that only seminaries can provide. A database of priests who would be potential recruiters for this program is being compiled. Valento said eight or nine young men interested in the priesthood have applied as a result of this new program. Five of them have been accepted. Valento knows of no other schools with programs directly aimed at recruiting would-be seminarians.

Valento also said there would be an emphasis on recruiting that stresses the opportunities the school's Army ROTC program presents. It is a segment of prospective students that Valento is terming "military-aligned students" --- individuals who have served in the active military or are with the National Guard or a state's military reserve units. These are attractive applicants because they receive pay and tuition assistance from their branches of the service.

He also said the new major in cybersecurity, available at only a few other colleges, is attracting attention. Thirty applications have been received and 25 of those folks have been admitted.

Kenney, the AD, is working with Valento and others on sports programs that would attract partial-scholarship athletes eager to pay some of their costs for the opportunity to be Division I athletes. Expanding the roster of the women's lacrosse team and launching men's and women's distance track teams are underway. Creating a men's lacrosse program is a passion of Kenney's. Lacrosse was a thriving sport in New York State long before it became popular everywhere else. Long Island, and that is where Kenney grew up, was sending top players to Johns Hopkins, Syracuse, the Atlantic Coast Conference schools and West Point and Annapolis decades ago. The sport has had an outsized appeal to high school athletes in the Corning/Elmira region for at least 40 years.

Sr. Margaret said the decision to remain Division I in athletics was, at least partially, driven by the notion of expanding the sports program and recruiting athletes that would be seeking to play at the NCAA's highest level but do it for the kind of subsidy a partial scholarship might bring. Kenney was freshly arrived in the wake of the decision and he quickly embraced it and began considering sports expansion. But frankly, St. Bonaventure is far behind as it regards partial-scholarship athletes as a recruiting tactic. Mount St. Mary's in Maryland has for years proudly touted that a significant portion of its students participate in Division I athletics. The Mount's undergraduate enrollment is more than 1,800, larger than Bonaventure's these days, and it has nearly 500 graduate students. Many other colleges have been wooing student-athletes in this manner. Even at the Division I level, not all student-athletes are on full scholarships, and it varies from college to college. A wrestler at the University of Iowa might have a full scholarship, given the interest in the sport in that state, but some baseball players or golfers or tennis players there are likely on partial scholarships.

All of the thought and energy being thrown at the enrollment crisis at Bonaventure is hardly a one-year exercise. It is a deeply complicated introspection of how the school remakes itself on behalf of attracting more undergraduate students, college transfers and graduate students. Substantial adjustments will be required on numerous platforms. There will be winners and losers among the university's various constituencies. The process of change will be long-term, open-ended. All of that said, some things must remain: The spirituality of the place, the welcoming atmosphere, the specialness of the institution, the ether that breeds lifelong affection for the school, those defining qualities that don't show up in a business plan.

A crisis is a crisis only when enough people recognize it. Trouble can arrive gently, kind of creeping up on you. Bad times aren't only the product of an avalanche. So is it fair to wonder if that is what happened at St. Bonaventure as it regards dangerously low enrollment? That leadership was slow to respond, failing to aggressively confront a challenge that was flashing danger signals for years? The people running the school were hardly inert in the past seven or eight years. A beautiful science center was constructed, presenting the opportunity to better educate students who would be candidates for the STEM jobs the employment market presents these days. Same with the new business school. It must be assumed those projects were undertaken in the belief they would attract students who might otherwise choose another school, students who are aware that the needs of potential employers have changed, and to meet their demands, curriculums must be adjusted.

Jack McGinty, Class of 1965, is a self-described "proud Bonnie." In an urgent and gravelly voice, the highly successful Pittsburgh attorney said he was worried about the demographics in Bonaventure's core market four years ago, when he stepped down in 2012 after eight years as chairman of the board of trustees. "Grow or fail" was clear to him back then, he said. McGinty is a trustee emeritus these days but still very active on behalf of the school, including as a substantial donor.

"The Western New York demographics have gone to hell in a hand-basket," he said. The situation is just as bad south of the New York state line. "No one lives north of Interstate 80 in Pennsylvania anymore," McGinty said. "Towns there ... St. Mary's, others ... there is no one left there. That means fewer people who can withstand the tuition (at a private school such as St. Bonaventure).

"Half of my friends when I was there were from the New York City metropolitan area. We've lost ground there. Bonaventure can grow. It has to grow."

McGinty is part of Pittsburgh's Rooney clan, the folks who founded and still own the Pittsburgh Steelers. As a young boy, McGinty got to know about St. Bonaventure because Art Rooney's Steelers would train there in the late summer and McGinty would come up from Pittsburgh to watch the practices. McGinty's uncle, Rev. Silas Rooney O.F.M., was Art Rooney's brother.

The Steelers train these days at St. Vincent College, the small Bene-dictine school in Latrobe, Pa., and McGinty is knowledgeable about the place. McGinty said that six years ago, St. Vincent started to adjust the curriculum to emphasize STEM courses. McGinty quickly adds the school was built "on a liberal arts model." So for him, there is no reason Bonaventure can't make these same significant adjustments.

"St. Bonaventure has to commit to science programs," McGinty said, firmly.

He was asked if he believes St. Bonaventure will survive the enrollment challenge.

"It will take good leadership," McGinty said. "Margaret is leaving the place better than she found it. The faculty have to wake up, change the curriculum. That is always an uphill battle. Everyone has to recognize we have run in to this headwind. Change is hard. We've been sucker punched by the enrollment issue. And we lost some ground with the basketball scandal."

The next president? "Look for someone to improve the school's academic standards," McGinty said. "Someone who can improve the enrollment and make changes with the faculty and the curriculum."

McGinty and Schmidt have a good relationship, and McGinty likes the way Schmidt finds players. "Like (Jaylen) Adams, he finds these kinds of kids," McGinty said, "and he gets a kid there, lets him experience the warm atmosphere, even kids from the city." McGinty said Coach Jim Crowley does the same thing on behalf of the women's basketball program, finding these under-the-radar ballplayers, whether they are from Wisconsin or Buffalo, and molds a winning program with them.

If the administrators at St. Bonaventure were slow to react to enrollment decline, then they were not alone. Jonathan Henry is the vice president for enrollment at Husson College, a small school in Bangor, Me., and something he said to the Huffington Post has gotten a lot of mileage:

"I think it is fair to say 30 percent of these private schools won't exist in a decade."

What schools?

"Predominantly white, non-urban colleges will struggle and non-white students require additional aid," the Wall Street Journal reported. "Declining freshman enrollment is most pronounced at baccalaureate institutions with fewer than 4,000 students," according to the National Association of College and University Business Officers. Institutions with at least 4,000 students that grant masters and doctoral degrees will be less impacted.

Dwindling enrollment began at least a half-decade ago. The Wall Street Journal reported that between 2010-2012 freshmen enrollment at 25 percent of the nation's private, four-year colleges declined 10 percent or more. The Journal also reported that between 2010 and 2013, 45 schools have merged with another institution. It was not only Bonaventure and Hilbert College that considered a merger to stretch resources and attract more students.

The causes for what confronts smaller liberal arts colleges come in waves. There are presently fewer high school graduates than a decade before, so there are fewer candidates for colleges generally. Online education is keeping many students off campuses. The back-breaking burden of student debt is a major disincentive. Family incomes are still stretched as a consequence of the recession, which wrought fewer jobs and stagnant wages for those who managed to remain employed.

Dealing with an enrollment crisis is messy. Consider Rider University, a private school located in the wealthy community of Lawrenceville, N.J., just a few miles from Princeton. In October 2015, Rider announced it was cutting 20 positions, 14 of them full-time faculty positions. It also said it would eliminate more than a dozen academic majors, including philosophy, piano, art history and French. The school president said the declining enrollment has created a nearly $8 million revenue gap in the overall budget. Nearly 300 students had been majoring in the programs that will be eliminated. There are 3,700 students there and tuition and fees are $38,000. Enrollment at Rider is off by 9 percent since 2009. A faculty member declared: "Morale is completely destroyed."

La Salle University, an A-10 rival of the Bonnies, also has problems. Enrollment in 2015 was 16 percent less than in 2014. The school's new president, Colleen M. Hancyz, said: "Our sector is facing a crisis at the moment across the nation." The university laid off 3 percent of its workforce. Tuition, fees and room and board at La Salle total more than $53,000 per year. The 2015 incoming class was 725. The decline in Catholic high schools and students opting for public universities were the primary causes, the school said.

Amid the stress of the enrollment challenge inside Hopkins Hall and beyond, it should be heartening that the university gets solid reviews. U.S. News & World Report ranked Bonaventure No. 5 on its 2015 list of best college values. The total cost of $42,817 for tuition, room and board, and fees is comparatively modest for a private school. The average cost of attendance, after the various incentives that are available, is $18,577. Aid benefits 95 percent of the students, and 84 percent of them return for their sophomore years. The graduation rate is 20 percent higher than the national average.

According to Valento, 14 New York City-area guidance counselors were flown to Olean for tours of the school. The cost was covered by one of the school's most generous graduates. One of those guidance directors, Joseph D. Korfmacher, has a blog: mrkcollegeknowledge. His assessment was rather remarkable. Portions of his overall impression:

"So I cannot express this enough, I love everything St. Bonaventure is about. This is a strong, supportive community of administrators, faculty and students who are there to prepare for a successful future, but are there for each other as well. Students hold doors for each other, they smile and ask how your day is going, but at the same time they are focused on their academics, and work hard to do well in the classroom.

"Their basketball games are a must-see event, with the entire community attending, rooting on their Bonnies.

"Finally, St. Bonaventure is just a school and community with good values. Yes, their network is expansive, where graduates are getting competitive jobs all over the country, but their mission is to form the entire person during their four years there … and this is something I can tell you they do very well."

You would have to believe that if you could squeeze the essence of that message and fit it on a billboard on the New Jersey Turnpike or on one of those banners that small planes tow over ocean beaches, there would be an uptick in interest in the college.

Dan Collins, presently a vice chair of the board of trustees at St. Bonaventure, said Valento has made a strong first impression with the trustees.

"The board is very pleased," Collins said. "Bernie seems to be aggressively moving in a number of areas." Collins also said the early data looks better than a year before.

"If we could assume last year was the bottom," Collins said, "that would be good. But we have a steep climb upward." He said Valento's performance has dispelled any concerns about institutional knowledge, that he has a clear sense of what makes the place special at the same time he is instilling the urgency to make the changes required for future success in attracting students.

Collins said adjusting the curriculum will mean tough decisions, and the faculty should be well-aware of that. A committee that numbers somewhere around 100, involving administrators, faculty and students, is considering what to change, what to cut and what to create. Collins is the board's liaison with this committee, and there are weekly hour-long phone conferences to assure the process is advancing.

Collins is clear about the challenge: "Creating new programs means ending some current programs." He knows this will bring reactions ranging from white-hot anger to devastating disappointment. And he is confident the faculty knows this is coming.

CHAPTER 15:
DRAMATIC RECOVERY

RICHMOND

One might think that the press row beneath the basket on the visitors' end of the Reilly Center court would not be an advantageous place to watch a game. But it is. You appreciate the physicality of Division I college basketball, the speed of it. You hear the players talk among themselves. You understand how fast and strong the guards play, both on offense and defense, and how quickly the ball moves around the perimeter, how hard it can be to cover a three-point shooter. Most of all, you can better understand the war that takes place in the lane and beneath the basket.

With 1:02 to play in the first half against Richmond, a mid-season "must win" after St. Bonaventure had fallen to 4-3 from 4-0 in the Atlantic 10, Jaylen Adams bolted down the lane and toward the basket. He could have just laid it up off the glass but he went for the rim and the slam. At the top of his leap, Adams was hit hard by a Richmond defender coursing like a missile. The ball bounced off the rim, and both players went sprawling.

It was a jarring collision, a foul but clean. The Richmond player, Marshall Wood, ended up beyond the baseline. Adams was propelled outside the lane and pointing up court. Both players quickly picked themselves up.

Marcus Posley came up to Adams, put his arm around his teammate and, with a smile on his face, talked to him. You couldn't hear what Posley said, but you could imagine it might have been something like, "Hey man, I appreciate your style, but you don't have to get yourself killed." Adams hit his two free throws to cut the Spiders' lead to 36-33. Richmond would lead 39-33 at halftime.

Maybe the best thing about those seats beneath the basket is watching how Dion Wright has made himself in to a wonderful player. Wright is not that big. He is listed as 6-foot-7 and 220 pounds and that might be a bit generous. But Wright was huge against Richmond, scoring 19 points, grabbing 14 rebounds, and blocking two shots as the Bonnies steadily pulled away from the Spiders in the second half to earn an 84-68 victory. It gave St. Bonaventure a 5-3 mark in the A-10 and placed them in a tie for fourth place with George Washington. The Bonnies now stood 13-6 overall.

Posley and Adams joined Wright to provide the formula that Mark Schmidt said was key to the team's success. They combined for 63 points and all three were key to Bonaventure scoring the first 11 points of the second half and never looking back, steadily growing the advantage to 65-53 with 5:15 to play on a Posley three-pointer. Posley would finish with 26 points and Adams dropped 18 on Richmond.

Much has been made of Wright's ability to slither inside and get points. His nickname is The Worm. His greatest advantage might be that he is a quick jumper, as opposed to a great leaper. Certainly, that benefits him and the team on the offensive end, but against Richmond, his rebounding was spellbinding to watch. Wright gauges where the ball might be headed on a shot and leaves his feet earlier than the opponents. He is an assertive rebounder, claiming the ball with both hands, and securing it, and looks immediately for the opportunity to start a break.

Thirteen of Wright's rebounds came on defense. His only offensive rebound was claimed in the first half, so Wright played a significant role in slowing Richmond down offensively in the second half, forcing numerous one-and-done trips. Wright also was often matched against 6-foot-7 Terry Allen, the Spiders' talented forward, or 6-foot-9 T.J. Cline, their other big man.

Wright also provided the most declarative basket of the game, a play that brought the season's biggest crowd yet --- 5,264 --- to its feet. With 4:08 to go in the contest, Wright grabbed a rebound on the defensive end and started dribbling up the court. He picked up speed and raced past the retreating Richmond players and never stopped, finishing with a booming dunk that gave the Bonnies a 68-55 lead. It was a statement loudly delivered by a player who is one of the least talkative members of the team.

Schmidt told reporters after the game that the second half was the best 20 minutes of defense the team has played all year. "When we play well defensively, we can compete with any team in the league," Schmidt said. He also noted that his team outrebounded Richmond 40-34.

The Bonnies played a lot of zone defense in the second half, and it worked. The Spiders, one of the nation's most efficient teams offensively, were just 9-for-33 in the second half, a totally uncharacteristic 27 percent from the field.

Bonaventure missed just nine field goal attempts in the second half, remarkable and a helpful thing in all regards but key defensively in this game, since it is much easier to set up a zone following a made basket. The Bonnies had nine blocked shots, and five of them were created by Jordan Tyson, who saw 20 minutes of action.

Chris Mooney, the former Princeton player and the Richmond coach for 10 years now, said: "Hats off to St. Bonaventure. Their second-half aggressiveness was the difference. Their guards are hard to defend and Dion Wright had a great game. Bonaventure just played better in the second half."

Mooney also said the Spiders were "too stagnant" against the zone. "We didn't shoot well and their length on the back end hurt us," he explained. "Their zone helped slow us down offensively."

One other reality might have hurt Richmond in the second 20 minutes, though Mooney, to his credit, chose not to mention it. Richmond went two overtimes to beat George Washington, 98-90, on the road in its last game. That was a Thursday night and the game was late, a 9 p.m. tipoff. The game ended close to midnight. That gave Richmond just Friday and Saturday to travel to Olean and prepare for the Bonaventure game, which was a 3 p.m. start on Sunday. The loss dropped Richmond to 3-5 in the league and 11-9 overall.

The Richmond coach also commented on "the strength and explosiveness of Posley," who got 19 of his 26 points in the second half. Posley, listed at 6 feet, is powerfully built, especially in his upper arms and shoulders. Those media seats under the basket also provide a perfect view for appreciating Posley's bursts through the defense that result in baskets and trips to the foul line. Lots of good guards these days cradle the ball to prevent steals on layup attempts. But Posley secures the ball with one arm, and sometimes both arms, against his chest, giving himself a millisecond between leaving his feet and readying the ball for some sort of shot. It seems a remarkable example of athleticism and grit.

St. Bonaventure also received an unbridled endorsement from one of the announcers on the telecast. The color man was Tom Pecora, who had been the coach at Fordham but was fired at the end of the 2014-15 season. Pecora had taken the Rams to Olean, including a trip that ended in defeat in his final season. But Pecora gushed over the place, crediting everything from the campus to the fans, especially the students, who make the Reilly Center a distinctive venue. At one point, Pecora told viewers: "If you have a son or daughter looking for a college, have them consider St. Bonaventure. It's a great school, with great spirit.""

ST. JOSEPH'S

For many years, Philadelphia is where St. Bonaventure's basketball dreams went to die. The 1969-70 team that should have won the national championship suffered its only regular-season loss at Villanova. In 1978, the Bonnies lost a first-round NCAA Tournament game at the venerable Palestra to Penn ... a ridiculous place to play a tournament game because the Palestra is Penn's gymnasium. Playing Temple on Broad Street, whether at the old McGonigle Gymnasium or the newer, much-larger Liacouras Center, was always a disaster, though the Bonnies managed to win their last Atlantic 10 contest against Temple, which was headed to the American Athletic Conference, when Matthew Wright scorched the Owls in Philly. The Andrew Nicholson-led team that would win the A-10 tournament in March 2012 and make the NCAA tourney, fell to La Salle at the Gola Arena in a regular-season contest. And St. Joseph's just seemed to own the Bonnies, whether the games were played at the Palestra, the old Spectrum, Hawk Hill or the Reilly Center.

Then things began to change. Mark Schmidt's Bonnies have had success against La Salle and St. Joe's in recent seasons. In the 2014-15 season, Bonaventure lost at home to La Salle but beat the Explorers in the conference tournament. Bonaventure defeated St. Joe's home, away and in the conference tourney in Brooklyn last season. In fact, the Bonnies had handled the Hawks in eight of their last 11 meetings. But managing that this season seemed highly unlikely. The Hawks stood at 18-3, their only losses to Florida, Villanova and Virginia Commonwealth, as they prepared for a visit from the Bonnies. St. Joe's was on the doorstep of the Top 25 and seen as a sure-shot selection for the NCAA Tournament.

Philadelphia likes to think of itself as a college basketball hotbed, with six Division I teams, the whole Big 5 thing, very well-regarded coaches who seem to truly respect one another, play charity golf tournaments together in the off-season, and battle one another for the bounty of big-time recruits who live and play in the city and the suburbs. But really, it is a pro town, even if you count the preposterously lousy and totally mismanaged Sixers. The Phillies were a sellout every game, at least until the key pieces of the roster got old at the same time. You can almost hear the shrieks from wrists being slashed when the Eagles go down.

Villanova and St. Joe's draw very well. Some Penn students and old grads support their program but the Palestra has lots of empty seats when the Quakers get in to Ivy League play. Drexel and La Salle really struggle to attract fans, and Temple people are having a hard time getting excited about the Owls' new conference, the American Athletic Conference, which means games against Tulsa and Tulane and other schools that mean nothing to Philadelphians.

St. Joseph's shut down the old Alumni Memorial Fieldhouse on campus for the 2008-2009 season, playing home games at the Palestra, and completely rebuilt the building's interior, creating the new Michael J. Hagan Arena as well as adding amenities such as meeting rooms and weight rooms. The end result is a 4,200-seat gymnasium that is shiny and new but looks and feels tight, snug. Red seats surround the court on four sides, and there are a lower and upper deck. The rows of seats are steeply banked, and the upper deck practically hangs over the court. The St. Joe's fans are both astute and full-throated. The place is loud.

The Bonnies were facing a team that had won 14 of its last 15 games, the only loss a three-point setback at home to VCU. DeAndre' Bembry, the 6-foot-6 junior forward from Charlotte, has been one of the conference's several-best players since his freshman season, but the Hawks were getting terrific performances from Isaiah Miles, a 6-foot-7 forward who worked hard in the off-season and dropped more than 20 pounds for his senior year. He had become a leading scorer and a threat from behind the arc. Aaron Brown, also a senior, was the shooting guard. The Hawks were notable for their defense, especially guarding against the deep ball.

St. Bonaventure was a 6.5-point underdog, according to the betting lines.

The Bonnies tested St. Joe's defense right from the start and took a 14-7 lead after consecutive three-pointers from Marcus Posley, Idris Taqqee and Dion Wright. Taqqee and Jaylen Adams hit from long range and the game was tied at 25. Nelson Kaputo made it a 35-32 game when he hit a three-point shot and then Adams drilled another three. The Bonnies led 38-32 and had shredded the Hawks' defense with eight three-pointers. They ended the half leading 42-35, but Adams, Posley, Jordan Tyson and Denzel Gregg each had two fouls.

The Hawks had no answer for Adams. The sophomore from Baltimore makes the game look easy. He never seems rushed. He glides along the court. He makes creative drives through the lane and delivers baskets amid the chaos inside, and always appears open from the outside. His jump shot is poison for the opponent, and he is one of the reasons Bonaventure is among the best foul-shooting teams in the nation and tops in the A-10 at 78 percent.

Nothing seems to trouble this guy. Adams said before the season that he had worked hard on his game in the summer and was eager to get going. Despite the loss of Courtney Stockard to a foot injury, Adams liked the composition of this Bonnies team. Adams has a brother, Brendan, a sophomore who is the starting point guard at Calvert Hall High School in Baltimore, and on video seems to play a game that is similar to Jaylen's. The dinner table conversation in the Adams home must be lively; Jaylen played at Calvert Hall's rival, Mount St. Joseph's High School. Troy Caupain, a junior at the University of Cincinnati, is a cousin of Adams, and joined Jaylen and Brendan in the summer workouts. Caupain, who resides in Midlothian, Va., dropped a career-best 25 points on Memphis in a game in late January.

Adams seemed to arrive in Olean almost casually. There was no apparent fervor from the fan base for Adams, no desperate threads on the Bona Bandwagon to have him signed. The only notable quality to his being recruited was that Bonaventure now had two guys named Adams, one a Jalen from Michigan and the other Jaylen from Maryland. Jalen was supposed to be a big-time recruit, and Schmidt called him "the most-explosive player" that he had brought to Bonaventure. Schmidt decided Jalen would remain Jalen and the other one would be called Jay.

Jay Adams had committed to Jacksonville University in his senior year in high school but then de-committed when the coach who had recruited him was fired. In an interview before the start of the season, Adams said the only school besides Bonaventure that had any interest in him at all was Mount St. Mary's, in nearby Emmitsburg, Md.

Unfortunately, nothing came of Jalen Adams, and he left after his freshman season. Jay Adams, however, was handed the keys to the offense before a game was played in the 2014-15 season, something that stunned many Schmidt-watchers. Dion Wright, as just one example, was glued to the bench for most of his first season.

Before he was lost to a broken finger two-thirds of the way through the 2014-15 season, Jaylen Adams could have been --- should have been --- the A-10's rookie of the year. His sophomore season has been scintillating, and it was on full view against St. Joseph's on this February night.

Posley scored on a jump shot and a drive in the early minutes of the second half but Bembry answered with two baskets. Adams hit another three-point shot and the lead was 53-46. St. Joseph's rallied. Miles scored and was fouled by Posley, his third, and Miles's free throw made it a 53-52 game. The Hawks fans, now boisterous, sensed that their winning streak would be preserved.

Wright answered with a hook shot in the lane, and then Bonaventure impressively dismantled one of the best teams in the league. Taqqee, having the best game in his career, hit a three from the corner. After making the shot, he headed up court but delivered a triumphant hoot at a nearby Hawks' fan who apparently had questioned Taqqee's accuracy.

But this night belonged to Adams. He hit his next three shots in a row, all from distance, the last one coming as the 30-second clock was about to go off. That one lifted the Bonnies to a 73-60 advantage with 5:30 to play, and some of the Hawks fans left their seats and headed out in to a strangely warm, rainy and foggy evening.

The lead would grow to 78-60 with 3:55 to play, and the Hawks cut it to 78-68, with 1:51 showing. Adams drove, grabbed his own rebound, made the shot and was fouled to make it 81-68. He made two free throws with 57 seconds to go and the game ended 83-73. This was certainly Bonaventure's most impressive victory of the year, a road triumph over a team that had been red-hot.

After the teams shook hands, Bona's players and coaches walked to a section behind one of the baskets and applauded their fans, who had made their presence known.

The line for Jaylen Adams in the box score was remarkable: 31 points, 10-for-21 and 6-for-12 from behind the arc, 5-for-5 for free throws, 2 re-bounds, 7 assists, 3 steals and 1 turnover. And he played all 40 minutes. It was his best game in his still-young career. In fact, it was as close to perfect as the sport allows. And 4,027 largely unhappy people were there to see it.

Watching this kid play, it is remarkable, even bizarre, that he wasn't more heavily recruited. Lots of schools keep an eye on Baltimore because of the talent there. Bonaventure enjoyed the services of a fine player in the late-1970s, Delmar Harrod, who came out of Mt. St. Joseph's.

Bonaventure hit on 13 of 34 three-point shots. St. Joe's was just 8-for-25. The Bonnies turned the ball over just twice for the game, and took 69 shots to just 57 for the Hawks. Turned the ball over twice ... in a very tough matchup on the road. That is coaching or skill or luck, but no team commits just two turnovers.

Phil Martelli, the longtime St. Joe's coach, said he would know whether his club was a contender in the Atlantic 10 after a visit to Rhode Island and the home game against the Bonnies. The Hawks handled the Rams in Kingston, 64-55, and despite the loss to the Bonnies, St. Joe's remained a contender. Building an 18-3 record never happens by accident.

Martelli walked off the court with his head down. When he met with reporters, he began by saying, "I told my team the better team won tonight." He mentioned his team's play on the defensive end and missed layups on offense, and there were a handful of them. "We needed to score in the high 70s and we didn't get there," the coach said. Martelli said the play of Taqqee "was a surprise." Also, Martelli's scouting report had indicated that Adams is not a great scorer on the road. "But it was a wonderful, wonderful game he played," Martelli said.

"We played well for a long time," Martelli said of the team's winning streak. "We didn't play well enough tonight."

Schmidt was clearly elated with this victory. "I am proud of our effort, coming in to a place like this … getting the win," he said. "Jaylen was terrific." Schmidt also said his team did a good job keeping the Hawks out of transition, where Bembry can be a huge menace, given his size and speed.

Of the 34 three-point shots, Schmidt said: "I told them don't fall in love with the three, but if it is open, you have to take it."

Given Adams's outburst, it would be easy to overlook the game

Wright played. He had 18 points, including two baskets from three-point range, and was 4-for-4 from the line. He also had 11 rebounds, four of them on the offensive end. Wright's activity inside had to have eased things a bit for the outside shooters.

The win raised Bonaventure's overall record to 14-6 and 6-3 in the conference, good enough for a fourth-place tie with George Washington. They would play struggling St. Louis next at home, then travel to Fordham. GW comes to Olean on Feb. 13. Those three games will go a long way in determining Bonaventure's status in the conference, and any hopes for a postseason tournament bid.

CHAPTER 16:
WINNING UGLY

ST. LOUIS

There were 15.9 seconds to play, a tiny shred of time separating St. Bonaventure from an ugly win or a spirit-sapping, momentum-killing defeat. St. Louis University, one of the Atlantic 10 Conference's weakest teams and a 15-point underdog on this Super Bowl Sunday afternoon, had bedeviled the Bonnies all game. The Billikens had done just enough scoring, particularly on the inside, and played well enough defensively, to not just stay in the game but to forge their largest lead, 50-42, with 8:56 remaining in the second half.

If the Bonnies fell to St. Louis on this day, it would render irrelevant their impressive triumph at St. Joseph's four days earlier. Gone would be all the attention they drew from that win in Philadelphia over a Hawks' team that had been 18-3 and riding a seven-game conference winning streak. Gone would be the fourth-place tie in the Atlantic 10 Conference, the 38th-best national Ratings Power Index, and the sense that this was a team capable of a special season.

Those were the stakes when the Bonnies prepared to inbound the ball under their own basket with the score 62-62, and the 15.9 seconds showing on the scoreboards. A crowd of 3,712, made modest by Super Bowl parties and the misplaced confidence that the Bonnies would race past the Billikens, watched nervously.

Jaylen Adams prepared to pass the ball to Marcus Posley for the trip down court that would mean victory, defeat or the vagaries of an overtime. But before that happened, Posley looked directly at Adams and then pointed to his wrist and tapped it, as if Posley were wearing a watch.

Posley received the ball and leisurely dribbled up court, with the St. Louis defense choosing not to press. With eight seconds left, Posley dribbled to his right, looking for a chance to drive the lane. Posley made his move with about four seconds to play, and saw the St. Louis defense stiffen to deny him an entry point. Posley then drove even more to his right and, still not in the lane, drew a defender and made a pass to his right to Adams that was more like a pitchout in football. Adams, steps behind the three-point circle, gathered the ball and launched an arcing shot. The ball hit nothing but net, just as the backboard light flashed orange to indicate the game was over, and the Bonnies had a 65-62 victory that was as crucial as it was blemished.

Mark Schmidt had positioned himself at the end of his bench and was kneeling at the baseline, giving himself great perspective to see Adams get the ball and drain the shot. Schmidt shook his fist in triumph and then turned and headed to meet Coach Jim Crews and his players, who never went away and looked at several junctures late in the game that they would steal a win.

Bonaventure's record was now 15-6 and 7-3 in the A-10, tied with George Washington for fourth-place in the conference. Two full games ahead of Davidson, Duquesne and Rhode Island, bunched at 5-5 in conference play. The Bonnies would next travel to the Bronx for a mid-week game against an improved Fordham team and then host George Washington on Saturday, which likely would be a sellout on alumni weekend and one of the most critical games at the Reilly Center in years.

After making the basket, Adams was rushed by his teammates, who are becoming expert as it regards the buzzer-beating celebration. So too is Schmidt, who would say later, after the press conference, that he told his players to be certain they got the last shot in regulation, to be sure there would be overtime if the win did not happen in regulation.

Amid the happiness on the court, Adams could be seen tapping his wrist, just as Posley had done before the decisive trip down the floor. Adams was asked at the press conference what the gesture means. "Winning time," Adams said, smiling. "It's time to win, someone has to make something happen, someone has to make a play."

Posley was Marcus the Miracle-Maker last season, for his stealing a win at Duquesne and his back-to-back buzzer-beating downcourt rushes that nailed Davidson and VCU. According to Schmidt, Posley was the first option against St. Louis. If he thought he could get to the rim, then Posley was supposed to drive. If not, Posley was to find Adams. Given how Adams has played this season, especially his 31-point explosion at St. Joe's, one is not surprised that he made the dramatic shot. There is a touch of magic to what the Bonnies have accomplished so far this season.

When he met the media after the game, Crews was not crestfallen. He surveyed the room and indicated he was surprised that a place as out-of-the-way as Olean drew as many reporters and photographers as it did. The Olean Times Herald and the Buffalo News always have one or two writers there plus photographers and video producers. There is always a contingent of students from St. Bonaventure's Russell J. Jandoli School of Journalism and Mass Communication, writing for print, social media and online blogs and other sites, and others producing photos and video. They are quite impressive, these student journalists, not at all reticent to press Schmidt or the players he brings to postgame interviews.

Crews called the contest "a good college basketball game." "We did a good job on Posley, Adams and Wright," he said. "We made it hard for them but they found a way to chip away." Crews also said his players failed to finish scoring opportunities inside the lane. He also said he admires what Mark Schmidt has done at Bonaventure. "We're competing. We're growing, getting better," Crews said of the Billikens.

Adams called the game "a dogfight" in his remarks to the media. It was that. St. Louis took a 19-12 command, helped by production from Jermaine Bishop, an impressive young guard, and a driving score by Mike Crawford. A dunk by Denzel Gregg on a nice feed from Posley, and drives by Idris Taqqee and Posley made it 19-18 with 4:50 left in the first half. A three-point goal by Bishop pushed the Billikens to a 25-20 lead, but Bona's would take a shaky 28-27 lead at the half on a three-pointer from Posley.

The Bonnies were shooting poorly. They were 11-for-29 overall and 2-for-13 on three-point attempts. They had little offense despite grabbing seven offensive rebounds in the first 20 minutes. Gregg played just six minutes in the first half and, typically, both Jordan Tyson and Derrick Woods had two personal fouls while playing just a combined 18 minutes.

The Bona players sort of strolled on to the floor as they came back from the locker room. They looked listless, rather than driven to overcome a lousy first half against a heavy underdog and frantic not to waste what they had accomplished in Philadelphia. Then they began the second half in a sleepwalk. St. Louis had its biggest lead at 50-42 on two free throws by Miles Reynolds with 8:50 to play.

Ash Yacoubou scored inside and then made a pair of free throws and the Billikens were still up, 55-49, with 5:53 remaining. Bonaventure seemed in real trouble. Robey's score inside gave the Bills a 57-51 lead.

Adams was fouled and made both shots and Gregg scored off a steal and then a pass from Posley. When Adams was fouled at the 3:34 mark and made both shots it forged a 57-57 deadlock. A three-point shot by Posley, made possible by a scramble inside for a rebound, pushed Bona's in to a 61-59 edge with 1:02 to go. When Reggie Agbeko made one of two free throws for St. Louis, it was 61-60 and Posley made it 62-60 after making just one of two foul shots. There were 26 seconds left.

Crews came up with a beautiful play after a timeout that found Mike

Crawford running alone in the lane and scoring to tie it at 62. That set up Posley and Adams for the finish. The Bonnies managed to survive.

"We didn't play a great game," Schmidt said at his press conference. "We won this on our defense and rebounding and showing determination. When you don't play your best and manage to win … that's a good thing."

Then Schmidt conceded a reality that hung in the room like a vapor, that his team had left its energy and swagger and determination in Philadelphia: "We couldn't let St. Joe's be the reason we lost today."

The Bonnies outrebounded St. Louis 40 to 29, and struggled despite 13 offensive rebounds. Adams finished with 19 points, Posley had 15 and Wright had 14 points and 10 rebounds. The Bonnies had 16 turnovers, including back-to-back trips when players dribbled the ball off their feet. Sixteen turnovers in an A-10 game is a suicide pact.

Away from reporters and in a hallway outside the arena, Schmidt brought up another problem, and not for the first time. He had warned his team of a letdown after the St. Joe's win, that they could not look past St. Louis. "I needed someone to say, 'OK Coach, I got it.' I needed a leader to make sure that didn't happen," Schmidt said. "We don't have that kind of leader."

This is a recurrent theme, something that clearly riles the head coach. He has some terrific players, guys who one could argue show their leadership by example, the way Dion Wright does rebounding and scoring inside against bigger opponents, the way Posley and Adams shoot so confidently in taut, tension-filled situations. What Schmidt wants and doesn't have is a personality that would bend the team to his will, a player who is a surrogate for the head coach and his assistants. He believes he doesn't have that, and it drives Schmidt crazy.

Schmidt talked about this before the season even began. I asked him who was the greatest leader among the players he has had. "Charlon Kloof," Schmidt said instantly, of the player who was at Bonaventure for just three seasons, who Schmidt somehow found in a prep school in the Canary Islands, a kid who was born in Suriname, moved to the Netherlands and caught the attention of college coaches on a scrap of land called Gran Canaria and the town of Las Palmas.

Schmidt certainly put in the miles to find Kloof and bring his talents and leadership to Olean. "I thought the Canary Islands were just off the coast of South America," Schmidt recalled. "It isn't." No, the Canary Islands, a seven-island Spanish archipelago, is off the coast of the North African nation of Morocco. There might be more exhausting and complicated travel than getting from Olean to the Canaries, as the islands are known, but you'd really have to work hard to find it.

Kloof, who has a Dutch heritage as a result of being born in the South American nation of Suriname, was a product of the Canarias Basketball Academy. Ballplayers from Europe who are accepted at the academy, will reside there and be exposed to U.S. style basketball. The founder and president of the academy is Rob Orellana, who was an assistant coach at a number of programs, including St. Francis College in Brooklyn and Fairleigh Dickinson in New Jersey. His program has been sending ballplayers to U.S. colleges since 2007.

Kloof, who played at Bonaventure for three seasons beginning in 2011, was worth the journey made by Schmidt. He was a starter for two seasons and part of a third and was the point guard on the team that won the A-10 Tournament in 2012 and went to the NCAA Tournament and lost to Florida State in the first round. Kloof speaks several languages, majored in finance at Bonaventure and displayed the leadership qualities that Schmidt is always seeking.

"He was the first player to practice and the last to leave," Schmidt said. "He was impressive from the first day he got here. He was the leader on the floor and in the locker room. The other players were quick to respect him." That would have included the star of the team, Andrew Nicholson.

Schmidt described Kloof as having the conscience of a coach. Schmidt yearns for that kind of leadership this season.

One other takeaway from the St. Louis game: Marcus Posley is clearly banged up. Tim Kenney had shared weeks ago that Posley had a hip injury. Posley had to leave the game with the Billikens to have his right ankle taped, and he was clearly limping, not badly but tellingly, in the second half. "He's playing through some things," said Schmidt.

Despite all the challenges, Schmidt's team had found a way to win another game, another conference game. It was a victory that would allow Schmidt to watch the Super Bowl without having to think, re-think, second-guess what he could have done better if St. Louis had prevailed. "It will make the beer taste better too," Schmidt said.

CHAPTER 17:

TROUBLE IN THE BRONX

FORDHAM

I t is difficult to understand why Fordham's basketball program has struggled for so many years in the Atlantic 10 Conference. It is a terrific university, with a beautiful campus, which might not be located in the sweetest stretch of the Bronx but there are lots of fine urban universities across the country that have sketchy neighborhoods they must call home. Fordham is large enough and so richly financed that it has a second campus at Lincoln Center in Midtown, which is home to some graduate programs, its Gabelli School of Business and Fordham College of Law. The Society of Jesus might drive the rest of Catholic clergy crazy but they are hugely respected as educators. There are generations of upper-crust New Yorkers brandishing Fordham degrees.

So why don't the Rams fare better? The program has a rich history, but has waffled for years now. The Rams run through basketball coaches at an alarming clip. The school's I-AA football team does very well. The Rams were 9-2 in the regular season in 2015, including a win over Division

I Army and a 5-1 record in the Patriot League, and made the I-AA Football Championship Series, losing to 7th-ranked Chattanooga. It should be easier to find seven or eight quality basketball players, especially when you call New York City home, than 40 or 50 talented football players.

The Rams have yet another new coach. He is Rich Neubauer, and his resume drips of success. In 10 years as the head coach of Eastern Kentucky University, Neubauer managed five 20-win seasons and two trips to the NCAA Tournament. Neubauer, who grew up in Louisiana, played at La Salle University and was a top assistant to John Beilein, the current Michigan head coach, when Beilein was at West Virginia. Eastern Kentucky is a member of the Ohio Valley Conference, which includes Murray State, Western Kentucky and some other gritty basketball schools. It's a tough league, and Neubauer more than held his own. He prospered.

The Rams were 9-2 before A-10 play began but the competition was very unimpressive. They lost to Texas-Arlington on the road in the non-conference opener and fell to the worst Boston College team in memory in the last game before A-10 play. In between, Fordham won nine straight, all of them at home, but it included the likes of Queens College, Coppin State, Fairleigh Dickinson and Central Connecticut State. The Rams did handle Manhattan and St. John's in that stretch.

Fordham was 3-7 in the A-10 when St. Bonaventure arrived at venerable, cozy Rose Hill Gymnasium the evening of Ash Wednesday. The Rams' conference wins were over La Salle, George Mason and UMass. After the drama and angst of the St. Louis game, it would do the Bonnies well if they took an early lead and cruised to another conference victory. George Washington awaited them on Saturday afternoon in Olean.

The announced attendance was 2,021 and, as usual, about half of those folks were Bonaventure fans from the New York-New Jersey-Southern Connecticut metro area. They weren't in for an easy ride. Fordham has a 6-foot-8 forward, Ryan Rhoomes, who had been a fine rebounder in prior years but had improved his offense in this his senior season. And he was causing problems for the Bonnies. He had six points in the first 11:27 and gave Fordham an 18-16 edge. A steal by Nelson Kaputo led to a three-point jumper for Jaylen Adams, and the Bonnies had a one-point lead.

But Rhoomes, helped by 6-7 sophomore Christian Sengfelder and freshman guard Joseph Chartouny, was making a mess of the Bonnies on the interior. Dion Wright's three-point goal gave the Bonnies a 29-25 lead but Rhoomes scored on a breakaway and Sengfelder followed with a score to cut the Bonnies' advantage to 31-29 at the half.

It was hardly a pristine first 20 minutes. Bonaventure shot 50 percent from the field but just 3-for-9 from behind the arc. Fordham's offensive stats were even worse, but the Rams owned the boards, 17-12, and Rhoomes was in charge on the interior, scoring 14 points and grabbing six rebounds. Dion Wright had seven points to lead the visitors, but Jerome Tyson was playing decently, with six points and three rebounds. Jaylen Adams, Marcus Posley and Denzel Gregg each had just six points.

The Bonnies found a spurt after Fordham grabbed a 32-31 lead. Posley nailed a three-pointer and Tyson scored on a rebound basket. Posley then came up with a steal and a driving basket and when Wright blocked a shot and then got a pass back from Adams for a score, Bonaventure had a 40-32 lead with 16:34 to play in the second half. It was by far the liveliest stretch the Bonnies had managed.

Fordham's offensive play had become ragged and another three from Wright gave the Bonnies a 48-38 lead. It wouldn't last. This has become something of a pattern for the Bonnies. When they have a chance to put the chokehold on an opponent, they ease up instead. This lapse was evident in the early minutes of the second half at Syracuse and has showed itself at other junctures in the season. And Fordham was not Syracuse, yet the Rams escaped and Bonaventure would pay for it the rest of the way.

Amid a spate of Bonnies' turnovers, Fordham rallied. Chartouny scored on a layup, and hit a three-point jumper. When Rhoomes made a jumper, it was 51-49 with 8:59 to play. Bonaventure got quiet offensively, and Fordham had found another gear. At this point, Bonaventure was struggling on both ends of the floor.

But Adams and Gregg hit three-pointers and it was 57-51 Bonnies. After a turnover by Gregg and a driving basket from Fordham's Antwoine Anderson, from Rochester's Bishop Kearney, the Rams trailed just 57-56.

In the next 2:50 of play, the game belonged to Fordham. Wright would make a jumper and Posley would hit a three-pointer, while the Rams were getting three-point goals from Nemanja Zarkovic and David Pekarek. When Pekarek, a 6-foot-7 forward, hit a jump shot, Fordham led 64-62. After a turnover by Adams and a score inside by Rhoomes, it was

66-62 with 3:09 to play.

The Bonnies were in a muddy scramble with a team that has struggled all season, and a loss to Fordham could be more than a blemish as it regarded the A-10 season. If Bonaventure was thinking postseason, and they had a right to be, a defeat in the Bronx would be ugly and problematic.

Adams made a pair of free throws and the Bonnies pulled within two, 66-64. The next stretch of play was an exercise in futility. Posley drove for a basket but Rhoomes blocked it. Rhoomes missed two free throws and Posley missed a three-point shot. Then Chartouny fouled Wright as he tried to score off a rebound. Wright made both shots and it was tied at 66. There was 1:29 to play, and neither team could risk a mistake.

But neither team was playing well enough to win it. Pekarek missed a three-point attempt. Idris Taqqee turned the ball over. Anderson missed a three-point shot and it was 66-66 at the end of regulation. It would be overtime.

Whatever the magic, the clutch shooting, the stunning play that provided the victories over Richmond and St. Joseph's, it was totally missing against St. Louis and now Fordham. There was no crispness in the efforts at both ends of the floor for the Bonnies on this night. Fordham was no better, and that was the only good fortune the Bonnies could claim.

Taqqee hit a shot for Bonaventure and Rhoomes answered for the Rams. The teams were tied with 4:20 to play. Both teams stumbled around for the next minute-and-a-half, missing shots and turning the ball over until Posley was fouled with 3:20 to go. He made just one of the shots and it was 69-68.

Tyson fouled Rhoomes, who had a genuinely fine performance on both ends of the court, really messing up the Bonnies on the interior. Rhoomes made both shots and Fordham led 70-69 with 2:49 left. Adams, hardly enjoying a stunning evening, fouled Chartouny, who made both tosses and the Rams were up 72-69. With 1:50 left, Rhoomes fouled Gregg, and he made both shots. It was 72-71, Fordham.

Chartouny missed a driving layup and Posley, who despite being just 6-foot manages to get rebounds when they really matter, pulled down the miss and was fouled. He made both, the Bonnies led 73-72, and 1:20 remained to be played.

Chartouny missed a shot, Posley rebounded and with 47 seconds showing, he missed a jumper. Then Anderson turned it over. The Bonnies called a timeout with 44 seconds left.

The strategy was evident to anyone watching. Bonaventure would use up as much of the 30-second clock as they could manage. The Rams would be reluctant to foul, because made free throws would leave them down by three with little time left.

With four seconds left on the shot clock, Taqqee, on an assist from Adams, made a jumper and Bonaventure had a 75-72 lead with 18 seconds to go. Chartouny --- and why he was taking so many shots in overtime when getting the ball inside to Rhoomes would have made sense --- missed a three-pointer. Posley was fouled with three seconds left, missed the first shot, drained the second one, and the Bonnies slinked out of Rose Hill

Gym with an ugly 76-72 victory.

The Bonnies rarely have 17 turnovers, but that was the number in the Bronx. "We were really trying to force things, and we had too many turnovers," Coach Mark Schmidt said. "We found a way to win, and that's a credit to our guys and their mental toughness." He also said the Rams came in with a good game plan, and that the Bonnies were fortunate to win.

Of the 17 turnovers, 13 came from Posley and Adams, which is rather stunning. Also surprising was how Fordham did not depend on Rhoomes at crunch time. He ended with 23 points and nine rebounds and was 10-for-13 from the floor.

The Bonnies will have to wash this one away quickly, since a difficult George Washington team will be the next opponent on a Saturday after-noon homecoming game.

CHAPTER 18:

WARM INSIDE

GEORGE WASHINGTON

All that would have been forsaken if St. Bonaventure University had decided to demote its athletic programs to Division II or Division III instead of Division I and end membership in the Atlantic 10 Conference was on vivid, gripping display for the critical game against George Washington on a late Saturday afternoon in mid-February. The Reilly Center was crazed and jam-packed, the first sellout since Andrew Nicholson's final game in 2012. The official attendance was listed as 5,480.

Rooms were difficult or impossible to find at the Fairfield Inn, the Microtel, the Best Western and the Hampton Inn in Olean/Allegany. Even by Western New York standards, the weather was imposing: Snow from lake-effect squalls left modest accumulations on highways and the streets in the towns. The cold was unspeakable, with real temperatures at minus-five degrees tumbling to minus-12 degrees late in the evening after the game. Wind chills were estimated at minus-25 to minus-30 degrees.

For sure, alumni swelled the crowd. It was billed by the school as '80s Alumni Weekend, and those folks were there. But there were alumni from several generations, drawn by a game of consequence at that juncture of a season where the real contenders for a postseason are determined. I met a 1954 grad in the lobby of the Hampton Inn, delivered to the ball-game by his family. There was a group of 2007 grads, fanatical followers of the brown-and-white despite being denied real basketball excitement in their years there, a particularly fallow stretch of time basketball-wise. They flew in from Boston and Washington and made the drives from Geneva, Rochester and Buffalo. Dan Collins, Class of 1973, the vice president of the board of trustees and a key player in the decision to remain Division I, was in the Reilly Center lobby hours before the game and waiting for his daughter Maura, who is not a Bonaventure grad but a hearty supporter nonetheless. She traveled from Alexandria, Va., to attend this game.

Bobi Cornelius, Mark Schmidt's secretary and the individual who provides the ballast of calm and order to what can be the chaotic coaches suite, left the afternoon warmth of her Shinglehouse, Pa., home to take in the game. Also in attendance were Andrew Nicholson himself, DaQuan Cook and Youssou Ndoye, teammates on the 2012 team that won the A-10 Tournament and played its heart out against a third-seeded Florida State team in that first-round NCAA Tournament loss in Nashville. All three play professional basketball these days, Nicholson with Orlando in the NBA, of course; Ndoye with the San Antonio Spurs' team in the NBA's D League, and Cook in the freshly created Canadian NBA circuit. The NBA's all-star break freed them up to be in Olean.

The students, of course, jammed the lower-level stands, including the particularly raucous group that sits behind the basket at the visitors' end of the court or stands in the limited space behind the press tables at that end of the floor. The 4 p.m. start of the game had given them time to liberate their vocal chords at the Burton, the Rathskeller, the on-campus beer joint, or any other place that looked warm and convivial in the piercing cold.

The weather did not discourage the essential, faithful fans who reside on both sides of the state line near Olean. Many of those loyalists were filling Reilly Center seats in the darkness of the post-scandal years and the balky, early years of the Schmidt era. In fact, many of them were there when even a portion of the student body wouldn't bother to go to the games. The local fans would certainly not miss a key game in a season that has begun to feel a bit remarkable, perhaps memorable. Their trucks, vans and SUVs were in the parking lots early on this day.

This was a big-time college basketball setting: A sellout, a game of great consequence, a very tough opponent, a national TV audience, an opportunity for those who pin dreams to a not-a-chance team and school to keep dreaming. Maybe not Allen Fieldhouse big-time, or Chapel Hill big-time, but an environment that is consistently gaudier than what shows itself at all Atlantic 10 venues excepting, maybe, Dayton and Virginia Commonwealth. UD Arena is big with a savvy but polite and knowledgeable fan base. Lots of season ticketholders. VCU is a huge school, heavy on commuters, and has a pep band that has impressed even Mark Schmidt. Yet Olean is the place and St. Bonaventure is the school that was forced to weigh whether the future should be Division I.

The Bonnies' conference season of streaks and slumps had arrived at a critical juncture. After the losses to Duquesne, Dayton and Virginia Commonwealth, the Bonnies had recovered with wins at home against Richmond, at St. Joseph's, at home against St. Louis and at Fordham. The win at St. Joe's was a thing of beauty. The victories over St. Louis and Fordham were gut-busters. Now came George Washington, 18-6 overall, including a victory over highly ranked Virginia, and 7-4 in the A-10. A week earlier the Colonials won at VCU, 72-69, and then were hammered at home by St. Joe's, 84-66. GW was rated a contender for the A-10 title before the season began, a big, talented and veteran team that would battle Dayton, Davidson and Rhode Island for conference supremacy. The Colonials were coached by Mike Lonergan, a hugely successful coach at Catholic University and then the University of Vermont. In five years, Lonergan had made GW a winner, and he had beaten the Bonnies three times in four meetings, including a clubbing in Washington a year earlier.

This would be the 12th game in the 18-game conference schedule for both schools. There have been plenty of alumni weekends at Bonaventure that meant little. This wasn't one of them. The Bonnies, a surprise to pundits, their fans and maybe themselves, were in fourth place with an 8-3 record in the A-10 and 16-6 overall. They had shown themselves as a team that can outscore very good opponents (Davidson, St. Joe's), be as tough as jerky when games become low-scoring grinders (Rhode Island, for sure), be death-wish leaky on defense (the loss at Duquesne), and be almost miraculous (Jaylen Adams's long three-point buzzer-beater to deny St. Louis).

The only constant has been the Bonnies play very hard, and if you wanted your team to have one quality, that isn't a bad one. They are skillful, tough-minded and self-confident. They are also small inside, which Dion Wright can make a non-issue with his consistently gritty play, young in key roles, which Jordan Tyson, Derrick Woods and Nelson Kaputo often struggle to overcome, and beat up, Marcus Posley, for sure, with hip and ankle problems, and Adams, with the wear-and-tear that comes with playing huge minutes that are punctuated with suicidal drives to the basket. Posley, Adams and Wright give this team a presence that can be wicked on opponents.

The size of the Colonials, or their "length," as coaches and broadcasters now describe it, was a concern for Schmidt and his assistants. Four of their starters are 6-foot-6 or bigger. They start three seniors. Their points come from an assortment of skillful players. Patricio Garino is a key piece, a 6-foot-6 senior who handles the ball very well and can score inside and outside. Tyler Cavanaugh, a 6-foot-9 junior from Syracuse, leads GW in scoring at just under 17 points per game and nearly eight rebounds per game. He is another big player who can put the ball on the floor and make moves. He gets lots of help inside from Kevin Larsen, a 6-foot-10, 265-pound senior who grew up in Denmark but prepped in Maryland. He provides 12 points and eight rebounds a game and is second in the A-10 in double-doubles. Joe McDonald is the senior point guard and Yuta Watanabe, from Japan and the Thomas More School in Connecticut (where the Bonnies' Denzel Gregg prepped), was playing his best ball of the season, providing double figures in points in four of GW's last five games.

Moreover, the Colonials really needed a win in Olean. A loss would leave them a full two games behind Bonaventure in the conference standings with six games left in the regular season.

Jordan Tyson, who did not even play in a game until Dec. 19 when he returned from a torn tendon in his wrist, was now the starting center. To this point, his major contribution was being something of a deterrent to drives in the lane and scores inside. He was delivering just two points, three rebounds and a blocked shot in 16 minutes per game. Denzel Gregg started in place of Dion Wright, who was late for a meeting and, surely, confirmed again for Schmidt something Skip Prosser once told him:

"Somehow, you can't just ENDURE the kids, you have to ENJOY the kids."

How much Schmidt enjoyed having a key piece, a senior, a guy who leads the conference with 11 double doubles, sitting on the bench for the start of a crucial matchup, was not asked.

The first eight minutes of the game were not a showcase for either team. It was a 4-4 game with 12:21 to go. But Gregg provided a dunk on a drive and then scored on a rebound, and Posley nailed a three-pointer. The Bonnies led 11-7 at the 9:42 mark. Bonaventure showed signs of breaking away late in the first half. They opened a six-point lead, 17-11, on a nice drive by Idris Taqqee and two free throws by Posley at the 4:25 mark. Wright, who ended up playing 15 minutes of the first half, hit a jump shot that pushed his team to a 24-17 lead with 30 seconds left. A drive by Garino made it 24-19 at the half.

Just watching the action, a Bona fan would worry about Cavanaugh and Garino. While Garino had just one score, his size and his handle were worrisome. Cavanaugh was very solid in the first 20 minutes, using his size and ball skills to provide eight points. The most encouraging sign for the Bonnies was their ability to deal with GW's size. The freshman Tyson was a major reason. He had six rebounds, two of them offensively, in the first half. While Larsen was grabbing seven rebounds, three of them on the offensive end, and scoring five points, Bonaventure had a 24-21 advantage in rebounds, 12 of them offensive rebounds.

The fans were as boisterous as their numbers, including one female Bonaventure student standing behind the baseline on the visitors' end of the floor. Maybe she was a Marine or a steelworker before she came to Bonaventure, but her language would have shamed not just Thomas Merton and St. Francis but Amy Schumer. Her inventively profane observations, screamingly delivered, targeted the officials and, for some reason, GW's Cavanaugh. If the referees could hear her, she might have been tossed from the place. If they heard her and chose not to take notice, their restraint was admirable.

Among its many challenges, Bonaventure received just two points in 11 minutes from Jaylen Adams, who picked up two fouls early in the first half. The sophomore made up for it with a remarkable second half. His two three-pointers gave the Bonnies some breathing room at 30-19. A drive by Posley and a three from Idris Taqqee gave the Bonnies a 35-23 command. Then Tyson punched away a shot attempt inside by Cavanaugh and then turned toward the GW forward screaming and smiling. Cavanaugh went face-to-face with Tyson but nothing came of it.

A basket from distance by Nelson Kaputo gave the Bonnies a 40-28 bulge with 13:20 to play, but Bona was flirting with foul trouble, racking up four personals to just one by the Colonials in the second half. A three-point basket by Garino cut the lead to 40-35, and GW was back in it.

Adams restored some order with a stunning drive and a steal that he turned in to a slam and a 44-35 lead with 10 minutes remaining. Garino hit another three-pointer, but Wright responded with a jumper and Adams converted a spectacular drive to make it 48-38 with 7:59 showing. Then Posley came up hobbling, aggravating either the hip injury or a tweaked ankle. He headed to the bench and Bonaventure showed a lineup of Gregg, Wright, Adams, Taqqee and Tyson.

Posley put himself back on the floor and then Adams drained another three to give Bonaventure a 51-38 lead. Garino, clearly stepping up, hit a three-pointer. Another driving layup by Adams gave the Bonnies a 55-42 lead with 5:15 to go. A nice drive by Gregg made it 57-42. If this brought comfort or confidence to the large crowd, it was misplaced. GW came back with a roar.

Garino drove for a basket, Matt Hart came off the bench to hit a jumper and Wright fouled Cavanaugh behind the arc. He hit all three free throws and it was a 59-53 game with 1:53 to go. Taqqee missed the front end of a one-and-one and GW scored on a fast break to cut the lead to 59-55. What had been a 15-point Bonnies' lead was reduced to four points. But the Colonials missed shots from long range as Adams hit two free throws and Gregg went three-for-four in two trips to the foul line. A final drive by Garino made it 64-57, but only 10.6 seconds were showing and Lonergan shut down his defense and conceded.

Lonergan met with the media following the game. Almost always, coaches open these sessions with a statement, a capsulized explanation of why their teams won or lost. Lonergan came in, sat down at the table in the front of the room, and said nothing. After an uncomfortable few moments, someone asked a question and the GW coach opened up. "We backed off their guards in the second half," he said, indicating that wasn't a strategic decision. "Adams is really good."

Lonergan was asked if he could remember one of his teams recording 20 offensive rebounds and still losing. "It's a kind of misleading statistic," he said, "because we shot so poorly." He also noted his team was turned over 16 times.

"Our basketball IQ was very low today," Lonergan said. "In the first half, we had poor shot selection. Bonaventure is not very big inside but they pushed us around. They are physical, athletic. St. Bonaventure was the tougher team today."

Mark Schmidt throws around compliments as if they were manhole covers. Before the season began, he was asked if he liked this team, this version of the Bonnies. "I didn't at first," he answered. "I'm liking them a little more." But he was clearly cautious. When he met with reporters after this victory, he was uncharacteristically effusive over the performance his players had given.

"It was a big game. George Washington is one of the elite teams in the league," Schmidt said. "It was a home game, it was homecoming. It was not a pretty game … but I couldn't believe how hard we played. We defended. We were physical. We made plays when we needed to."

Then he added: "It's a great day."

For his first several years in a job that is now in its ninth season, some Bonaventure fans didn't know what to make of Schmidt. He wasn't homegrown, not a Bonaventure graduate, like Larry Weise, Jim Satalin and Jim Baron. The common refrain on the Bonnies fan boards was that Schmidt "just didn't get the place." That began to change after Schmidt and the Bonnies defeated George Washington in a game in Washington in 2011. Schmidt was asked by a Washington reporter about Bonaventure having a large and loud contingent of fans in the Smith Center, basically taking the place over, stealing one of the benefits that a home team should expect.

Schmidt's answer is, at this point, well-remembered: "They are like a cult, but in a good way. They are everywhere. We went to Arkansas-Little Rock and we had fans there. They are great fans. The alumni love the place. I went to Boston College, and I love Boston College, but not like this."

And it is not just Schmidt. His assistant coaches always go out of the way to acknowledge Bona fans at road games. They did it at Hagan Arena after beating St. Joe's. When the Bonnies beat UMass to get to the finals in the A-10 tournament at the Convention Center in Atlantic City in 2012, Dave Moore, the top assistant, waded in to a crowd of Bonnie celebrants, hugging fans and slapping fives.

For the second time in seven games, Schmidt shared his feelings about his job. The first was after Bonaventure rallied from a 45-18 first half deficit and dropped 61 points on Dayton in the second half. It was a loss, but a large crowd in the Reilly Center stood and cheered their team in the closing seconds. "There was never any booing," Schmidt said of the devastating first 20 minutes. "It makes me proud to be the coach of St. Bonaventure."

This time, after winning before a homecoming sellout, Schmidt said: "The crowd gave me goose bumps. It was unbelievable. The Reilly Center is an unbelievable venue for college basketball."

Tyson and Adams joined Schmidt at the press conference. Adams scored 17 points in the second half, many of them on drives that were downright artful. Tyson didn't score, but his seven rebounds and his play against Larsen were significant, and Schmidt wasn't going to waste an opportunity to make Tyson feel good about himself. At one point, Tyson said: "I feel like I'm getting better."

Schmidt said of Tyson: "He is improving and we need him to improve."

CHAPTER 19:

A DISASTER IN PHILLY

LASALLE

Under the somewhat yellowish lighting at Gola Arena, tucked in to the compact and dense campus of La Salle University, a refuge for generations of sons and daughters of blue-collared immigrants in a challenged stretch of North Philadelphia, St. Bonaventure's marvelous season took a big hit. The Bonnies lost to the Explorers, and it wasn't as close as the 71-64 score would indicate.

How did this happen? How could a team that had rattled off five straight conference wins and put itself in place to be among the top four in the Atlantic 10 Conference and the valued byes it would bring in the conference tournament, lose to last-place La Salle?

The Bonnies made it look easy. Mark Schmidt could speak to how it happened: "We didn't play," he said. "We deserved to lose. We weren't ready to play. La Salle played better than we did. We didn't show up ... didn't get the effort we had to have. La Salle played harder than we did."

That is how it happened. For why it happened, there were no ready answers. Why weren't they prepared to play? The Bonnies looked like a tired team. Maybe the skill and energy needed to unfurl a five-game win streak in the meat of the season had caught up with a team whose best players often see 35 to 40 minutes. Maybe they had hit some wall of mental or physical fatigue?

"Fatigue had nothing to do with it," Schmidt snapped, angry at the suggestion.

Whatever the cause, it was a bad loss, maybe a loss that could end up defining the season. The Bonnies were 10- or 11-point favorites coming in to this game. They had everything to play for, and La Salle was 1-12 in the A-10 and 5-18 overall. When the game was over, the Bonnies would get on their bus and head to the airport for their charter flight to Dayton. Little time to prepare for a noon tip-off Saturday against the Flyers, who were also in Philadelphia this Wednesday night and lost at St. Joe's. How not to be trailing 45-18 at the half at UD Arena will be one of the challenges.

The day before the La Salle game, when the Bonnies were busing to Bradford and a charter flight, escaping a heavy, wet snow storm, Schmidt was cautious about this game. He had been watching tape of the Explorers and he judged them "a scary team." Jordan Price, a bruising big guard, had hurt the Bonnies the year before, when La Salle won at the Reilly Center. Schmidt also liked the skills of Yevgen Sakhniuk, a forward/center from the Ukraine, who was tricky inside. Johnnie Shuler and Cleon Roberts were decent shooters. Among the Explorers' shortcomings was an ability to score. They managed just 48 and 62 points in their two games against St.

Joe's and 60 against Duquesne. They had scored 61 at home against Dayton, and that was enough for a four-point victory. La Salle's only league victory before the Bona game had come against the powerful Flyers. For sure, stuff happens.

With the kind of firepower St. Bonaventure can deliver, this game should have been highly winnable. Moreover, the Bonnies couldn't afford to lose it, not at this juncture, not after what they had accomplished so far.

The Gola Arena provided a strange setting. La Salle listed attendance as 1,329, and that seemed very inflated. There were a hundred or so Bonnie fans behind the team's bench. The place was empty enough that you could hear the sneakers squeaking on the floor and plays being called out, like at a scrimmage.

For the Bonnies and their fans, this one looked like trouble from the start. Idris Taqqee and Dion Wright had turnovers in the first 53 seconds. After Price and Roberts nailed three-pointers, Schmidt called a timeout at 18:29. When the Bonnies came back on the floor, Denzel Gregg had replaced Wright. Another three from Price made it 11-2 La Salle. Johnnie Shuler's three gave La Salle a 14-5 lead at 15:03. Another Shuler jumper and La Salle was up 16-6 at 12:52. When Shuler dropped another three-pointer, La Salle's seventh three-ball in a bit more than 12 minutes, the Bonnies trailed 25-15.

Then Bonaventure showed some life. Taqqee scored and Adams got inside on a drive. Posley was fouled as he attempted a three-pointer, and he made two of three. Then Adams forced a steal and drove for a dunk, and

Wright scored on a rebound to tie the game at 25-25. A three-pointer from Posley gave Bonaventure a 30-28 lead with two minutes left. Karl Harris gave La Salle its eighth three-point goal of the first half and a tap-in by Tony Washington lifted the Explorers to a 35-32 lead at intermission.

If you were a Bonnies' fan, you could allow yourself some optimism that it was just a three-point game after a very shaky, uninspired first half. You would have to be concerned that a poor rebounding team such as La Salle would hold an 18-14 advantage and be shooting the long ball at a 50 percent clip. The Explorers turned it over 11 times in the first 20 minutes, a lethal pace, but Bonaventure had seven TOs.

La Salle opened its lead to 37-32 but Posley provided a pair of three-pointers and a drive to give the Bonnies a 40-37 edge. Bona's led 42-41 at the first timeout. If Bonaventure was going to pull away, as it had at critical moments in its five-game win streak, this would be a good time.

It did not happen. Roberts nailed a three-pointer and Price converted two free throws to give La Salle a 54-51 lead. As the teams huddled during a media timeout with 8:25 to play, Dave Moore, the Bonnies' assistant coach, who has advanced to a walking boot as his torn Achilles tendon mends, stood at the edge of the circle, shaking his head, distressed at the situation, and the toll that a loss would exact.

Bonaventure battled the rest of the game, but La Salle's big edge in rebounding and a defense that had dogged Bonaventure from the start assured the outcome. Washington and Sakhniuk suddenly had become the inside presence that La Salle had missed all season. They provided the points that gave the Explorers a 62-58 lead.

The Bonnies' last chance was a three-pointer from Posley that gave them a 63-62 lead with 2:10 to play. But Washington scored on a feed from Price and then Price drove for a basket and the Bonnies were down for good, 66-63, with 1:07 left. In the last 30 seconds, Price would power himself to another basket inside, Posley would be called for an offensive foul, and Amar Stukes would hit two free throws.

Bad timing for St. Bonaventure that La Salle Coach John Giannini was able to say of his team after the game, "That's the team that I thought I would see all season." His bigger guys played well and his guards defended wonderfully against Posley and, especially, Adams, preventing them the kind of blazes in to the lane and to the rim that had been a hallmark of the Bonnies so far.

Fifteen of Posley's 21 points came on three-pointers. Adams ended with 12 points. Wright had 16 points. Adams played all 40 minutes, and did so with signs of discomfort, including his wincing and massaging his hamstring at one point. Posley and Wright played 37 minutes, and Posley continues to be pestered by hip and ankle pains. Denzel Gregg managed just three points in 20 minutes.

In the three games before La Salle, Schmidt had praised his team for its toughness and its defense. They held GW to 57, Fordham to 72 (in an overtime game) and St. Louis to 62. "Defense is a staple and offense is fickle," Schmidt has said, and of course he is absolutely right. But something is amiss with the Bonnies' offense at the moment.

Idris Taqqee scored on a layup with 10:47 to play in the second half against the Explorers. The next field goal for Bonaventure was a three-point basket from Posley with 4:41 to go. La Salle was not able to put the game away in that barren stretch of time for the Bonnies. But that absence of an offensive punch certainly assured Bonaventure wouldn't take control of the game and pull away.

The drop in offense, after scoring 97 against Davidson, 88 at UMass, 88 in the loss at Duquesne, 61 in 20 minutes against Dayton, 84 against Richmond and 83 at St. Joseph's, leaves the Bonnies more vulnerable. It makes one wonder just how compromised physically Posley and Adams might be, because their abilities to both shoot outside and make things happen on drives have been the keys to much of the Bonnies' success to date.

Schmidt's formula for this season began with Posley, Wright and Adams combining for 55 points each game. They combined for just 49 in this 71-64 loss, one that could haunt the Bonnies and their hungry fans.

CHAPTER 20:

A GEM IN DAYTON

I lived and worked in Dayton for two years early in my newspaper career. I was an editor on the sports desk of the Dayton Journal Herald, the morning newspaper. Cox News also owned the Dayton Daily News, which was the larger of the two papers and also produced the Sunday newspaper. The Journal Herald is long gone, the victim of the slumping readership that has devastated that industry. My oldest daughter was born in Dayton. I enjoyed living there.

Dayton is a good-sized city of 141,000, and much-larger Cincinnati is only an hour's drive south. The people are unusually pleasant … perfect models for "Midwestern nice." The region has some beautiful suburbs, such as Centerville, Kettering and Beavercreek. The region churns out lots of good athletes, some of whom head off to play football or basketball at big-time colleges, and the most fortunate ones become Buckeyes. Baseball Hall-of-Famer Mike Schmidt is a Daytonian. Manufacturing, especially the old National Cash Register company, drew lots of people from Kentucky and Tennessee to Dayton before and especially after World War II, so hearing a deep southern accent in Southwestern Ohio is not unusual. The place calls itself The Gem City. The population is crazy for the Cincinnati Reds.

The University of Dayton is a major presence in the region, a cornerstone of the area's economy, a major employer, and a point of pride. Flyers basketball is a significant recreational outlet, for the students, for sure, but also for the region's residents. Their enmity for Xavier University, 50 miles to the south, knows no bounds. Dayton's reputation as a college basketball hotbed is the reason that when the NCAA expanded the tournament field to 68 from 64, those last four teams selected engage in "play-in" games in a bracket now known as the First Four. The games are played at UD Arena and draw the usual 13,000-plus, prompting broadcasters to now describe Dayton as Basketball Town USA. The rich, it seems, do get richer, and the Flyers are the evidence, season after season.

I saw some games at UD Arena when I was residing in Dayton, including a hugely memorable upset of No. 1 ranked De Paul by St. Joseph's in an NCAA tournament first-rounder in 1981. De Paul's star, and the best player in America that season, was Mark Aguirre. When a layup by the Hawks' John Smith dropped through the net as time expired, eliminating DePaul, Aguirre grabbed the game ball, stormed off the court, found an exit door at the arena, and walked the two miles to his downtown hotel, wearing just his uniform and sneakers. According to lore, the game ball ended up in the nearby Miami River.

Bucky Albers, a terrific reporter and columnist for the Journal Herald and the Dayton Daily News, said Tom Blackburn, the legendary coach of the Flyers, once told him: "You can't call yourself a college basketball coach until you have awakened in Olean, N.Y. on a Sunday morning."

The Flyers and their fans awakened on the morning of Saturday, Feb. 20, and were eager to wash away their last game and to punish their next opponent. After rattling off nine straight A-10 victories, Dayton was whacked on Hawk Hill, losing 79-70 to St. Joseph's. It was on the same Wednesday evening that the Bonnies fell at La Salle. If you were a Bonaventure supporter, nothing about this matchup should have felt good. Losing to the Explorers had to be as dispiriting as it was costly, and the first 20 minutes against the Flyers in Olean would still be a fresh memory. Dayton would be hell-bent to make things right in its world, erasing the memories of the loss in Philadelphia and keeping pace with VCU and St. Joe's atop the conference standings and embellishing an overall record of 21-4. The Flyers were already an NCAA tourney shoo-in, so their task on this day would be dressing up the resume, positioning for a high seed. A sellout of 13,455 gathered at the UD Arena for the noon tip-off.

Mark Schmidt was truly heartened by his team's second half against Dayton in Olean. The first half was a nightmare, and it should have been. It wasn't simply that the Bonnies played poorly, it was just as much a case of how good Dayton was. But the second half was a tonic. Bonaventure responded to the challenge in unforgettable fashion, and 61 points in one half is a hell of a statement, no matter the opponent.

Before he had even landed in Ohio, Schmidt was asked how do you beat Dayton? Won't there be a hangover from the first meeting? Schmidt didn't buy it. "We could have lost by 30, we could have lost by 50, but we didn't," he said, firmly. "The way we came back against them should mean something.

"We can play with them. We know we can compete with them."

And the Bonnies did. They raced off to a 15-5 lead. It was all Wright, Adams and Posley. Wright hit a baby hook to start the game, Adams hit a three, Posley drove for a basket and Adams hit another long ball. Another hook shot and a three-pointer from Wright provided the early advantage.

Dayton came back. Steve McElvene, the Flyers' 6-foot-11 freshman center, from right next door in Indiana, hit a pair of free throws and a basket inside to cut the deficit to 15-11. Minutes later, on a drive from Scoochie Smith, Dayton was within one, 22-21. It was starting to feel like a heavyweight fight.

Schmidt had sent out a new starting lineup for this matchup. Idris Taqqee and Jerome Tyson did not start. Denzel Gregg and Derrick Woods did. Gregg, alongside Wright, would provide additional firepower. Woods was a bit less foul-prone than Tyson at this point. Gregg drew some fouls and stole some attention from Wright on the inside. Late in the first half, Woods hit a pair of free throws, Wright scored inside off a pretty feed from Nelson Kaputo and Gregg scored inside to put the Bonnies ahead, 31-25. Two free throws from Posley and the lead was 33-26 with 4:35 to go. Both teams were racking up fouls at a fast rate.

Dayton began to really push the ball after defensive rebounds and it was resulting in trips to the foul line and quick baskets. Dyshawn Pierre drilled a three to cut the Bonnies edge to 35-34 with 1:40 left in the half. Two free throws from Smith gave Dayton just its second lead of the half, 36-35, with 59 seconds remaining.

Then Adams converted two free throws and drilled a three-pointer to give the Bonnies a 40-36 halftime lead.

Schmidt was right. His team could compete. In fact, his team had a first-half advantage that was 31 points better than the first 20 minutes in Olean: The 27-point deficit plus the four-point Bona lead at the half in Dayton.

What must have been worrisome for Schmidt and his coaches were the driving baskets and trips to the foul line that Dayton guards Scoochie Smith and Charles Cooke were managing. The Flyers hit only a pair of three-pointers in the first half, and beating the Bonnies down the floor clearly was a tactic, and it was working. It also worked in the first 20 minutes in Olean. Gregg and Posley each had three fouls at the end of the half, and Wright had a pair.

The Bonnies, however, were making an impression. David Kaplan, the college basketball analyst for NBC Sports Network, called the Flyers and the Bonnies "two of the heavyweights in the league." Not bad, since Bonaventure was picked anywhere from seventh to ninth in various pre-season polls.

The next 20 minutes were an exercise in true grit. Bonaventure got baskets inside from Wright and Woods. Smith and Cooke delivered three-point goals. Posley hit a three, Smith answered again with a long ball, and

Adams drove for a basket and hit the free throw that came with it. Adams had 19 and the Bonnies led 52-45 with 16:30 to play. It was quickly 52-51, however, as Cooke made two free throws, McElvene, who had a strong game overall, scored inside, and Pierre drove for a basket.

The Flyers took a rare lead at 53-52 on a drive and free throw from Cooke, as Dayton continued to play fast. But Adams answered with his own three-point play and then Wright blocked a shot inside, ran the floor and put back a rebound. When Adams again scored inside, it was 59-54 Bonnies with 10 minutes to play.

Kaputo, the freshman guard, has struggled in the conference after some highlight moments in the non-conference schedule. His minutes have gone down. After McElvene again scored inside to trim the Bonnies' lead to 59-56, Kaputo drilled a three-pointer. A drive by Cooke and two free throws from Pierre and it was 62-60 with 8:18 left, and then Woods threw the ball away. There was no margin for error moving forward, and the Bonnies had seven team fouls, putting Dayton in to the bonus.

It was at this point that Kaputo dropped another three ball, and the Bona lead was 65-60.

Cooke drove once again for a basket and was fouled. On the play, Adams got up slowly. Moments later, Posley was fouled but he missed both free throws. He made up for it with a steal and a basket and it was a five-point lead once more, 69-64, with five minutes to go. Smith and Pierre both pierced the Bona defense with drives and the lead was just 69-68, with 3:40 showing.

Denzel Gregg did not exactly fill up the box score on this day, but he supplied big-time minutes. The biggest was the three-point goal he provided that put Bonaventure ahead, 72-68. Pierre, the conference's Litigant of the Year --- he filed a suit against his own school for suspending him in the first semester for bad behavior --- made two free throws to cut the margin in half.

The next two minutes were drenched with drama and will be recalled by Bona fans for years to come. There was a loose ball on a Bonnies' offensive possession and players for both teams scrambled for it. Dayton ended up with it but Schmidt argued that there had been a change in possession, and the ball belonged to his team. The call did not go his way. Dayton had the ball with 1:10 left. McElvene scored inside and the game was tied at 72.

Bona called a timeout with 53 seconds to play. The rest of the game belonged to Jaylen Adams. With 36 seconds to go, Adams found just enough room to fire off a three, and he hit it. The lead was 75-72. Cooke missed a jumper with 21 seconds showing and Bonaventure claimed the rebound and called time out. Dayton was desperate now, and Kyle Davis fouled Adams, who hit the two free throws.

After a UD timeout, Cooke tried a three with 11 seconds to go and missed. Adams, of course, was the rebounder, who was fouled and made the free throws with two seconds to play. Game over. Bonnies prevailed, 79-72.

In a span of 36 seconds, Adams scored the last seven points, Dayton lost its second straight and its first at home this season, and the Bonnies, who could have been walking dead leaving La Salle, instead had their biggest regular season victory in years. By beating the 15th-ranked Flyers, Bonaventure recorded its first road victory on the home floor of a ranked team in its history.

It was the first time in 78 games that Dayton had lost back-to-back games. That's remarkable, but it must be noted that the Flyers did not have Kendall Pollard, a tremendous player but out with what is being described as a bruised knee. He did not play against St. Joe's either. Nonetheless, this was just Bona's second win at UD Arena and its first in 14 years. Dayton came in to this game with its highest ranking in 49 years … that is the magnitude of this Bonnies triumph.

Tom Archdeacon, a columnist for the Dayton newspaper, had a name for Adams: Superman. For his part, Adams just wanted it noted that he had a good time. "This is just a crazy environment --- the atmosphere, the noise, everything --- I just love it," he said.

Adams had another one of those lines that would boggle the mind of a basketball junkie, if not for the fact that it was this baby-faced sophomore from Baltimore: 8-for-19, 5-for-9 from behind the arc, 10-for-10 from the foul line, 6 rebounds, all on the defensive end, 6 assists, 2 steals and 0 turnovers.

While Adams was indescribably good, and timely, he did have help. Wright played all 40 minutes and had 15 points, eight rebounds, an assist, a steal and a block. Posley had just three field goals, one of them a three-ball, but he got to the line, went 5-for-8, and doled out three assists. His ability to drive to the basket kept the UD defense honest. Gregg had eight points and four rebounds. And Tyson and Woods combined for eight rebounds.

Dayton Coach Archie Miller, who was gracious when he won in Olean, and certainly worried about a two-game losing streak and the injury to Pollard, tossed superlatives toward Adams. "He's one of the best guards I've ever coached against," Miller said. "To do what he was able to do and never come out of the game was incredible. When you have a guard who can do what he did in that environment, he could beat anyone in the country."

Schmidt's claim that his team could play with Dayton must have been wonderfully delivered to his players in the 63 hours between walking off the floor in North Philadelphia and the tip-off at UD Arena. Of Adams, he said: "Jay's just terrific. He has a really calming influence on our team. Nothing is really too big for him."

As he did after the loss to Dayton in Olean, Schmidt reverted to pugilism to describe what the Bonnies had accomplished: "When you come in here," he said of Dayton, "you got to be prepared for a fist fight."

CHAPTER 21:
PAYBACK FOR DUQUESNE

In the Atlantic 10 Conference, which is rich with tremendous, high-scoring guards, the duo of Derrick Colter and Micah Mason is as formidable as any. The two of them combined for 50 points in Pittsburgh when the Dukes ended Bonaventure's four-game winning streak to start conference play. In this rematch at the Reilly Center, Colter and Mason combined for just 29, but Duquesne got points on the inside and claimed a remarkable 48 rebounds, 22 of them on the offensive end, and owned a 45-37 lead after Eric James scored inside with 16:14 to play.

The Dukes steadily pulled away from the Bonnies in the last 10 minutes at the Palumbo Center, and this one was beginning to look like a carbon copy. Mason and Colter were taking lots of shots but missing most of them, yet Duquesne was getting double-digit contributions from four other players and absolutely owning the backboards on both ends. Schmidt was glad for the media timeout, because there was no vividly clear path to victory for his team at this juncture.

Then L.C. Gill nailed a jump shot to keep Duquesne ahead at 48-41.

This day began with drama of another sort at St. Bonaventure. Sr. Margaret Carney, who weeks earlier announced she would resign in the summer after 12 years as president of the school, released a statement in the morning that disclosed she had been diagnosed with a form of blood cancer, multiple myeloma. The statement displayed the kind of grit the 74-year-old nun exhibited as she tackled all the other challenges she faced in her time in office. Carney said her schedule might ease up a bit but that her doctors had assured her she would be able to fulfill her duties. She noted that her travel might be curtailed some on behalf of a compromised immune system from the treatments she would receive.

Carney stressed that the illness has nothing to do with her decision to retire in July. The diagnosis came after her announcement that she would be stepping down. I met with Sr. Margaret a few hours before the game and she was in great spirits, far more open and at ease than when I spent time with her earlier in the season. She was dressed in a colorful suit and was directing some of her staff as she began to deal with all of the files and documents that would be cleared from her office. Despite the discovery of her illness, she seemed unburdened by her decision to retire and eager for the sabbatical she planned. She looked happy.

Sr. Margaret was at the ballgame, and waded in to the student section of the bleachers, where a number of the folks were holding placards with the message # CarneyStrong. Carney ended her short statement regarding her diagnosis with distinctive grace: "It will come as no surprise to anyone that I intend to do everything possible to win this battle with cancer. I will also find in this many opportunities to ponder the fundamentals of the faith with which I was gifted in baptism. This is the faith I will do my best to honor and live by in the months ahead. Adding your prayers and support is what I ask for and what I will need."

Whatever was said when Schmidt huddled with his team lit something of a spark. Jaylen Adams fed Jordan Tyson, who would play big minutes in this game, and the big freshman converted. Then Denzel Gregg drove for a basket and was fouled. The made free throw cut the lead to 48-46 with 12:53 to play. A three-pointer from Dion Wright pulled the Bonnies within 52-51.

The Dukes quickly answered. Mason hit a three-point shot but Adams was fouled and made the two free throws. Lewis scored on a rebound basket but Tyson was fouled and made both of his shots. After Mason made a three-point goal, Darius Lewis scored inside and the lead was back to five.

Duquesne will surely miss Mason and Colter, both seniors, but the Dukes have a major piece in Lewis, a 6-foot-11, 245-pound junior from Lexington, Ky., to build around. And Lewis isn't the only inside presence for Duquesne. James and the 6-foot-8 junior Gill did damage in this game. Coach Jim Ferry will have six players 6-foot-8 or taller returning next season. And as Mark Schmidt often points out, everyone has good guards, you can always find guards. Finding two that match the talents of Mason and Colter will be more of a stretch, however.

Mason hit a three-pointer to give Duquesne a 65-59 command with 8:29 to play, and if Mason or Colter were to find a hot hand at this point, then the Bonnies would be cooked. The Dukes' guards did not.

Adams hit back-to-back threes and Bonaventure had clawed back to a 65-65 tie. Adams was fouled trying another three-pointer and made two of the three shots and the game was tied at 67. It was 69-69 when Dion Wright scored inside. Then Marcus Posley, who had a quiet game, hit a three-pointer and the Bonnies took a 72-69 lead. They never trailed again.

Tyson, certainly playing one of his best games, scored on a rebound and was fouled. His made shot gave Bonaventure a 77-72 lead with 54 seconds to go. When Wright made one of two free throws it was a 78-74 game, but TySean Powell, a sophomore and another good-looking big man for the Dukes, scored on a rebound and it was a two-point game with 11 seconds left.

The Bonnies seem to have chronic problems on inbounding the ball, and when Adams was tied up in just such a moment, it seemed that Duquesne could have one more possession to tie or win the game. But the possession arrow signaled Bonaventure and Dion Wright was fouled and made both free throws to give the Bonnies an 80-76 edge with eight seconds remaining. That would be the final score.

It would seem Ferry has Duquesne headed in the right direction, even with the losses of Colter and Mason. Ferry is a stylish guy, who seems to always have a kerchief in the breast pocket of his well-tailored suits. In a level voice, Ferry told the reporters that it was a "hard-fought game with a tournament environment to it."

Ferry said both teams played well defensively and free throws were the decisive factor down the stretch. He said his team didn't get to the foul line much in the second half, while the Bonnies rallied with the help of free throws. Speaking of Wright and Gregg, Ferry said, "We couldn't keep them out of the lane."

Then Ferry concluded by saying, "Nineteen and seven, fifteen and thirteen, that's the difference between us." Whatever problems the Dukes are having with the rest of the Atlantic 10, there really isn't much that separates these two teams. The conference schedule-makers always have the Bonnies and Dukes playing home-and-home. "They think we are rivals," Schmidt said. "And we are."

Jaylen Adams would finish with 24 points, but half of those came on free throws. Posley had 11. Wright was his usual presence, scoring 15 points and grabbing eight rebounds and playing for all 40 minutes. The Bonnies also got a combined 15 points from Derrick Woods and Tyson. Tyson also had seven rebounds in 27 minutes. Despite Duquesne's dominance on the backboards, most of that came in the first half. Also, both teams had the same number of points in the paint: 32.

Wright joined Schmidt at the media session. Wright said: "We are a far better rebounding team than we showed in the first half." He also said Lewis was a formidable presence inside. "It was tough going in there," Wright said. "but I tried to make the most of it."

It is a measure of the Bonnies' efforts this season that the 11-4 record resulting from the win over the Dukes tied the school record for A-10 wins in a season. The 1999-2000 team also had 11 wins in the conference. This year's team still has three regular-season contests to go.

Schmidt called the game a great victory. "We played hard," he said. "We showed great character. The offense missed some shots. And we were killed on the boards in the first half." The Dukes managed a 28-16 advantage in rebounds in the first 20 minutes. Schmidt had praise for Duquesne's talent and the team's "mental toughness."

Mason had averaged 24 points in his previous five games. "From a defensive standpoint, we needed to stop their runs," Schmidt said.

Schmidt was back in his office at 7:30 a.m. the next day. He was asked if this is his best team after nine years at Bonaventure. "We had more talent with the Nicholson team (in 2011-12)," he declared. "But we have a better backcourt this year. We have better guards."

It is hard to keep count of how many times Schmidt says "Anybody can beat us, but we can beat anybody." He points this out for a bunch of reasons, foremost because it's true, that it is critical for his players to operate with that mindset, and to remind that despite their place in the standings and the season they are crafting, there is no margin for error. In that regard, the loss at La Salle makes Schmidt's pronouncement more than just coach-speak.

CHAPTER 22:
DODGING A BULLET

The more you see of it, the more certain you are that being a Division I college basketball head coach is a brutal way to make a living. The salaries might be hefty, but the job never ends, and from October to the conclusion of the season in mid-March or later, it is seven days a week, 12 or more hours a day. The sense of control, the notion that the head coach is the master of his destiny, is illusory. Control is ceded at various times to athletic department budget-makers, a referee having a bad night, your point guard's history professor or the hormonal late-night urgings of your star forward. The head coach and his assistants will spend a combined 60 or 70 hours planning and practicing the game plan for the next opponent, and then it is largely turned over to young men thrust in to a frantic, heated environment that demands split-second decision-making and flawless execution.

The coaching staff can plan exquisitely, make all the right in-game decisions, and lose ... lose in ways that are devastating.

Just ask Derek Kellogg. Fifteen minutes earlier, his University of

Massachusetts team had lost to St. Bonaventure, 85-83. Now he had arrived in the cramped, unremarkable space that is the post-game media room at the Reilly Center to tell a dozen or so journalists how it happened and how it made him feel --- a preposterous task since everyone assembled had seen Kellogg's team play a wonderful game only to lose in excruciating fashion, and if you didn't feel badly for Kellogg, if you couldn't see he was hollowed out by the defeat, you were a dolt.

Kellogg was the star guard on the best teams in UMass history, top-ranked teams that lost just 11 A-10 games in the four seasons that ended in 1995. This defeat was the Minutemen's 11th conference loss this season. They had fallen, convincingly, to the Bonnies in Amherst, Mass., earlier this season. But in this game, played before nearly 5,300 fans who assembled for the final home appearance for seniors Marcus Posley and Dion Wright, sorting victory from defeat was a major undertaking.

Jabari Hinds, who would finish with 25 points, scored on a layup to give UMass an 83-81 lead with 29 seconds to play. Then Marcus Posley, by strength of will and remarkable athleticism, split the UMass defenders, bolted down the lane, ball-faked once, laid the ball in for the basket and drew the foul. His made free throw gave the Bonnies an 84-83 lead with 13 seconds to go.

Hinds missed a jump shot and Dion Wright grabbed the rebound and was fouled. With just seven seconds remaining, it seemed the Bonnies would escape. Both teams were in the bonus. Wright missed his first free throw but made the second, and it was 85-83. There were 4.6 seconds to play.

Massachusetts spread the floor and hurriedly moved down court. Bonaventure was loosely spread but seemed well-positioned. Suddenly, Donte Clark bolted to the corner in front of the UMass bench and received a pass. He set himself for the shot just as Wright ran toward him, leaping with one arm raised, looking like some sort of giant bird of prey. Clark fired and caught nothing but net as the buzzer blared and the orange lights flashed on the backboards. Three-point goal. Game-winner, 86-85, Minutemen.

Immediately, the referees rushed to the scorer's table to view film of the final shot. Mark Schmidt walked toward them, waving his arms to indicate the shot came after the buzzer sounded. Kellogg and his players stood nearby. The call came in less than a minute or so, but it felt longer, as it does when you are waiting for the cop to come back to your car with the speeding ticket. The ball had not left Clark's hands before the buzzer. The Bonnies won, 85-83.

Kellogg is one of the more fashion-conscious coaches, but at this moment, his sharp double-vested blue suit couldn't conceal his weariness and frustration. He exhaled loudly as he sat down in the media room. The Bonnies have won hard-fought, tightly competed games at home this season. And in the wake of most of them, certainly not all of them, the losing coaches have been remarkable for their class and professional demeanor. Three nights earlier it had been Duquesne's Jim Ferry: Anguished loser of a taut, nerve-wracking game but pure class. Same with Jim Crews, who was able to call his St. Louis team losing on a buzzer-beating shot by Jaylen Adams, "A great college basketball game." The same can be said for Kellogg.

"St. Bonaventure is a very good team," Kellogg began. "They have a propensity for winning tight games. They did a nice job down the stretch. St. Bonaventure was fortunate to win. It was a hard-fought game."

Jaylen Adams had been brilliant in the previous two games but the Minutemen held him to 14 points. "We tried to keep Adams out of the lane," Kellogg explained. "We did a good job on him. He is a great player."

Then Kellogg was asked about the grind that is the Atlantic 10 Conference regular season, the overall quality of the teams in the league, the tough, close games, and doesn't that make a team battle-tested for the conference tournament and the postseason (though UMass would have to catch fire and win the A-10 tourney to have a postseason).

"Coming to Olean at any time hardens you for anything," Kellogg said, drawing laughter. "I never thought Bonaventure would go away." It was a key observation, because Kellogg's team had buried the Bonnies with a six-minute blitzkrieg in the first half, going from a 21-17 deficit at the 9:37 mark to a 39-21 command with 3:57 to play. Trey Davis, a six-foot senior from Texas, did some of the damage from long range. He would finish with 26 points on the night. And in that stretch of time the Bonnies had problems with Rashoon Holloway, a 6-11, 335-pound freshman, on the interior. He ended the night with 10 points and four rebounds, and if he loses some weight and replaces it with muscle, Holloway will continue to make life difficult for Derrick Woods and Jerome Tyson in the coming seasons.

That 18-point command, that stretch of luminous play, weighed on Kellogg. It should have been a huge factor, a guarantee of a road victory, something to build on as Brooklyn and the conference tournament await. Instead, it was just 45-35 UMass at the half, and the Bonnies would tie the game with less than four minutes gone in the second half.

So how do you measure the toll of a game such as this, for Kellogg, for his assistants? On paper, it's just numbers: UMass goes to 12-16 overall and 5-11 in the conference. Trey Davis and Jabari Hinds combine for 51 points, but both are seniors. They aren't building blocks for next season, they are lost production that will somehow have to be replaced. Your team plays about as well as it can play, does so in front of a near-sellout crowd that is pure emotion because of Senior Night and the kind of season that is a rare gift amid an Olean winter.

More heart-wrenching is the fact that on the last play, the key play, the play that decides the outcome, you and your team do everything right. You find a player alone in the corner, you get him the ball, he takes the shot, does so under great pressure, and makes it. You win, but you don't. You were off by a tenth of a second, by the blink of an eye. You were a heartbeat away. Usually, you lose because your kids fail to do the things you have been coaching them to do since practice began more than four months ago. Today, they did nearly everything correctly, and you still lose. This is your life, Derek Kellogg.

Mark Schmidt arrived in the press room and he brought Posley and Idris Taqqee with him. Posley is a constant presence at these postgame interviews. Not so much for Taqqee, but that will change. He is having a strong sophomore season, delivering in unexpected ways. He gets a lot of respect from his teammates.

The Bonnies had four players in double figures. Posley ended with 22, Dion Wright had 21, and 11 rebounds, a spectacular performance; and Taqqee had 19. Denzel Gregg quietly had nine points and six rebounds in just 21 minutes. The Bonnies outrebounded UMass 32-23.

Since he had been waving off the made field goal at the buzzer, how was he so sure it was late? "I had no idea," Schmidt said, laughing, then quickly added, "but my assistant coaches said it did not beat the buzzer."

The coach emphasized how important it had been to reduce the 18-point lead that UMass had late in the first half. If they had not trimmed that deficit in the first half, then there would not have been such a quick comeback in the second half.

"We had too many turnovers in the first half," Schmidt said. "The first five minutes of the second half were key, but we were never able to get over the hump. But we found a way. Idris never had five threes before. Marcus made a great drive at the end."

Schmidt and the players were asked about the Bonnies trailing by five, 79-74, with 3:06 to play and a media timeout. "There was no panic in the huddle … maybe me, but not the players, they stayed confident," Schmidt said. "We've had good luck in tight games, so we were confident."

Then the questioners turned to Taqqee. He saw serious minutes as a freshman last season and was credited for his defense and rebounding.

He is a tough and athletic 6-foot-4 guard, but scoring points was seen as an added bonus. That's changed. Taqqee has developed a jump shot. He used it to drop 13 at St. Joseph's and he had 19 on this day, and the Bonnies needed every one of them, obviously. Taqqee was 7-for-10, 5-for-7 from beyond the arc.

Someone had asked Kellogg about Taqqee, and how the UMass defense wasn't accounting for him. The coach said that after Taqqee hit a couple of three-pointers in front of him, it caught his attention. In Philadelphia, Taqqee had nailed a jumper and then turned and chirped at some St. Joe's fans who were giving him a hard time. Taqqee apparently had a message for Kellogg as well, and someone asked Taqqee about that.

The sophomore said that the Minutemen were defending Posley and Adams and leaving him alone. "So I was getting no respect," Taqqee said. "I've spent too much time in the gym not to get respect." Later, Taqqee said he will do anything to win, and that defense and rebounding remain his top priorities.

Toward the end of the press conference, Schmidt was discussing all the close games the Bonnies have had, and how well they have had to play to win so many of them. Then he tried to make a point about the challenges of getting a group of young men, ranging in age from 18 to 23, to all work for a single goal. Then, out of nowhere, the whole conversation took a delightful, quirky bent.

"The male brain isn't even fully developed at age 18 to 23," Schmidt said. "So these guys aren't fully developed. The male brain doesn't fully develop until age 25." Schmidt wasn't smiling when he said this.

Sitting right next to Schmidt, of course, were Posley and Taqqee, Specimens 1 and 1A, and by now they were laughing and whispering between themselves, lab slides come mirthfully alive. Now smiling himself, Schmidt repeated the fact to reinforce his point: That coaching is exasperating, that the difference between winning and losing is scant. Schmidt, however, seems to be correct. There have been studies that indicate that the male brain does not fully mature by age 23, while the female brain matures earlier. The age of 25 does seem to be the typical timeframe for full brain development for men.

There were, unsurprisingly, no questions from the sportswriters on this matter. No one asked Schmidt for his source. But since Schmidt is a native New Englander, they should have guessed that he was, maybe, possibly, no one has any idea, referencing the Young Adult Development Project by the Massachusetts Institute of Technology in 2008.

Maybe it's not all X's and O's for Mark Schmidt. But on this day, his disregarded team, the one overlooked by all the basketball savants in the preseason, was 20-7 overall, 12-4 in the Atlantic 10, winner of eight of its last nine conference games and now fully assured of no lower than fourth place in the Atlantic 10. That earns the Bonnies the critical double bye in the A-10 tournament.

The Bonnies received four votes for the Top 25 in the coaches' poll. Their daily RPI ranked them 34th, squeezed between Seton Hall and Princeton. Teams rated 30 to 32 are Notre Dame, Arizona and Wisconsin. Pitt is rated lower than Bonaventure, as are Wichita State, Providence, Florida and Vanderbilt. Not bad for a place scrambling to stay in business.

Schmidt could surely wrap his brain around that.

CHAPTER 23:
REMARKABLE IN ROCHESTER

It seemed a reasonable decision many months ago. St. Bonaventure's students would be on their so-called mid-spring break on March 2 when St. Joseph's came to Olean for the final home game of the season. So the school's athletic department leadership decided to move the event to Rochester, a Wednesday night game at the Blue Cross Arena. The Bonnies have been hosting a game in Rochester for a number of years. Often it is an early-season non-conference game, though they played a conference game against George Mason there the season before.

Playing in Rochester recognizes that the city and its region have sent generations of students to Olean, more in prior years than presently, unfortunately. As Bonaventure's enrollment has sagged, St. John Fisher College, a Division III school located just outside Rochester in the town of Pittsford, N.Y., has surged: 2,700 undergraduates and a 1,000 or so graduate students, many drawn by practical courses of study such as pharmacy, nursing and executive leadership. Bonaventure is desperately hunting for students. Reminding folks in and around the Flower City that Bonaventure and the

Rochester region have a rich history makes all sense, and doing it with one game a season at the Blue Cross Arena is both easy and practical.

But things change. What made sense at the time Mark Schmidt was tearing up the course at Bartlett Country Club in Olean and Tim Kenney was settling on his new home in East Aurora had been overtaken by the present --- and pleasant --- realities of this season. The Bonnies were 21-7 and 12-4 in the Atlantic 10 Conference, assured at this point of no worse than the four-seed and a double bye in the upcoming conference tournament in Brooklyn. They were clearly one of the conference's best teams at this point, clustered with VCU, St. Joseph's and Dayton. They were a hot and dangerous squad, winners of eight of their last nine A-10 games and now being discussed as a contender for an NCAA tournament berth. Bonaventure toggled between the "last four in" and the "last four out," depending on which bracket bloviator was the last to tweet out his science, but it was heady stuff for Bonnie fans and recognition that their team was having a season for the ages.

As soon as the warm glow of the hard-fought victory over UMass had dimmed, the reality landed on Bonnie fans: The school had ceded the advantages, the atmospherics of the Reilly Center for the neutrality of the Blue Cross Arena. The opponent, rattlesnake-tough St. Joe's, would know as much about the place after the first shoot-around as the "home" team. The crushing presence of the fans in the tight confines of the Reilly Center would be gone, replaced by the wide-open spaces and the softly banked seats of a site that can accommodate more than 12,000 for basketball. If the

Bonnies and Hawks attracted half that many on a mid-week night, it would be a pleasant surprise. At this point, the most important game is the next one, the one that will decide if the season was hugely memorable or just a cheap trick, and the university had willingly ceded a significant advantage.

Finally, the hometown fans and the alumni had filled nearly 5,300 seats for the game against Massachusetts and they were loud and rowdy. The only reason for moving the game to Rochester --- no students on campus --- had been overtaken by the performance of the team and the high stakes the season now presented. And all of that was now at risk because of an innocent call made months ago.

In the end, Rochester would be a basketball Valhalla.

It was a bitter and grey day. The Genesee River ran high and fast through town, the color of caramel. By late afternoon, the bar at the Radisson Hotel on Main Street was three-deep with Bonnie fans, and more kept coming, abandoning workplaces after 5 p.m., toasting what had been a wondrous season to this point, and, likely, sustaining themselves for the kind of tough matchup that St. Joe's was certain to provide.

A month had passed since Bonaventure handled the Hawks in an almost routine fashion in Philadelphia. Amid that stretch of time, the Bonnies would lose on a Wednesday night at last-place La Salle and then resurrect themselves with their best away-game victory in years, maybe a decade or more, at Dayton. They were 6-1 in that stretch of the schedule, and nine of the last 10. No surprise, St. Joe's had kept the exact pace. The Hawks were tripped up by high-scoring Davidson, 99-93, in North Carolina, but stopped Dayton in Philly, 79-70. St. Joe's entered the game at 13-3 in the conference and 23-6 overall --- a resume that had them pegged by the forecasters as a certain NCAA tourney entry. The Bonnies were in fourth place in the A-10 but a game behind the Hawks. For the Bonnies, the season could be made or lost in this matchup.

You look at the best of the St. Joe's roster and you see that Coach Phil Martelli doesn't have to wander far to attract top ballplayers to Hawk Hill. His best player, junior swingman DeAndre Bembry, is from Charlotte, N.C., but he was at The Patrick School (the high school powerhouse once-known as St. Patrick's High School in Elizabeth, N.J.) when Martelli started recruiting him. Isaiah Miles, the jump-shooting 6-7 forward, is from Baltimore. The senior guard Aaron Brown and freshman guard Lamarr Kimble are from Philadelphia, and Shavar Newkirk, also a guard, is from Cardinal Hayes in New York.

Before the game, in a brief center-court ceremony, Mark Schmidt presented a basketball to Marcus Posley that showed he had topped 1,000 points for his less-than-two years at Bonaventure. There would be more scoring. Posley's first three ball of the night gave his team a 9-8 edge. A pair of drives by Posley, sandwiched around a three-point goal by Brown, gave the Bonnies a 15-14 lead, but Posley picked up a second foul and went to the bench. This hinted of real trouble. A three by Bembry and a drive by Kimble gave the Hawks a 21-17 lead, but a rebound basket by Denzel Gregg, an old-fashioned three-point play by Idris Taqqee and a hook shot by Gregg made it 24-20 Bonnies.

Then Posley and Gregg spurred their team. Posley hit a three, scored on a drive and then was fouled as he attempted a three and dropped the free throws. The lead was 32-24. Gregg scored on a drive, Posley hit a three-pointer and Gregg made a pair of free throws. Gregg hit a jumper to make it 41-28 for the Bonnies at the half, and fans began to believe Bona's mastery over St. Joe's might continue. The Bonnies beat the Hawks three times in the prior season. A win on this night would make it five in a row and seven of the last nine.

The Bonnies had scored on 17 of 33 first-half possessions. Posley had 18 on 6-for-7 from the field and 3-for-3 from long range. Gregg had 10, which was good because St. Joe's refused to let Jaylen Adams go off as he did in Philly, where he scored 31 points. The Hawks had doubled up their defense against Adams and committed against the ball screens designed to free Adams for long jumpers. That worked. Adams had just three points in the first half and Wright had just four. Gregg's contribution had been essential.

The next 20 minutes were remarkable, and left the nearly 6,700 in attendance gasping. And that is saying something, because Posley provided indelible memories last season with his back-to-back buzzer-beaters against Davidson and VCU and the 36 points at Duquesne, including 12 points in the last 2:35 of regulation to rally his team from an 11-point deficit and to an eventual overtime victory.

Schmidt would declare after the game that he had never seen anything like this in all his years as a head coach or assistant coach. That it was Posley who provided it just proves the serendipity of college basketball recruiting when you are St. Bonaventure and not Villanova or UConn or Michigan State. Posley grew up in Rockford, Ill. He was a teammate of Fred Van Fleet, another good-shooting six-foot guard. Van Fleet is now a senior and a starter at Wichita State. Posley headed off to Ball State in Muncie, Ind., a member of the Mid-American Conference.

Posley had a more-than-decent first year at Ball State, starting a number of games and averaging a little more than six points per game. But the coach who recruited him was fired, and Posley decided to move on. "I didn't want to have to replay my freshman season," Posley has said, meaning he did not want to have to convince another coach that he was a good enough player to start.

Posley ended up at Indian Hills Community College in Iowa. Posley had a very solid season at Indian Hills, scoring nearly 14 points per game on a top-ranked team that routinely sends its players to big-time Division I programs. Posley's performance brought him a lot of attention and the Bonnies were fortunate to bring him to Olean. He has never disappointed.

Posley is a nice young man. He is majoring in international relations with minors in business and management. He is soft-spoken and articulate. In the wake of Jerome Tyson's wrist injury, Posley was the one starter who believed the Bonnies could play small, the way Dayton did the year before, and win. Posley has a good demeanor. When a ball bounded in to a crowd of grade school-aged cheerleaders at a game at the Reilly Center and Posley went to retrieve it, he did so with a big smile on his face and made sure none of the kids were hurt.

How is it that a player as skillful as Posley, certainly one of the best players in the A-10, did not end up at a Big 10 school? Probably because no one in that conference would invest in a JUCO guard who is six-feet tall, no matter the numbers he produces.

St. Joseph's tore in to the Bonnies' advantage in the early minutes of the second half, getting it down to 43-37 on an Aaron Brown three-pointer. The Bonnies pushed back, getting a basket and free throw from Derrick Woods and a three-pointer from Dion Wright. It was 49-39 when Posley was tagged with his third foul. When Wright hit another three-point goal and was fouled and converted a four-point play, the lead was 53-41 with 15:52 remaining.

But the Hawks wouldn't go away. They pushed the ball in to the offensive zone on each possession. A three-pointer from Papa Ndao cut the lead to 53-48. Newkirk scored on a drive, Brown hit a jumper and then Miles hit a three to give St. Joe's a 55-53 edge with 12:42 to play.

It was tied at 58 with 11:33 to play when Posley began a whirlwind stretch. A pair of free throws and two determined drives by Posley gave Bonaventure a 64-58 lead. Wright hit his third three-pointer, Posley again willed his way to the rim for a bucket and Adams converted a steal in to a layup. Then Posley, maybe 18 inches, maybe two feet, behind the arc, hit a three-point basket to give the Bonnies a 74-60 lead. When Dion Wright hit two free throws, it was 76-60 with just 7:55 left, and it appeared the Bonnies had overcome the best the Hawks could deliver.

Posley then delivered 14 straight points, two of them tape-measure long balls, the last one providing a 92-77 advantage with a bit over two minutes to play. It was a good thing, because the Hawks were unwilling to die. Gregg, who played a wonderful game, was cramping up. Since he is very reliable from the free throw line, it is about the only explanation for his missing four straight shots, giving St. Joe's a flicker of a chance. When Brown scored on a drive, St. Joe's was within 93-88 with 39 seconds left. Wright shut the door on the Hawks with a pair of free throws and a dunk off a break against the Hawks' press.

When it was over, when it was clear the Bonnies had won nine of their last 10 conference games and carved a pathway that could result in their being the No. 2 seed in Brooklyn, the performance by Posley came in to focus. He had scored 47 points, the most by a Division I player this season. He was four points shy of the school record, the 51 points Bob Lanier scored against Seton Hall in 1970. Lanier dropped 50 on Purdue in the title game of the Holiday Festival in New York that same season.

Posley was about as close to perfection as a basketball player could be: 15-for-19 from the field, 6-for-7 from three-point land, 11-for-12 from the foul line. That it came in a game with such consequences adds to its luster. The last A-10 player to score that many points was Doug West of Xavier in a win over Dayton in 2008.

When Hawks' Coach Phil Martelli arrived in the media room after the game, he scanned the box score in silence for a half-minute or more. When he looked up, Martelli said:

"It was a wonderful atmosphere. Congratulations to the Bonnies fans. They truly made it a home court at a neutral site."

Martelli then focused on Posley's performance. "Obviously, the Posley numbers jump out at you and we have to look at the man in the mirror and see what all of us could have done," he said. "But the other number is the turnovers (13) for us. Turning the ball over was a real issue for us."

Martelli's next observation was made ruefully: "It wasn't the individual defense but the accountability on the defense. We didn't prepare them well enough and that's on me. What are you going to do about (Posley)? We did a nice job on Adams and we didn't do enough on Posley."

Someone asked Martelli what it is like to be a coach and watch a player torch your team, the way Posley did. "Does it make you feel powerless?" Martelli was asked. "Not powerless," he said, without elaboration, and then reminded that his team had enough of a persuasion on the game to score 62 points in the second half.

Wright and Gregg were essential as well for the Bonnies. Wright had 22 points and six rebounds. Gregg had 14 points and six rebounds.

Schmidt has said that finding a big but mobile forward is a priority as recruiting moves in to the spring season. He said it in the context of finding good guards, that it is not all that difficult, that there are plenty of fine guards to go around. That practically every team has sharp guards. That might be true, or partly true, but having guards such as Jaylen Adams and Marcus Posley is a once-in-a-decade experience for a school such as St. Bonaventure. Because if one of them doesn't nail an opponent, chances are the other one will. In Philly, it was Adams who went off like a madman, scoring 31, as the Hawks concentrated on Posley. Then Posley was simply off-the-chart in Rochester. Martelli made his choices as it regards bearing down on either Adams or Posley, and it backfired in both games. And St. Joe's is very good, more than just Bembry and the much-improved Miles. The Hawks play two point guards. Newkirk, the sophomore, was a two-time all-New York City point guard. Kimble, the freshman, was a first-team all-state player from powerful Neumann-Goretti High School in Philly. Brown, the 2-guard, is from hard-scrabble Darby, just west of the Philadelphia city line. He signed with West Virginia, did not get the playing time he wanted, and transferred to St. Joe's. He is a senior now, and big for a guard at 6-foot-5 and 220 pounds.

Neither Posley nor Adams have the basketball bloodlines of those three guards. But they have absolutely manhandled the Hawks' backcourt. The tandem of Posley and Adams is something to be savored by fans of the team. Adams was held to just six points by the Hawks this time but provided seven assists.

The loss of Posley to graduation is almost impossible to measure. Tracking his scoring is easy to do, but there are no metrics for how badly a player wants to win, no statistics that indicate a 47-point starburst is coming in a must-win situation, in an unfamiliar building, against a tough opponent in a once-in-a-decade opportunity.

There are guards, and then there are Posley and Adams, and they are very rare.

CHAPTER 24:
NO BLUES IN ST. LOUIS

ST. LOUIS

This could be the credo for the perpetual underdog: If you don't shoot yourself in the head, someone else will.

St. Bonaventure took care of business on a Saturday night in St. Louis, beating the Billikens, 76-67, and recording its best regular-season ever in the Atlantic 10 Conference. Then things got even better. St. Joseph's fell at home to Duquesne. Dayton knocked-off first-place Virginia Commonwealth. As a result, the Bonnies, Dayton and VCU concluded the A-10 regular season with records of 14-4. St. Joseph's fell to fourth place at 13-5.

For the first time, Bonaventure was co-champion of the Atlantic 10 Conference.

The Bonnies had won 10 of their last 11 games, the stumble against La Salle the only defeat. They would go to Brooklyn and the conference tournament as the No. 3 seed and beneficiaries of a double-bye in the A-10 tournament. Their first game would be at 9 p.m. on Friday, the third day of the event. Duquesne and La Salle would play on Wednesday. The winner would play No. 6-seed Davidson on Thursday, and the survivor of that game would meet Bonaventure in the quarterfinals on Friday night.

Would the 14-4 league record and the overall record of 22-7 assure the Bonnies a spot in the NCAA Tournament field? Could the selectors actually deny a spot to a school that had a share of its league's championship, especially a league as tough as the A-10, if the worst happened and Bonaventure was one-and-done in Brooklyn?

Joe Lunardi isn't convinced. Lunardi is a St. Joe's guy. He went to St. Joe's Prep. He went to St. Joseph's University. He is an assistant vice president of marketing and communications for St. Joseph's and he is the color commentator on the Hawks' radio broadcasts. He is also an NCAA bracketologist and he has the loftiest platform for his prognoses: The Entertainment and Sports Network. Joe Lunardi is ESPN's guy for predicting who should and should not make the field of 68 for the NCAA tourney each season. And Lunardi is not overwhelmed by St. Bonaventure's body of work, now that the regular season has concluded and the major conferences begin their postseason tournaments.

One clarification: The Barclays Center in Brooklyn is host to both the Atlantic 10 Conference championship tournament and then a first-round of play in the NCAA Tournament.

These bracket predictions start popping up earlier and earlier each season, it seems … like the Fourth of July. They are meant to be fun, for the most part, something to provoke conversation. Until very late in the basketball season, they carry little weight, certainly far less than the weekly college football and basketball rankings issued by the Associated Press and ESPN. But by this time of year, the two weeks that the mid-major conferences and then the "power" conferences, the Big 10, the ACC, the Big East, the Southeastern Conference, the Big 12 and Pac-12, hold their tournaments, the several best of the bracket scribes get huge attention. Lunardi is one of them. So is Jerry Palm, for example, who works this voodoo on behalf of CBS Sports News. There are others as well.

Lunardi took his first crack at the 2016 NCAA bracket on Aug. 5, more than two months before teams could even open practice. For the A-10, he had Dayton as a 10-seed and Rhode Island an 11-seed, but as one of the First Four, who would have to survive a "play-in" game against Georgia. By Jan. 4, George Washington was introduced as a 7-seed and Dayton had risen to a 5-seed. Dayton held fast in the Feb. 5 bracket, but now VCU was in as a 9-seed and St. Joe's had appeared as an 11-seed.

The lineup had changed somewhat by March 2, the day of the St. Joe's vs. Bonaventure game in Rochester. Virginia Commonwealth was a 10-seed, Dayton was a 7-seed, and St. Joe's was an 8-seed. Two days after the Bonnies handled St. Joseph's for the second time, they finally showed up in the bracket as a 12-seed but would have to tangle with Michigan in a play-in game --- a First Four game, as the NCAA describes it. Dayton was a 7-seed and VCU a 10-seed but the Hawks stayed fat and happy as an 8-seed that would face Pitt in the East Region in Brooklyn.

Joltin' Joe advanced Bonaventure to a No. 11 in the bracket of March

7, but it would have to survive a play-in vs. Connecticut. Dayton remained a 7-seed and VCU bumped up to a 9-seed. The Hawks slipped to a No. 9, but in Brooklyn and against Colorado. Easy trip for the Hawks and their fans.

How did St. Joseph's and Bonaventure play down the stretch, the defining portion of the regular season? St. Joe's went just 6-4 in its last 10 games. The Hawks lost at Davidson and, in its last home game, against Duquesne. In a span of 28 days, St. Joe's lost twice to the Bonnies, once at home in comfy Hagan Arena and once at what actually was a neutral site. In the A-10 regular season, the Hawks finished in 4th place, and the Bonnies were in a three-way tie for the league championship. The Bonnies were 14-4 in conference play and 22-7 overall. St. Joe's ended at 13-5 in the A-10 and 24-7 overall. Obviously, all that math had little or no influence on Lunardi, who sees the Hawks as a far more convincing case than St. Bonaventure.

Palm's bracket of March 6 would be more warmly received by Bona fans. He has the Bonnies an 8-seed in the East and playing Oregon State, a No. 9, in Brooklyn. Dayton is a 6-seed and will meet a play-in selection in Providence. St. Joe's is a 9-seed and would meet Wisconsin in Oklahoma City. VCU would be a 10-seed and face No. 7 Texas Tech in Denver.

Lunardi was scrambling as March 8 dawned. Blood was spilled hours earlier when Iona defeated Monmouth for the Mid-Atlantic Collegiate Conference tourney title, Hofstra was dispatched by UNC-Wilmington in the Colonial Conference, and Valparaiso went down in overtime to Wisconsin-Green Bay in the Horizon League. Three favorites, three regular-season champs, and one or all of them had been likely to make the NCAA field by winning their tournaments. Room had to be made for Iona, Wilmington and Green Bay. One or more teams that had been safely placed hours earlier would be impacted. One of them was St. Bonaventure. Lunardi decided that the Bonnies had to take one of the bullets. They would have to survive a play-in game against UConn as an 11-seed. Valparaiso would still make The Dance, as a No. 12 vs. No. 4 Indiana in Oklahoma City. Monmouth would have to play itself in as well, needing to hurdle Syracuse in another battle between 11-seeds.

St. Joseph's remained bullet-proof. The Hawks would be a 10-seed and meet Texas, a 7-seed, in St. Louis.

Palm was steadfast regarding Bonaventure, keeping them an 8-seed and facing Oregon State at the Barclays Center. Dayton was a 6-seed in Providence and would face an 11-seed play-in survivor. He also had both St. Joe's and VCU as "on the bubble." St. Joe's was a 9-seed vs. 8-seed Wisconsin in Oklahoma City and VCU was a 10-seed and would face Texas Tech, a 7-seed, in Raleigh.

This is an elaborate way of saying that making the NCAA tourney is a crapshoot, unless you win your conference tournament or you finish first in the Ivy League regular season. The Ivies don't play a conference tourney. If you manage not to disband during the season and you are in a Power 5 Conference, it seems you will still have a chance. A 10-member NCAA Selection Committee will make the decisions. The chairman for the 2016 field is Joe Castiglione, the athletic director at Oklahoma, and the vice chair is Mark Hollis, the AD at Michigan State. Athletic directors and conference commissioners often comprise the committee in most years. There is an undeniable bias toward the power conferences, if anyone reviews recent history.

Who knows if anyone of relevance, if anyone even remotely tied to the selection process, pays attention to a guy such as Lunardi. Nonetheless, he has enough of a profile, enough of a solid track record, enough of a reach that one could imagine his proposed bracket having a vaporous quality as the selectors ponder the choices, something that seeps under the closed door of the meeting room. For sure, every year there are coaches, players and their fans who are infuriated and crushed by the committee's verdicts. You can only hope it isn't your school.

There was little drama to the Bonnies victory over St. Louis in front of a Chaifetz Arena audience that was far fewer than the announced 7,812. Nothing that came close to the pitched battle in Olean, where the Billikens threatened to run away and hide in the second half only to be tied with seconds to go and then beaten on a Jaylen Adams three-pointer at the buzzer. The Bonnies played a solid if not exactly inspired game. They did reach Mark Schmidt's magic formula for success: Adams had 23 points, including 4-for-8 from three-point range. Posley had 18 points and Dion Wright added 16 points and eight rebounds. The goal is a combined 55 for the star trio and they bagged 57 in this game.

St. Louis did cut the Bonnies' lead down to three points, 60-57, in the second half but the pace of the game did not favor the Billikens, who often struggle to score and average only about 64 points per game. The Bonnies' 41-33 command at the half meant the Billikens would have to score big in the final 20 minutes, and that is not their style.

The Bonnies outrebounded the bigger Billikens, 39-36, but St. Louis had 24 points in the paint. Posley buried St. Louis down the stretch, hitting a three-pointer and then scoring off a drive to extend the advantage to 72-61 with less than two minutes to go.

Schmidt was clearly thrilled with the win and the way his team has played in the last 11 games. "To win the most games in school history in the conference, to win 22 games is a great feat for our guys," Schmidt told J.P. Butler of the Olean Times Herald. "I'm really proud of what they've done. No one thought they could do it, and they proved people wrong. And they kept on doing it and doing it and doing it."

The TV in the Bonnies' locker room was turned on as soon as the team was off the court. The draw was the VCU at Dayton game, which went to overtime. When Dayton hit a late shot to win it, Bonaventure knew it had a piece of the A-10 championship.

"It's been a special season, and the guys, they deserve everything," Schmidt said. "The excitement on their faces when the ball didn't go in (a desperation heave by VCU that did not come close) ... that picture is worth a thousand words," Schmidt said. "I'm really proud of what they've accomplished."

It was also a special season for Schmidt. His peers, the 13 other head coaches in the Atlantic 10 Conference, selected him as coach of the year. When your team is predicted to finish 8th in a 14-team league and you end up winning a share of the league title, you did something right. The A-10 has gained great respect nationally in the last seven or eight years. The arrival of Davidson two years ago has made it even more bruising. The preseason prediction that Bonaventure would be in the bottom half of the league this year was not out of line. Schmidt had known quantities in Posley and Wright, both seniors and both significant contributors in the 2014-15 season. Adams had missed the last third of his freshman season last year with a broken finger, so for many observers within the conference, he remained a question mark. Schmidt thought he had a source of scoring in Courtney Stockard, a junior college transfer, but he broke his foot even before practice began in October. Schmidt and his assistants were excited about the possibilities of Jordan Tyson at center, but he would be out until late December with a torn tendon in the wrist. That meant Derrick Woods, a 6-foot-9 forward and a true freshman who was not even on campus for summer workouts because he was finishing a high school course to be fully eligible, would have to be a starter.

So Schmidt had to finesse a lineup that was pocked with both holes and question marks. And he did just that, adopting a hurry-up, score-in-bunches offense in an effort to offset a lack of size that would surely cost the team on the defensive end. "We have to play fast," Schmidt had decided. Posley, Wright and Adams flourished in the tempo, and Woods and Tyson at least held their own. Denzel Gregg, the 6-foot-7 junior from Syracuse, also stunningly athletic, was a steady source of scoring and rebounding off the bench. Nelson Kaputo, who was playing in high school in Canada a year before, provided ballhandling and some long-range scoring off the bench, though he seemed to tire and be a bit less impactful as the season wore on. Whatever the reason, his playing time has diminished.

Lastly, Schmidt and his coaches saw potential and talent in sophomore Idris Taqqee, who at 6-foot-4 was athletic enough to defend bigger players, to grab some rebounds and, as the season progressed, provide scoring, including from three-point land. Taqqee was a starter for almost all of the season.

Basically, Schmidt was honored by his peers for maximizing the hand he had to play, and that is quintessential coaching. Teams with decidedly more talent --- Dayton, George Washington, Davidson, Rhode Island, for sure, and Richmond and St. Joseph's, most likely --- fell to the Bonnies. Schmidt is a master of the X's and O's and a motivator. He is also a tough critic of his players. He sees potential in players that other coaches overlook, and he makes those players better.

Dion Wright is a classic example. No one was recruiting him as he ended his high school career in California. He went to a talent showcase in Las Vegas and a guy who played for Xavier when Schmidt was an assistant there saw Wright play. That former player called Schmidt and said Wright looked good enough to play in the A-10. As Wright himself recalls it: "Next thing I know, I am on a plane to Buffalo."

Wright played very little as a freshman until a late-season game in the Reilly enter against Charlotte, then a member of the A-10. The Bonnies jumped all over Charlotte and opened a huge lead early. Wright saw a lot of playing time in that game, about 11 minutes, and he clearly recalls it. "I remember that," he said in an interview. "I had 15 (points) and four (rebounds)." He remembers it because that was the only extended opportunity he had all season. But Wright steadily improved, made himself a great rebounder and a potent scorer on the interior. Late in his junior year, he started hitting three-balls and he has become even a more effective long-range shooter this season.

The only downside to this day of Atlantic 10 Conference awards announcements was that Wright went unrecognized, and the Bonnies would have gone nowhere this season without him.

Along with Schmidt being named coach of the year, Adams was named to the conference's first team and Posley to the second team. Gregg shared the Sixth Man of the Year award with Jabarie Hinds of UMass. Wright was overlooked and did not make even the third team.

Wright could have been bitter, clamorously aggrieved. To his credit, he chose not to be.

"That's all right," Wright said. "I've been overlooked my whole life."

CHAPTER 25:

BUSING TO BROOKLYN

It has been an exceedingly interesting time for Tim Kenney, St. Bonaventure's first-year athletic director. He was a top assistant AD at the University of Massachusetts but longed to direct his own program. Kenney took interest when Steve Watson, the AD who hired Mark Schmidt --- and Jim Crowley, the man who coached the Bonnies' women team to the Sweet 16 in 2012 and made them a first-rate program in the Atlantic 10 Conference --- was hired to be the athletic director at Loyola University in Chicago.

Watson was a tough act to follow, for whomever replaced him. He was not a Bonaventure alum, but his father was a high-ranking academic administrator at the university and was dean of the business school when he died from a stroke in 2011 at the age of 67. His mother, Suzanne, was a lecturer in the Department of Computer Science. Not long after, Steve Watson's brother, also named John, just 45 years old, collapsed and died. The younger John Watson was a marketing professor at the school and, like his father, did color commentary for Bonaventure basketball games. The

Watsons were something of a first family at the institution. And they were home-grown, residents of nearby Franklinville, hardy and happy Western New Yorkers.

There is more than a little self-centeredness, an insularity, connected to St. Bonaventure University. It isn't pervasive or overwhelming, it isn't even mean-spirited, but it is there. At its root is the suspicion that if you are not from the place, then you will not be able to understand it, and therefore not serve it well. It is the very reason that alumni and fans were not sold on Schmidt for several years. That they believed he did not appreciate the essence of the school and the tight-knit region it calls home. Then the wins started piling up and Schmidt became a comfort to the Bonaventure faithful. At the conclusion of the basketball season these days, alumni, students and fans of the program fear that Schmidt will be hired away by a bigger, richer program and for more money than Bonaventure could pay. So these days, given the inequities of the contemporary sports scene, Schmidt is embraced by the fan base, and some, and rightly so, see him as a savior of the men's basketball program.

Tim Kenney's passage from risky stranger to just-one-of-us is barely underway.

The Bonnies Bandwagon is the fan board for following the school's sports teams. But the observations, the dialogues are wide and deep, and range far beyond the athletic programs. Anyone who is a decision-maker, a ranking officer of the school, is fair game. Sr. Margaret Carney, the school president, has been buffeted during her 12 years in the office. But when she announced she was retiring, and later when she put out the word that she was suffering from cancer, the riders of the Bandwagon were genuinely gracious, even prayerful, on her behalf.

Oftentimes, the only thing that connects the various posters, especially the regulars, is their affection and concern for the place. But the points of view can be jarringly, bitterly wide-ranging. That makes the Bandwagon similar to most every sports-driven online venue. Most other collegiate boards don't fret the future of their school, however. There are consistent contrarians on the Bandwagon. Regulars who are desperately unhappy with the management of the university. Even-minded types who are deeply devoted to the basketball program, realize that Bonaventure is challenged in a number of ways, and are unwaveringly supportive despite those challenges. There are wide-eyed optimists, hardened skeptics, and gentle souls who simply were stamped by spending four years at the place and ache for it to prosper. A season like the one being stitched together in 2015-16 is a tonic for the vast majority of the Bandwagon regulars.

Steve Watson was well-regarded by the university, its officers, the student body and alumni. His decision to move on to Loyola was a disappointment to supporters of the school's athletic programs, but understood Chicago might be a more bountiful landscape than Olean. Whomever succeeded Watson was going to be measured and prodded, and Kenney has felt all of that. The fact that Kenney's wife, Maureen, is a native of Grand Island, a town north of Buffalo, brought some comfort to fans. But it didn't last all that long.

Kenney is a 45-year-old native of Long Island. He was a very capable athlete growing up and went to the University at Buffalo, where he was the star of the swimming team and an All-American. It is difficult not to like Kenney once you have met him. He has a big smile, an Irish face and high energy. Mark Schmidt and he seem to have created a great relationship in short order. "He has lots of ideas," Schmidt said, and left the impression that was a good thing.

Among Kenney's professional achievements is an ability to find alternative sources of funding for college athletic programs. Accomplishing that at a major state university, a research center, where much of the funding is public, is one thing. Doing it at St. Bonaventure is another, but supplementing university funding with new streams of external monies for sports programs is an established requirement these days. Athletic programs, even at Alabama and the Notre Dame, are not self-supporting. Well-heeled alumni, booster clubs and corporate sponsors are essential sources of revenues. Kenney's biography indicates that revenue support for the UMass Athletics Department was at an all-time high when he departed for Olean.

Kenney arrived on campus when the deliberation regarding remaining Division I was winding up. His first challenge was a decision to place two rows of 24 seats each on the floor of the Reilly Center across from the home and visitors' benches. Fourteen of the 48 seats were reserved for students. Season tickets for these seats would be $710. The seats sold out, raising revenue of at least $25,000. It would seem to be a simple and profitable tactic. Not so.

There was a clamorously negative reaction from some of the Bandwagon regulars. The negativity stretched from concerns that the seat-holders would be trampled when students and others storm the court after a buzzer-beating victory to the loss of the home court advantage that comes from having rowdy students, some dressed in costumes, a banana is a regular attendee, standing all game long on the floor and right along the sideline and hassling the opposing players.

Amid the furor an impression was left, perhaps from Kenney's office, that the front-row seats were created to deter the students from court-storming, something they did last season after Posley's driving basket that clipped VCU at the buzzer. And that this was a directive from the Atlantic 10 office. That simply gave more energy to the debate, which went on for weeks, and allowed some of the second-guessers to decide Kenney was a bad choice for the AD job.

There was other banter, including some criticism about a new scorer's table with a 32-foot LED display for graphics and for advertising. With all the challenges confronting the school, these criticisms, spawning heated and varied reactions, seemed overdone. As the season progressed, the critics quieted.

Along with a new job, moving his family from Massachusetts, finding a school district with a swimming program for one of his kids, and buying a house in East Aurora, Kenney was experiencing a painful hip injury that required him to use crutches and then a cane for months. Kenney said the cause was micro-fractures, and they likely were the result of his playing lacrosse as a student.

Kenney's role is significant and challenging. Uppermost will be his involvement in the strategy to expand the sports program to recruit more athletes and raise the enrollment, the greatest challenge confronting the university. It will require Kenney to sell his ideas to the board of trustees and the other key administrators, even while the president's chair is empty and the faculty is restive about curriculum change and the costs of sports, especially coaches' salaries, and Mark Schmidt's in particular.

Early in the week leading in to the Bonnies' Friday night quarterfinal game in the A-10 Tournament, Kenney was in a van along with Steve Mest, the sports information director, and others, making the long drive from Olean to Brooklyn. Kenney was upbeat --- about the performances of the men's and women's basketball teams, his new job and the opportunities it presents. This is the guy who earlier in the year said of his role "passion trumps finances." And you could believe him.

Kenney seems to enjoy the challenges of using athletics to improve enrollment and provide revenue for the university. He described what he termed "a multi-layer analysis" for leveraging sports as a source for more students and new revenue. He mentioned "growth sports," and men's and women's lacrosse were included, but he allowed some sports have "no growth potential."

"We have no choice, the school has no choice," Kenney said, regarding new monies from athletics. Kenney said the prospects of creating a men's lacrosse program requires developing a template for credible revenue gains and the other implications. "We need to show quantitative results (for sports expansions) and sell it to the board," Kenney said.

"We have to create reasons for gifting," he added. "The passion for the university is real. We don't have to manufacture it. We have to take advantage of this basketball season. But when we go to people and ask them to give us money, we need to be able to say, 'Here's what we will do with it.' "

Nearly a year in to his job, Kenney seems genuinely happy. "I'm loving it," he said. "We can do things. We can have a big effect, in short order."

Schmidt, his coaches and his players were in a bus and making the same trip as Kenney, east through the Southern Tier and parallel to the Pennsylvania state line, and then plunging south through the Catskills, and places such as Milford, Pa., and Monticello, N.Y., near where streams from the Delaware River draw fly fishermen, and then through the knot of interstates that girds the New York metropolitan area. A six-hour haul, but time to think.

It is a drive that thousands of Bonaventure students, spanning decades and generations, made numerous times in their years at the school, going back and forth from homes in Long Island, Brooklyn, Queens, and North Jersey to Olean. The university needs more young people in those places to choose St. Bonaventure these days, and not Fairfield, Quinnipiac and SUNY-Binghamton, good schools and closer to home.

Schmidt was relaxed. He should have been. Perhaps his only regret was that his wife, Anita, and his two younger sons would be in Glens Falls,

N.Y., for the Class B championship. Olean High School is 25-0, and Derek, a senior and a shooting guard, and Mike, just a freshman and a point guard, are on that squad. The family's oldest son, Nicholas, now plays at Alfred University.

Schmidt rarely talks about himself. But when he was asked about winning the Coach of the Year Award, he seemed genuinely pleased. "Coaching is a fraternity," he said. "We all look out for each other. For your peers to recognize you like that, it's a good feeling." And Schmidt received some congratulatory e-mails from the league coaches and the others he will see in Brooklyn. When the conversation turned to the A-10 tourney, Schmidt rattled off comforts and concerns.

"We come in to the tournament playing well, confident, and that's good," he allowed. "But if you get off to a bad start, then all the good things of the past are just that, the past. Being off for a week (the win in St. Louis on the previous Saturday night and not playing until 9 p.m. Friday in Brooklyn because of the double-bye earned in the regular season) allows you to get healthy, to get your legs back. But if the team you play has already played a game or two games, then they have a comfort.

"They know the arena better. They know the sight lines. The rims are tighter in these NBA arenas, and they will have had a game or two games of shooting at those rims. And there is the pressure of the moment. But our guys are loose, and that's good in this kind of moment. We want to win the A-10 tournament but we have to worry now about winning the first game. Otherwise you are one-and-done."

Schmidt had said at one point late in the season that this year's team had "overachieved." He was asked about that. "The injuries we had before the season began were an issue," Schmidt said. "Losing Courtney (Stockard). The injury to Jordan (Tyson). We were down to just seven guys, basically. How do we make it through the season?"

One of the ways was winning close games. "We were able to close out games," he said. "In a good year, that's what you do. We made plays to win games. When you win close games, you convince yourself you can do it. In a bad year, you lose close games. Even in the first Dayton game, the players still believed they could win."

Schmidt added: "We had no idea we would do this. No moment was too big for these players. We have two guys who want the ball at crunch time. It's been magical."

Schmidt was asked about the tournament and the four players in their initial seasons --- Tyson, Nelson Kaputo, Derrick Woods and LaDarien Griffin. "All they know is this," Schmidt said. "They think this season is normal, because it is all they know at this point. I don't think they fully comprehend what is going on.

"But we wouldn't be where we are without the role players ... what Idris (Taqqee) does for us.

"Our guys have been good in this kind of setting."

Schmidt said the time off has made the team healthier, especially Posley and Adams. "They are getting better," Schmidt said. "They couldn't practice sometimes. Now they are healthy and back to practicing. Posley has more explosion, more lift on his shots."

Bonaventure would know its first tournament opponent when play ended Thursday. Friday night presented the first of three games at the Barclays Center --- three games if all went well.

CHAPTER 26:

ONE-AND-DONE AND SNUBBED

It was about 9 a.m. on Saturday, March 12, and another day of the implausibly wonderful weather that has chased winter from the East Coast weeks ahead of schedule. We were waiting for an Uber van to pick us up on the corner of Fulton and Duffield streets in the Park Slope section of Brooklyn and take us to Penn Station and a train back to Philly. Only about eight hours had passed since leaving the nearby Barclays Center, where St. Bonaventure had lost, agonizingly, to Davidson in overtime in the quarterfinals of the Atlantic 10 Tournament.

Then Coach Mark Schmidt showed up.

Schmidt, wearing a black nylon sweat suit with Bonnies stitched on the chest, had just grabbed a coffee from a nearby shop. His first words were: "Well, the sun came up this morning."

Maybe it was the large crowd of reporters and all of the TV cameras, maybe it was a degree of confidence that the close loss to Davidson would not hurt Bonaventure's hopes for the NCAA Tournament, but Schmidt was not disconsolate at the press conference after the game. He called it a great game and said Davidson made the key shots at the end. "We've been the ones doing that this year," Schmidt said. "We were up twice by double digits," he added. "We had our chances, but they made more plays than we did."

Posley and Wright accompanied Schmidt to the press conference. They had played magnificently, accounting for 64 of the team's points in the 90-86 defeat. Both had 32 points. Wright had an amazing 15 rebounds, six of them on the offensive end. Posley had seven rebounds and five assists. Twice Posley crumpled to the floor from hard contact, and both times got up and returned to play. Wright was in for 44 minutes and Posley for 43. Wright was asked about the defeat. "It hurts," said Wright, with typical brevity. "We played hard, my teammates played hard."

Schmidt was asked about his team's chances for the tournament. "We hope (to have our name called)," he said. "I think we are deserving. We'll see what happens. Our goal was to win our conference, to win the tournament. Our guys are loose at the big moments. They don't freeze up. But Davidson played better."

Schmidt was upbeat the next morning as well. He said he had talked to someone of significance who indicated that "there was a buffer" between where the Bonnies were likely to be seeded in the NCAA tournament and the teams that would just barely squeeze into the bracket. Schmidt was also thrilled that he would be in Glens Falls, N.Y., that night to see Olean High School's boys' basketball team play for the New York State Class B championship. Two of Schmidt's sons play on the team, one a senior and the other a freshman, and their mother was already there, passing up the A-10 tournament to see her sons compete. Schmidt had rented a car and would drive the nearly four hours to Glens Falls from Brooklyn. Olean won, and his son Derek, the senior, was voted the tournament's most valuable player. Schmidt was even interviewed on radio at halftime of the game. When asked about the Bonnies making the NCAA tournament, Schmidt answered: "I like our chances."

It would be another 33 hours or so before Schmidt, his team, an entire university and its fans would have their world rocked.

The Bonnies should not have lost this rematch with Davidson. They opened substantial leads in the second half and didn't protect them. That said, if not for the heroics of Posley and Wright, they would not even have been in this game. Jaylen Adams played 37 minutes but left no fingerprints. His face was masked by pain. He clearly labored. At one point in the second half, Wright, who was about to inbound the ball to Adams for a trip up court, yelled to the guard: "Come on Jay!" Schmidt said Adams played with a painful back injury; for sure, he was severely compromised. His line in the box score was so unlike the sophomore's usual performances: three points on 1-for-10 shooting and 1-for-5 from distance, 0-for-1 from the foul line, and that miss was costly; five rebounds, four assists, two steals. Davidson's guards had big games, with Jack Gibbs scoring 29 and Brian Sullivan 15. Jordan Watkins and Jordan Barham provided a combined 21 points off the bench. Some of that was the result of Adams struggling on both ends of the floor.

Idris Taqqee had nine points but Denzel Gregg, who was in foul trouble the whole game, was gone with five minutes left in regulation. The Bonnies needed much more from Gregg than six points and four rebounds in just 18 minutes.

Bonaventure managed a 37-32 lead at halftime when Taqqee hit a three-point goal and Posley followed with two more three-pointers. The Bonnies scored the first seven points of the second half to lead 44-32 and force a Davidson timeout at the 18:14 mark. At that moment, it felt like Bonaventure would get a handle on this game. When Posley hit a three-point shot it gave the Bonnies a 55-45 command. The lead was 60-49 with 11:50 to play when Wright scored inside.

When Adams returned from a three-minute break on the bench, it was 65-54 with 7:40 remaining. Then the Wildcats rallied. Forwards Peyton Aldridge and Nathan Ekwu scored inside. When Aldridge was fouled and hit both free throws it was a 70-67 Bonaventure lead with 3:16 to go. A three-pointer from Sullivan pulled Davidson to 73-72 with 2:10 left. Shortly after that, Adams missed the front end of a 1-and-1. Posley, however, scored on a drive and the Bonnies were still up, 75-72. Davidson took a timeout with 21 seconds to play.

All Bonaventure needed was one defensive stand. Instead, Aldridge was fouled as he took a three-point shot from the corner. Wright made a run-and-jump toward the shooter but hit Aldridge's hand as he released the ball. Aldridge then calmly nailed the three shots. I was sitting beneath that basket and next to Chuckie Maggio, a Bona junior from Rochester and a very promising young journalist. I remember turning to him before the ball was inbounded and saying that a foul on a three-point shot would be the worst that could happen.

The game was tied at 75. Bonaventure used its final timeout to draw up a last play. Schmidt said it was designed to get Posley into the lane, and if that was blocked, to get it back to Wright for a jump shot. Posley's driving layup missed.

All the momentum was with Davidson. Aldridge gave the Wildcats a 77-75 lead with a jumper. Posley answered, but Sullivan and Watkins hit long balls and it was 83-77 with 3:30 left in overtime. Two free throws from Wright and a jumper by Posley made it 85-83. Sullivan hit another three-pointer and it was 88-83. The Bonnies cut the margin to 88-86 on a rebound basket by Wright and a foul shot by Taqqee. Gibbs finished it with two free throws. Final: Davidson 90, St. Bonaventure 86.

Davidson Coach Bob McKillop called it, "A terrific college basketball game. Both teams emptied their tanks." Aldridge was asked about Wright: "He's a great player," the forward said. "He can take you on the dribble and he was knocking down shots."

McKillop said every player on his bench was thrilled with having another five minutes to play. Then he recalled Posley's buzzer-beating drive that clipped Davidson in North Carolina last season, and McKillop's hope that Posley wouldn't repeat that magic at the end of regulation in this game. The next night, Davidson was eliminated from the A-10 tourney by Virginia Commonwealth.

McKillop, a couple of hours later, made a great impression on two Bonaventure fans in the lobby of the Hotel Indigo in Brooklyn. The two young men, who graduated from Bonaventure nearly nine years ago and were dressed in brown, said hello to McKillop, who then walked toward them and put both his hands on the shoulders of one of them.

"Believe me, you guys are in," McKillop said, emphatically, meaning the NCAA Tournament. Then he added: "I grew up not far from here, in Queens, and the only place I wanted to go to was St. Bonaventure. But I wasn't a good enough player."

McKillop, who is 65, went to East Carolina University to play ball but transferred to Hofstra. He then coached high school on Long Island, went to Davidson as an assistant coach for a season, and then returned to Long Island to coach powerful Long Island Lutheran High School. In 1989, he headed south again, this time as head coach at Davidson.

One of those two kids McKillop talked to in the hotel lobby was my son.

Schmidt had said on Saturday morning that the plan to watch the NCAA Tournament Selection Sunday show would be a low-key and closed event. It would largely be players, coaches, administrators, other staff and family. Sr. Margaret Carney would be there. It would be held in the Hall of Fame suite at the Reilly Center. CBS-TV sought to have cameras in the room to capture the reaction of the Bonaventure players. That request was turned down. The thinking had been that if the news was not good, if the Bonnies were somehow passed over and not selected, that it would be best not to capture the sadness and disappointment for the viewing pleasure of a national audience.

On Saturday morning, I thought the school might have passed on a marketing opportunity, a chance to put Bonaventure in front of a national audience that would likely include tens of thousands of high school-aged teenagers who were, or soon would be, considering college choices. But on Saturday morning I did not believe that a team that had won at Dayton, twice beaten St. Joseph's, earned a co-share of the Atlantic 10 Conference championship and lost a hard-fought overtime game to a very good Davidson team in the conference quarterfinals would not be selected. The Bonnies were 22-8, had been exceedingly strong in the last weeks of the season, and were solidly placed on the brackets of most of the so-called experts. The team had done most everything right, and Posley, Adams and Wright had shown themselves to be exciting viewing.

Super Bowl Sunday, the Kentucky Derby and Selection Sunday are the three-worst examples of televised sports excess. The build-ups to the events are exhausting and boring. The endless would-be analysis rarely discloses anything substantive. By the time the horses bolt out of the gates at Churchill Downs on those May Saturdays in Louisville, most of them must be 4-year-olds. As always, the forced march to finally announce the selections dwelled on the top eight or nine teams. It was predicted that North Carolina, Kansas, Virginia and Oregon would be No. 1 seeds. Charles Barkley, who can be both astute and silly, decided North Carolina was the team to beat. He also said the Pac-12 Conference was underappreciated, but he quickly added that might be because he resides in Arizona and those are the teams he watches the most. He then butchered the task of predicting winners on a touch-screen display. At least that was entertaining.

St. Bonaventure had a few mentions. Some of it was under the heading of who might be in and who might be out. Syracuse, UConn, Vanderbilt, Tulsa and Monmouth were among others discussed as coin flips.

Finally, the outcomes of the selection process began to be announced. If you were waiting on the Bonnies to be called, the first sign of trouble was Tulsa being selected for a play-in game against Michigan as an 11-seed. Analyst Seth Davis quickly declared Tulsa a bad selection. UConn as a 9-seed in the South Region was discomforting. St. Joe's, which pounded VCU earlier in the day for the A-10 Tournament title, was being sent out west as an 8-seed, and St. Joe's being in the tourney was expected, of course. Vanderbilt and Wichita State being opponents in a battle of 11-seeds was not good news; both had been appraised as underperformers this season. And the bracket was filling up.

VCU was an 11-seed and would play Oregon State in Oklahoma City.

Hope for the Bonnies was waning. Still, you watched. Dayton was a No. 7 and would play 10th-seeded Syracuse, whose famed coach was suspended for nine games this season because he let his program run amok for years. The Orange were in.

There was one slot left, and it was plugged by Gonzaga, an 11-seed that would play Seton Hall in the Midwest.

The committee, and none of them had basketball backgrounds, according to TV analyst Jay Bilas, a Bonaventure advocate, had done its job: The royalty of NCAA basketball had been served.

Mark Schmidt's best team in nine years in Olean, his 22-win team with some high-profile victories, a team that rattled off 10 wins in its last 11 games in the regular season, the co-champion of the rough A-10, failed to make the NCAA Tournament. The one-and-done in Brooklyn cost him and his players and their fans.

Schmidt, it turns out, knew he was dead before all of the selections were even announced. His agent texted him and told him the Bonnies were not selected, and how sorry he was about that. The results of the Selection Committee had been leaked in the middle of the CBS telecast and it immediately blew up on Twitter. Bonaventure players were reaching for their phones and hearing the same message: No NCAA Tournament for them. Some of them started to leave the Hall of Fame suite. It was, in short, a disaster, a travesty. Not only did the 10-person selection committee, a gaggle of big-school athletic directors, open the door for a bunch of marquee schools that had mediocre seasons, and for a couple tagged with sanctions for violating numerous NCAA rules, they could not even keep it a secret.

The decision not to let the cameras in to the Hall of Fame suite was the only thing that went right that evening.

As televisions clicked off around the country, the selections for the National Invitation Tournament were announced. This used to be something of a big deal, back when the NCAA Tournament field was limited to 32 teams. The Bonnies won the NIT in 1977, back when it mattered, beating a very good Houston team led by high-scoring guard Otis Birdsong. Bonaventure was the first team named for the NIT on this Sunday early-evening show. A No. 1 seed in an eight-team group, the announcers even termed it "the Bonaventure quadrant." The Bonnies would host Wagner College, from the Northeast Conference. In a prepared statement, Schmidt managed to sound enthused.

"The NIT is a great tournament," he said, "and we hope to have a great crowd. Our goal now is to show (the NCAA) committee they made a mistake. Our goal is to make a run to Madison Square Garden."

Less restrained, he also said he wouldn't allow "10 guys in a conference room to define our season." His greatest challenge will be to get his demoralized, overlooked team to get juiced about the NIT. And while the NIT is now a shadow of the NCAA Tournament, its field of 32 includes some heavyweights: If the Bonnies handled Wagner at the Reilly Center in the opening-round game, the winner of Creighton vs. Alabama awaited. Virginia Tech and Brigham Young would also be potential foes if the Bonnies kept advancing.

Valparaiso, Monmouth and St. Mary's, which also had NCAA hopes, are in the NIT field. So are Davidson and George Washington from the A-10.

In the 36 hours after the NCAA field had been unveiled, the Kremlinologists of the basketball world were hard at work. Much attention landed on Tulsa. The Hurricanes are a member of the American Athletic Conference. This is certainly the weirdest contingent in all of NCAA sports.

It is a polyglot of schools that are geographically disparate, spread from Storrs, Conn. to Cincinnati to New Orleans to Tulsa. There are no real historic rivalries and the academic reputations of the schools swing wildly. It is a made-up conference, the lost tribe of the NCAA, schools that were abandoned when the Big East Conference imploded and morphed in to the "Catholic Eight," sending some institutions with football programs on searches for new homes, such as Pitt, Syracuse and Boston College to the Atlantic Coast Conference.

Perhaps the two biggest orphans are Connecticut and Temple, now part of the American Athletic Conference, and largely to house football teams. Unless Temple is playing Penn State at Lincoln Field in Philadelphia, there are few fans (though a home game against Notre Dame, a onetime thing in the 2015 season, was a sellout --- many of them fans of the Irish). The Owls did not draw well in basketball this season when AAC foes were the opponents. Getting Philadelphia-area fans excited about East Carolina at Temple on Broad Street in North Philly is a dicey thing to sell. There is some of that in Connecticut as well. Fans of the Huskies have a hard time getting enthused about a home game versus Tulane in downtown Hartford when the opponents used to be Georgetown and Syracuse.

Fran Dunphy, the well-regarded Temple basketball coach, must wonder at times how his universe has been altered. The Atlantic 10 had made sense for Temple, at least as it regarded basketball. But the school's hierarchy has become enchanted with football. There are talks of building an on-campus football stadium. So off to the AAC marched the Owls.

Tulsa's basketball season was just okay. The Hurricanes were 20-12 overall. Their best non-conference win was over Wichita State but they fell to Arkansas-Little Rock and Oral Roberts. The Hurricanes did beat a good Iona team 90-81 at home. They were 12-6 in the conference. Tulsa won twice against East Carolina, Tulane and Central Florida, split two games with Southern Methodist, Cincinnati, UConn and Temple, and lost to Memphis but beat South Florida. Tulsa was trounced by Memphis, 89-67, in the opener of the AAC tournament. So Tulsa also was a one-and-done in its conference tourney. It just didn't shatter its season.

Tulsa was seen as an NCAA Tournament longshot. So how did it get selected? Might it have been the persuasion of Joe Castiglione, the selection committee chairman and the athletic director at the University of Oklahoma? The theory is Castiglione urged that Tulsa be selected because he has a relationship with the Tulsa athletic director, Dr. Derrick Gragg. In an interview he once did with an online magazine, Gragg was asked who were key influences for him as he advanced in his field. He named Castiglione, who had hired Gragg as a compliance officer when Castiglione was the AD at the University of Missouri. Gragg has included Castiglione as one of his "great, great contacts."

That was the buzz. Is it true? Did Castiglione press hard, twist arms on behalf of Tulsa? Who knows? When Castiglione was interviewed by the Tulsa World after the selections were announced and was asked about St. Bonaventure, he denigrated its non-conference schedule. Castiglione also told the newspaper that Tulsa was the last team selected. "It was a really tough conversation but they edged out the other four teams (that included St. Mary's, Monmouth and Valparaiso, along with Bonaventure) because of their Top 50 wins, which were four," he said.

Regarding St. Bonaventure, Castiglione answered: "A really tough non-conference strength of schedule. The best team they beat in the non-conference was 80 or above."

The Tulsa World, the Hurricanes' hometown newspaper, had this to say about the team and the tournament:

Tulsa was a surprise NCAA Tournament entrant. The Hurricanes chances seemed dashed by a loss to Memphis in the AAC tournament. "We felt really good about our resume going in to the Memphis game," TU Coach Frank Haith said. "Regardless of the stuff everyone was saying, it's obvious the (NCAA selection) committee valued our league and what we accomplished in non-league and the league. What a blessing. God is good."

Many analysts called the Bonnies dismissal the biggest snub in the NCAA selection process. Some used sterner language, none more power-fully than Phil Martelli, the St. Joe's coach. He used the Monday forum of the annual Coaches Against Cancer breakfast at the Palestra, a big, well-at-tended event each spring in Philadelphia, to make his points. "Let me tell you how St. Bonaventure got screwed," was Martelli's introduction of the topic. Then he described the intrigue involving the Tulsa selection.

Martelli wasn't done. He went on radio, and more than once.

"I think what they did to St. Bonaventure was a disgrace," Mar-telli said on CBS Sports Radio's After Hours with Amy Lawrence. "They changed the criteria team-by-team. As much as I'm elated for our group, I'm a little bit down and despondent for the Atlantic 10 and for that terrific team at St. Bonaventure. They got mistreated by this committee."

"I have no idea," Martelli answered, when asked to explain how this might happen to a team with Bonaventure's record and key victories. "How you can look at this league and not recognize an RPI of 29 --- that team beat us twice. They tied for the regular-season championship in our league. They won at Dayton – an extraordinary win. And to have them on the outside looking in, it's just wrong. You can give me all the explanations that you want, and I'm not pigeonholing any team that they put in. But what they did to that group of kids is borderline criminal."

Martelli's words are about as staunch as it gets regarding a college coach and criticism of the NCAA in any capacity. While it changed nothing, it was wonderfully refreshing, far more honest and strident than most college coaches would ever dare. And everyone knew Martelli had absolutely nothing to gain by saying it.

A day or two later, Will Wade, the first-year coach at Virginia Commonwealth, unfurled a lengthy, almost tutorial explanation for why a school such as St. Bonaventure has a tough time lining up an exemplary non-conference schedule. It involves having the money to pay for a quality opponent to come to the Reilly Center.

So Schmidt had two conference foes going to bat on behalf of his 22-win team and conference co-champion.

Martelli is one of the reasons that Philadelphia college basketball can be a wonderful ride each season. He toggles between high-grade cranky and benevolent and caring, and he is old enough to know he can't be reined in. He also nailed the NCAA Selection Committee for overvaluing the Power 5 Conferences. At one point he said the committee had hijacked the tournament on behalf of the big-name programs.

No one is safe from Martelli's sharp tongue. Senior forward Papa Ndao was called for a technical foul with eight minutes remaining and St. Joe's ahead of VCU by nearly 20 in the A-10 tournament title game. Ndao (pronounced NOW) complained too loudly about a foul that was called on him, and he was slapped with a technical. When his teammates could not get him to settle down, he was being taken out of the game when he walked over to the official, gestured wildly at him and said something else. Ndao was tossed from the game, pushed away roughly by Martelli, and then escorted to the locker room, with an assistant coach upbraiding him every step of the way.

Martelli was being interviewed moments after the victory over VCU and talked about how everything had gone well for the Hawks in the tournament, and then added: "Even though Papa Ndao embarrassed all of us."

CHAPTER 27:
BITTER END TO A BEAUTIFUL SEASON

Practice had just concluded on a Tuesday night. Wagner and St. Bonaventure would play their first-round game of the National Invitation Tournament at the Reilly Center the next evening. There was talk of another sellout crowd, a show of support, perhaps, for a group of players who had been wronged. Two nights after the Sunday shunning, Mark Schmidt was still steamed, and the leaked outcome that arrived in the middle of the selection show, shattering what was meant to be a celebratory gathering and sending some of his players out of the room, some of them cursing loudly, left him incensed.

"I am so sorry someone sent that lineup out," he said. "It was terrible. It could not have been worse. I can't describe it. A couple of guys left upset. They lived for that moment. It was hard to handle. We thought we were in."

Schmidt was glad for the support he and the school received from Phil Martelli. "We have a very good relationship," Schmidt said. "He is passionate about the Atlantic 10. When he speaks, people listen." Schmidt said he was gratified by what the A-10 commissioner, Bernadette McGlade, had said. She was outraged by Bonaventure's not being selected and cited that no other team in the history of the tournament went uninvited when it was co-champion of its league and had an RPI below 30. She said she planned an investigation. It will be interesting to see if that really happens.

"It gives you a good feeling that they cared," Schmidt said.

He thought having "two football guys" directing the selection committee was a mistake. "That's like getting me to decide eight bowl games," Schmidt said. He also had a problem with two women being on the committee. "This wasn't a Title IX situation," he said. In fact, there was just one woman on the panel, Janet Cone, for the past 12 years the athletic director at North Carolina-Asheville.

Schmidt, his staff and the players did not bother to watch the telecast of the NIT selections. They took the players to the locker room and told them how badly they felt for them. An effort was made to pump them up about the NIT, to get them excited about the prospects of playing at Madison Square Garden. The fact that Bonaventure was a No. 1 seed meant that they would play --- if they kept winning --- the first three games at home. Keep winning, you get to stay home. Three wins at home and they would head to New York for the semifinals and a possible championship game.

The coach thought the discussion helped. He said, "Next day, everyone says 'Let's go.' "

Schmidt also said: "If someone told me before the season we'd be a number-one seed in the NIT, I'd have said, 'Damn, that's great.'"

He was asked how the assistant coaches, Dave Moore, Steve Curran and Jerome Robinson, were handling the situation. "They are disappointed but they understand the politics," Schmidt said. "You invest your whole life in something, and there are few opportunities to get (to the NCAAs)." Few opportunities if you are St. Bonaventure, but that was left unsaid.

There had been a bit of chatter on the Bona Bandwagon that Jaylen Adams might consider leaving Bonaventure for a bigger, gaudier program. Some of this, maybe all of it, came from Adams tweeting something along the lines of "I'll never be overlooked again." Schmidt was asked about this, and he didn't flinch.

"Poaching is always going on," Schmidt said. He mentioned Louisville and Drexel, a reference to Damion Lee, who had finished his undergrad degree at Drexel, using his last year of eligibility as a grad student at Louisville. "If you have a good kid," Schmidt said, "you almost have to re-recruit your guys, your good kids."

Then I asked Schmidt about his future.

"Everyone wants to be appreciated," he said. "I just want to do what's best for my family. I have a son who is just a freshman (at Olean High School). If I'm here next year, I'll be here 10 years. But if something came up, I'd have to listen."

Then Schmidt became more expansive. "It's not just what you can do for me. It's what can you do for the program," he said. "My name is out there ... the way it was when we won in 2012. I'm not saying I'm leaving. I love where we live. The new AD is good, very supportive.

"We need to raise money. Try to change Bonaventure from 'the little

Bonnies.' I don't want to come in seventh each year (in the conference). We need more money to make this program a consistent contender. Make kids know this is the kind of place they are coming to."

Schmidt's frankness on this topic, the clear indication he has these strong feelings and they are on the surface, was a bit of a surprise.

So was Wagner. The Seahawks, who play in the Northeast Athletic Conference, a low-major conference, were 23-11 overall and 13-5 in the league. They won their first two games in the league's postseason tourney before being bounced by Fairleigh Dickinson. They were given an eight-seed in the NIT and a bus trip to Olean. A crowd of more than 4,800 turned out on a weeknight, eager to keep the Bonnies' season alive after the jolt of not getting picked for the Big Dance.

In appreciation, the Bonnies presented a sloppy, listless first 20 minutes that summoned memories of the first half against Dayton in the Reilly Center. They were bullied inside by Wagner's 6-7 center, Mike Aaman, and riddled by the Seahawks' guards. It was an 8-8 game with nearly six minutes gone when Wagner showed it had come to play and had no concerns about the Reilly Center atmosphere. In fact, the Seahawks were having fun with it. When Wagner finally took a deep breath, the Bonnies were buried, 36-19, with just 3:45 to go in the first half.

Romone Saunders, a sophomore guard, had been murder. He had 13 points in the first half and missed only two shots. Wagner was 17-for-31 from the field and the halftime bulge was 40-26. Bonaventure was 9-for-30 from the field and hit just two of 15 three-point attempts.

The simplest explanation for the first-half performance was that Bonaventure was weighed down by the Sunday circumstances, that it had no stomach for the NIT. But simple is rarely correct. The Bonnies were outhustled and outplayed, and looked lousy in the process. Their responsibility was to show something to the people who came out on a weeknight to support them. And, a good performance in the NIT, making the trip to Madison Square Garden, would stick it to the folks who denied them a spot in the NCAA Tournament.

Wagner would win this game, but Bonaventure at least showed some life in the last 10 minutes. Wagner led 53-40 when Saunders hit another three-point shot and then put his finger to his lips to silence the fans loudly urging a Bona comeback. When Aaman scored inside, the Seahawks still led comfortably, 64-55, with less than eight minutes to go.

But Bonaventure had picked up the pace, deciding, at some point, it would not let this season end with a whimper. Posley's two free throws cut the lead to 65-60 and Denzel Gregg followed with a rebound basket to make it 65-62 with 4:25 left. Dwaun Anderson scored on a pretty set play and then got a rebound basket. Wagner was up 69-64.

The Bonnies were clawing at this point. Adams nailed a three-pointer to cut the lead to 69-67 with 3:05 to go. A jumper by Gregg made it 71-69. There was 2:12 left. Then Saunders, brilliant all night, made the play that ultimately secured the win for the Seahawks, nailing a three-point shot that gave his team a 74-69 lead with 1:45 to play.

Wagner held on, but the Bonnies kept pressing them. A long ball from Adams with 7.4 seconds to play made it 76-72. When Posley hit a three-pointer --- a shot he launched from a few feet behind the arc --- the Bonnies were within two, 77-75, but the clock blinked 0.8 seconds. Two free throws gave Wagner the 79-75 victory.

How good is Wagner? The Seahawks flew to Omaha and three nights later were absolutely hammered by Creighton, a 4-seed, 87-54.

Posley and Adams joined Schmidt in the meeting with the media after the game. The absence of Wright was striking, given it was his last game also. Maybe Dion had given all that anyone could have hoped for in four years, and answering the sometimes insipid questions of reporters would have been one burden too many.

"We didn't come out well at all," Schmidt said. "Wagner came out hard on us. They knocked us back. In the second half, we got back in to the game, but Wagner always had an answer."

Then Schmidt considered the entire season, saying again that the team had a great year but it was disappointing how it ended. "I'm proud of Marcus and Jaylen," he said. "We wouldn't be celebrating a great season without them."

There were two bittersweet moments at the end of the game, after the teams had shaken hands. Few of the fans had left, and as the Bonaventure players started to head off the court, those fans came to their feet and started applauding the team for its efforts this year, for providing the kind of season that doesn't come often to the Southern Tier or the rest of Western New York.

The second moment was even more moving. Posley headed off the court, the last Bonaventure player to leave for the lockers, and then stopped. He turned around, walked toward the center of the court, and, with arms extended, began to wave to the fans, and continued to wave until he reached the tunnel. The fans responded. The entire act didn't take 10 seconds, but it was sweet and genuine. The guy played just two seasons at St. Bonaventure, but he provided excitement and memories not to be forgotten and made an indelible contribution. And he did it with class and a smile. When asked at the postgame press conference what would be his warmest memory of his time at Bonaventure, he said: "The community."

It took just 120 hours, from the tipoff for the game against David-son in Brooklyn to the end of the game against Wagner, to crush a sea-son that even Mark Schmidt, not really a lyrical fellow, had called "mag-ical." One-hundred and twenty hours and the mingled sensibilities of the 10-member NCAA Selection Committee, which clearly served the big-name conferences and penalized St. Bonaventure, for sure, and Mon-mouth, to name two schools many thought would be selected. Joe Casti-glione, the AD at Oklahoma, chaired a group that included the athletic directors from LSU, Michigan State, Stanford, Duke and Creighton. That assured the Big 12, Big 10, the Southeastern Conference, the Pac-12 Con-ference, the Atlantic Coast Conference and the Big East Conference were, at the least, represented.

So how did that work out? The Atlantic Coast Conference, Big 10, Big 12 and Pac-12 each placed seven schools amid the 68. Five teams from the Big East made it. Thirty-three teams, half of the tournament field, came from five conferences. The Southeastern Conference had just three, same as the Atlantic 10. The mongrel American Athletic Conference had three selections: UConn, Cincinnati and Tulsa, the team that went 12-6 in its conference and had 12 losses overall and likely was the pick that bumped St. Bonaventure. Or it was UConn, which was 11-7 in the American. Or, God forbid, Syracuse, which waltzed in to the NCAA tourney with a 9-9 ACC record, a 19-13 overall record and a three-game losing streak. Weeks later, the Orange were in the Final Four, one more thing to churn the collective bile of Bona Nation.

A 22-8 overall record, a 14-4 conference record that included two wins over St. Joseph's and a win at Dayton, a share of the conference title and an RPI under 30 could not displace one school from the conferences with the strongest constituencies on the selection panel.

The overtime loss to Davidson in the conference tournament certainly hurt the Bonnies. But was it so damaging that it overrode the overall resume? Would Bonaventure still have been discounted if it had won the Davidson game? The Bonnies had beaten Davidson in conference play.

Did anyone in that supposedly secure room of 10 athletic directors dare to frame the discussion in this manner: Is St. Bonaventure one of the 68 best teams in the nation? Because the answer would have to have been obvious. Instead, it became an exercise to place the programs who always swell the roster of 68 teams. The committee contorted itself to get Tulsa, with 12 losses, on to the bracket, and Syracuse, which along with the University of North Carolina had shamed itself.

Somewhere, Dick Vitale, the clown prince of college basketball, the breathless booster for the perennial powerhouses, a man who publicly urged that the then-commissioner of the Atlantic 10 Conference expel St. Bonaventure when scandal tarred the place in March of 2003, when he never clamored for harsh penalties against the Orange, the Tar Heels or the Jimmy Valvano-led North Carolina State back in the day, likely was smiling. It would be Vitale's kind of NCAA Tournament, with Armani-clad coaches and prime-time players.

But for the people who care about the Bonnies' program and the university, these will be questions and an outcome that gnaw for years.

EPILOGUE

It was the first week in July, and Mark Schmidt was in North Augusta, S.C., right across the Savannah River from Augusta, Ga., and the closest thing to heaven-on-earth, the Augusta National Country Club. The rest of the city of Augusta has some hellish spots, however. The weather was mad-dog hot and humid and the event that drew him, Peach Jam 2016, something he has attended before, is nothing he especially enjoys. "I hate this trip," Schmidt said.

The Peach Jam is a non-stop procession of 16- and 17-year-old basketball stars playing in a five-day tournament of AAU squads from across the country. It is sponsored by Nike. It's a magnet for college coaches, and Schmidt really can't afford to miss it. As usual, Schmidt was on the hunt for players others had overlooked --- the undersized forward, the left-handed point guard, the deadeye shooter who is a step slower than you'd prefer --- and the evidence is now ample that Schmidt knows what he is doing. The very best players there already have their short lists of college choices, and St. Bonaventure, to be sure, is not on any of those lists. The head coaches of the perennial powerhouses, the teams that seem to always be No. 1 and No.

2 seeds when NCAA Tournament time comes around, are on hand to impress and stroke the superstars, the one-and-done guys, they are pursuing.

Schmidt will see some or all of his A-10 coaching colleagues as well as old friends, such as Chris Mack, the Xavier coach. But the whole thing is something of a meat market, a blur of players, most of them trying too hard to impress. Schmidt calls the hectic first-day of the event, when no teams have been eliminated, "Black Wednesday."

Sixteen weeks have passed since Wagner ended the Bonnies season in the first round of the National Invitation Tournament. Schmidt's anger and disappointment have not eroded in the period of time since The Snub, the decision of the NCAA Tournament Selection Committee that deemed Bonaventure unworthy of a bid. "Our numbers spoke for themselves," Schmidt said. "We should have been invited."

Schmidt is most distressed over the fates of Marcus Posley and Dion Wright, whose college careers ended with the loss to Wagner.

"Whenever I see those two guys, that will be what I remember," Schmidt said. "They deserved to be there. Marcus and Dion were not able to do something that would have been memorable for them.

"For Duke and Kansas, the tournament is always about winning the national championship. For us, just getting the opportunity to play in the tournament is what we thought we had earned. And we were denied that."

The trip to Georgia was not Schmidt's only flight south after the season ended. He was invited to discuss the head-coaching job at the University of Central Florida in Orlando. There he met with Dan White, the UCF athletic director, whose previous job was AD at the University at Buffalo. Schmidt said he had never met White before the interview, but White certainly had to be aware of what Schmidt had accomplished in Olean.

Was Schmidt truly interested in the position? "Yeah, I was interested," he said. "I wouldn't have gone down there if I wasn't. I have to do what is right for my family, so that's why I talked to them."

Days later, White hired Johnny Dawkins, who had been fired as the Stanford coach, to lead the UCF program. Dawkins will be paid $1.1 million in his first season with the Knights.

And just about the time Schmidt had returned from Florida, Athletic Director Tim Kenney disclosed he and Schmidt had already been discussing a contract extension. That deal was made, a six-year contract that would pay Schmidt handsomely. One report said the salary would be $825,000 a season. A source said that number was a bit high, that the annual salary would be around $750,000.

"It's closer to the higher number," Schmidt said, declining to be more specific.

Schmidt and Orlando do not seem an obvious match. A plain-spoken, rough-hewn son of blue-collar Attleboro in the treacly kingdom of make-believe, and no ocean beach to boot. It would extend Schmidt's golf season, for sure. But it is plausible that he saw no reason not to talk with UCF. What harm could come from it? Plus, it was added leverage in Schmidt's clearly stated insistence, made in the days after the Wagner loss, that the men's basketball program required more financing and he deserved a raise.

In any case, St. Bonaventure has doubled down on Division I, at least as it regards men's basketball. In all likelihood, some of the funding for Schmidt's new contract will come from wealthy and generous alumni. The grinding sound will be the teeth of faculty members, already distraught and angry over stagnant salaries and now confronting the tumult sure to occur as the curriculum is adjusted on behalf of attracting more students.

Schmidt and his assistants will have a longer bench in the 2016-17 season, a significant difference from November of 2015, when the season began without Courtney Stockard, who would miss the entire year, and Jordan Tyson. That left the Bonnies with just a seven-player rotation that included two freshmen.

There are three returning players who chewed up big minutes last season: point guard Jaylen Adams, three-guard Idris Taqqee and small forward Denzel Gregg. Adams and Taqqee were starters. Derrick Woods, who would be a sophomore, started 22 games as a 6-foot-9 forward/center. He shared time at that position with Tyson, who was healthy for all of the conference schedule.

However, Tyson decided to transfer after the season and is headed to Georgia State. Schmidt left the impression that both he and Tyson agreed a fresh start somewhere else made sense for the Ohio native.

Then, more than four months after the season had ended, Woods announced he was leaving Bonaventure. This one is difficult to understand, at least on the surface.

In August of 2015, Woods was being worked out by Dave Moore in an otherwise empty Reilly Center. Woods was fresh on campus because he had to complete a summer high school course to be eligible to play in 2015-16.

Schmidt watched a few minutes of the workout as he headed to a meeting in Tim Kenney's office and then said of Woods: "This kid has no idea how good he can be." And at the end of a season of 22 starts, a lot of minutes of playing time and some memorable performances, nothing argued that Woods would be anything but a steadily improving big man who would be around for three more years.

One theory is that Woods looked at a roster for the upcoming season that would include redshirt 6-foot-7 transfer David Andoh, Chinonso Obokoh, a 6-foot-9 center and a transfer from Syracuse University, and eligible to play immediately because he has his undergrad degree; and freshmen Amadi Ikpeze and Josh Ayeni, all inside players, and decided playing time would be reduced.

Just as likely is a difference of opinion between Schmidt and Woods over what kind of player Woods should be. Even before his freshman season began, Woods described himself as "a stretch four," a big forward who was mobile, ran the floor well and could score inside and on jump shots from 12 to 15 feet and out. And Woods did hit some outside shots, and a few of them came in pressure-packed moments in both non-conference and conference games last season.

Schmidt, however, did not share Woods' opinion of his being a stretch four. "He is a back-to-the-basket player," Schmidt said.

Taqqee and Gregg will be fixtures on the court, and the question of starting versus subbing will get worked out.

Matt Mobley, a 6-foot-3 two-guard, who sat out last season after transferring from Central Connecticut State, is viewed by the coaches as a big-time scorer and a worthy successor to Marcus Posley, a big challenge given Posley's remarkable two seasons with the Bonnies. The 6-foot-5 Stockard, a junior college transfer, will push hard for a starting role.

Kaputo, who played well as a freshman, will spell Adams at the point and allow Schmidt to move Adams in to the two-guard spot when the situation invites. Kaputo will get lots of playing time.

After that, the roles are less certain. Schmidt likes Obokoh's size, defense and rebounding, and any scoring he provides will be gravy. Schmidt spoke with Jim Satalin, the former Bonaventure player and head coach and a Syracuse resident, about Obokoh. Satalin told Schmidt that the senior is "a high-character guy, a hard-worker, and smart."

The Bonnies recruited two freshmen. Ayeni, who signed in the late spring, could be a steal. He is a 6-foot-8 forward from Baltimore who chose the Bonnies over an offer from South Carolina. Schmidt, and the players who worked out with Ayeni, love the kid's toughness. Tareq Coburn, a 6-foot-4 guard from Cardozo High School in New York City, is considered a good recruit, but playing time could be hard to find in his first season. Caleb McGuire, a walk-on, will return for his senior season.

Two other forwards will be seeking roles. LaDarien Griffin, who played decently in limited appearances as a freshman, is a work in progress, according to Schmidt. "He is improving and he is getting stronger," Schmidt said. Andoh, forward, who sat out last season after transferring from Liberty University, has to get back in to playing shape, according to Schmidt. Ikpeze, a freshman from Amherst, N.Y., is 6-foot-10 and 245 pounds, and would seem to have a bright future. To ensure that, and not to waste a year of Ikpeze's eligibility, he could end up redshirted. But with Tyson and Woods gone, Ikpeze might see time as a freshman.

The depth and the talent create a pleasant dilemma for Schmidt, who admits to preferring a rotation of eight players. "The more guys you play, the less rhythmic you are," the coach said. "There's likely a separation between the first eight players and the guys nine through 12." With the departures of Woods and Tyson, there are now 12 players on the roster.

The new recruits, the returning starters and the players who sat out last season have drawn enthusiasm that the 2016-17 club can build on the great success of the previous season. What must be measured, however, is the absence of Posley and Wright. It is difficult to overstate what is lost without them. Posley made miracles happen, and to some degree his very presence allowed Adams to be the impact player that he was in 2015-16. That said, Schmidt says it will be easier to replace Posley than Wright.

"Wright was a nightmare matchup game-after-game," Schmidt emphasized, a 6-foot-7 forward who ran the floor like a guard, handled the ball and drove off the dribble, muscled up against bigger interior players, and hit baby hooks inside and nailed three-pointers. And he was a tireless rebounder on both ends of the floor. Wright, Posley and Adams combined to be a three-headed monster for foes. Any one of the three, on any night, meant the difference between victory or defeat, especially as it regarded the wearying conference schedule. Two-thirds of that component is gone now, and accounting for that in the upcoming season will be a challenge.

There is talent, and then there is talent that is clutch, the players who show up when it counts the most. It forces one to recall the loss to Davidson in Brooklyn, the excruciating overtime defeat that cost Bonaventure its trip to the NCAA Tournament. Adams, dogged by a painful back, had just three points that night. Wright and Posley each had 32 points, remarkable play, and did it amid stifling pressure. And it was not enough. The good news is that Adams was a first-team A-10 selection and he is back as a junior next season. But some combination of Mobley, Stockard and Gregg will have to provide what Wright and Posley brought most every game. Not easy, and maybe impossible.

The end of the academic year brought interesting developments.

Tim Kenney concluded his first year as athletic director with a move that was acclaimed by the fans. Now hanging above center court at the Reilly Center is a state-of-the-art video board. The board, which measures 8.2 feet by 13.3 feet, is a gift from Al Horton, a 1966 graduate and a member of the board of trustees. This might soften the outsized clamor that resulted from the priority seating that moved the students off the floor on the sideline opposite the teams' benches.

Bernie Valento had a strong first year as the VP for enrollment.

By late May, 440 new students accepted offers to attend St. Bonaventure. Valento thinks the number will be 450 or a bit above that by late August, swelled by some transfers. That is a heartening outcome when compared to the 385 or so new students who arrived in the autumn of 2015. Valento believes new initiatives to recruit students, both undergraduate and graduate students, along with new academic programs directed at present-day marketplace needs and more online course offerings, will bring additional enrollment growth moving forward.

Jim Crowley ended his remarkable run as coach of the Bonnies' women's basketball program and accepted the head coaching position at Providence College.

Schmidt has offered a scholarship to another Baltimore kid, and this one is also a guard. Brendan Adams is going to be a junior in high school in the 2016-17 season, so his decision and arrival on any campus is a long way off. But he already has offers from Kansas State, George Washington and others. He is a bit bigger than his brother.

Sr. Margaret Carney concluded her presidency of the university in July, as planned. An interim president, Dr. Andrew Roth, arrived in August. He had been president of Notre Dame College near Cleveland from 2003 to 2014, where he increased enrollment from about 775 students to nearly 2,800. The board of trustees believes a permanent president will be announced in December 2016 and begin work at Bonaventure in the summer of 2017.

Finally, here are some numbers that are, frankly, mind-blowing, given the size of the school, its alumni base, its location and the huge advantages that St. Bonaventure's big-market Atlantic 10 Conference rivals all enjoy. One would have to believe that the data, to a large degree, affirms the devotion of the school's alumni and the Upstate New York fan base. It also says something about capturing the attention of just-plain basketball fans, no matter their connections, no matter their locations, who are charmed by a high-achieving underdog:

Basketball games involving Bonaventure in the 2015-16 season had more viewership than any other school in the 14-member conference, according to the NBC Sports Network, which is one of the broadcast affiliate for the conference. The four games telecast by NBC Sports involving the Bonnies had an average viewership of 78,500. The second-best was Virginia Commonwealth University's four games, which averaged 72,250. Third-best was the University of Dayton's four NBC-televised games, at 60,000.

Of the five most-watched A-10 games on NBC Sports this past-season, the second-, third- and fourth-largest audiences involved the Bonnies --- 99,000 for SBU vs. Dayton, 91,000 for Davidson vs. SBU, and 73,000 for St. Louis vs. SBU.

Logic, common sense, demographics, realties, money ... they all defy those numbers.

But then again, magic stoked a remarkable and historic season for St. Bonaventure.

Black magic ended it.

ACKNOWLEDGMENTS

This project began in mid-summer of 2015 as a phone call to Mark Schmidt, who amiably and politely indicated he was not at all eager to be the central figure in a book that would chronicle St. Bonaventure University's 2015-16 men's basketball season. "I am just not sure I want to put myself out there like that," he said. But in a face-to-face conversation in early August, a visit that also included a meeting with Schmidt, Athletic Director Tim Kenney and Director of Basketball Operations Matt Pappano, Schmidt agreed to give it a shot. And Schmidt held up his end of the bargain, allowing numerous and lengthy one-on-one interviews and phone calls, some in the early mornings, many late in the evenings and often when he was traveling. He was always candid and open, often passionate, often disappointed, sometimes angry, sometimes hilarious, never boring.

As someone who cares deeply about the school, and as a fan of the Bonnies, I had admired how Schmidt steadily improved the program. Seeing just how hard Schmidt and his staff must work to get the results they achieve increases that admiration.

I want to thank Coach Schmidt for all the cooperation he gave me on behalf of this book, and for his endless good humor through the process.

Matt Pappano, the director of basketball operations, has a groaning portfolio of tasks and duties, including non-conference scheduling, directing the summer basketball camps, assisting players with their academic responsibilities and preparing scouting and video on opponents, yet he cheerfully and capably was my liaison to the basketball office, setting up interviews with Schmidt, the assistant coaches and the players.

Assistant coaches Dave Moore, Steve Curran and Jerome Robinson were always informative, helpful and pleasant.

Steve Mest, the highly capable director of sports information, used his valuable time to assure I was credentialed for home and away games, as well as the conference tournament in Brooklyn. Bobi Cornelius, the secretary in Schmidt's office, was a continual source of assistance and good cheer.

Athletic Director Tim Kenney always found time for interviews, many of them devoted to subjects such as the tricky pursuit of new sources of revenue for athletics, especially the men's basketball program, and dovetailing expansion of intercollegiate and club sports with the drive to attract more students to the university. As a result, Kenney has become more than just an AD. He is a major strategist for the school, and a key member of the president's cabinet.

I owe a great debt to Dan Collins, a vice chair for the board of trustees and an executive with Corning Inc., who somehow found stretches of time to recount the complexities of the study that determined the university would continue to have Division I athletics and the plans and strategies that have been put in motion to steadily increase enrollment.

The same must be said for Bernard Valento, the vice president for enrollment. Just months in to a pressure-packed position, and temporarily living in the friary, Valento explained how he was reorganizing his department to attract more students to St. Bonaventure. Valento also has a major role in the revamping of the curriculum on behalf of courses of study that reflect the contemporary employment markets.

Sr. Margaret Carney made time for me amid an array of challenges she faced as the university president, including the enrollment slump, a decision to retire as president after 12 years, and a significant health issue. She is the embodiment of grace under pressure.

Jack McGinty, the Pittsburgh attorney and a trustee emeritus, explained why his alma mater needed to alter the curriculum. Two outstanding faculty members, Dr. Richard Simpson and Dr. Denny Wilkins, provided essential background information on some key issues.

And among the nicest experiences for me was being with some wondrous sports writers: J.P. Butler, the men's basketball beat writer for the Olean Times Herald; Chuck Pollock, the Times Herald columnist and sports editor, and columnist Bucky Gleason and beat reporter Mark Gaughan of the Buffalo News. It was a privilege to be in their company.

About the Author

Brian Toolan is a veteran journalist who worked for 43 years as a reporter and a ranking editor in the newspaper business. Positions he has held include sports editor and managing editor of the *Philadelphia Daily News*, business editor of the *Philadelphia Inquirer*, editor and senior vice president of the *Hartford Courant* and national editor of the *Associated Press*. He was editor of the *Courant* when it won the 1999 Pulitzer Prize for its coverage of a murderous rampage at the headquarters of the Connecticut Lottery. He directed coverage of the Virginia Tech shootings and the Minneapolis bridge collapse while at the *Associated Press*. He resides in New Hope, Pa.

46865832R00189

Made in the USA
Middletown, DE
10 August 2017